THE THEOLOGY OF THE OLD TESTAMENT

BY . . . . . OTTO J. BAAB

The THEOLOGY OF THE OLD TESTAMENT

New York   Nashville

ABINGDON-COKESBURY PRESS

THE THEOLOGY OF THE OLD TESTAMENT

SET UP, PRINTED, AND BOUND BY THE
PARTHENON PRESS, AT NASHVILLE,
TENNESSEE, UNITED STATES OF AMERICA

To the memory of
My Father

WILLIAM GEORGE BAAB

preacher, teacher, and ardent student of the Bible

Preface

THIS book is written for those whose acquaintance with the modern method of Bible study has not produced the expected religious results. They have some knowledge of the sources, dates, authorship, and content; but it is largely fragmentary knowledge, disconnected and detached from the faith men live by. Nearly twenty years of teaching, both in college and in theological seminary, have made clear that an emphasis which is placed exclusively upon a critical analysis of the biblical text and literary materials tends to produce both confusion and indifference. What is needed is the presentation of the material contained in the Bible in the form of living truths to which its writers were so passionately dedicated. This can be done only by a complete allegiance to the ideals of scholarly research and a frank acknowledgment of a religious motivation. Both are essential to an adequate understanding of the Bible.

It is fruitless for teachers of the Old Testament to exhort their ministerial students to do more effective biblical preaching while continuing to stress only questions of origin, unity, secondary sources, period of composition, and textual glosses or interpolations. The Protestant ministry will react to this type of teaching either by a superficial treatment of biblical texts or by a complete rejection of the critical method in favor of rank literalism. When laymen in the realms of science, business, and military leadership are declaring with deep earnestness that the world profoundly needs a faith rooted in the Christian religion, it is time to rethink the content and goals of biblical teaching in the light of its creation of such a faith. This book is the result of sober and protracted reflection upon this problem.

Preachers and writers upon religious subjects are particularly prone to reveal the limitations of their biblical knowledge with respect to the Old Testament. Having never surveyed the magnificent panorama of Israel's religion with quickened imagination, they have seized upon particular passages to support a vague feeling that the Old Testament is inferior in ethical and religious quality to the New Testament. An outstanding preacher recently in a sermon addressed to a sophisticated congregation mentioned the "primitive" character of the religion of Israel as compared with that of the New Testament. Information gathered from seminary students reveals an avoidance of the Old Testament in their preaching, probably based more upon lack of conviction regarding its religious truths than upon actual ignorance of its content—at least this is what their teacher would like to believe. If this is the situation among ministers, what must be the sad plight of laymen who depend upon the ministry for intelligent leadership?

Thus this book is planned as a guide to enable students of the Old Testament to integrate information they have gathered and to view it in relation to the major theological concepts of Israel's religion. It should also be useful to any reader who wishes to probe beneath the historical and textual facts in order to ascertain the meaning and abiding value of the Old Testament. It is hoped that its use will promote among ministers biblical preaching which is more effective because based upon a grasp of biblical theology, and among laymen religious living which arises from a new conviction that the Bible is indeed the book of truth and life. The limited number of books in the English language which survey the material in the Old Testament from this standpoint suggests that this book will meet a real need in the study and by the fireside.

The method has been to survey the books of the Old Testament canon in order to discover prominent and representative religious teachings and to present these teachings with as much fidelity to the purpose and meaning of their biblical sources as possible. Although questions of date, composition, and authorship have been deliberately kept in the background, they have constituted the frame of reference in which this investigation has been carried on. Ideas have been selected, not because of their personal appeal or because of their striking nature, but because they seem to be typical and are attested by a substantial number of witnesses. In some instances a book may be silent on a given theme. Thus the book of Esther does not mention the name of God. Where direct evidence from other sources, however, appears to be adequate, such silence on the part of one book has little weight. It has not been demanded of the literary witnesses that they be unanimous in order to establish the typical character of a belief, since the very nature of the Old Testament as a collection of writings expressing from a religious viewpoint the varied interests and needs of the Jewish community in its historical development makes such a procedure practically impossible. We are dealing, not with theological treatises, but with poems, hero tales, court records, prophecies, and laws. In such a collection religious beliefs may be implicit even though not

8

openly asserted. It is of course unsafe to assume that this is true unless direct and positive evidence from other sources is available.

Biblical passages are cited frequently to substantiate the positions taken. Those of special pertinence are quoted directly. For this purpose the 1931 edition of *The Bible: An American Translation,* by J. M. P. Smith and E. J. Goodspeed, has been used by permission of the publishers, the University of Chicago Press. The translation of the Old Testament in this edition, which has been reprinted from time to time, in large size without column divisions, is that of the original separate edition of 1927 and seems to me preferable to the slightly revised translation in the smaller two-column edition of 1935 and its successors. This translation, through continuous classroom use, has been found to be intelligible to the modern student, as well as reasonably accurate and readable. Students who prefer to use other versions, however, will have little difficulty in checking the citations. The use of transliterated Hebrew terms has been reduced to a minimum, although complete avoidance of technical terms has not proved to be possible.

This book attempts to permit the Old Testament to declare its own faith in its own way within the limits imposed by the need to translate that faith to readers who belong to a modern Western culture. In view of this purpose, interpretations have been excluded. Consequently, few authorities are noted or quoted, not because of indifference to their ideas, but because a survey of scholarly opinion is not the task. Nonetheless, grateful acknowledgment of the work of biblical scholars in the fields of textual, historical, and theological research alike must be expressed. My former teachers and present colleagues at Garrett Biblical Institute, as well as teachers at the Divinity School of the University of Chicago, have contributed to my understanding of the Old Testament and of biblical criticism beyond my power to repay. I wish particularly to name Professors Frederick C. Eiselen, Leslie E. Fuller, and Edwin E. Voigt of my student days at Garrett; the present generation of Garrett students who have sat in my classes and given encouragement by their interest in the Old Testament; my associates in the biblical field on the Garrett faculty—Professors Edward P. Blair, Albert E. Barnett, and Charles F. Kraft—whose helpful comments on the manuscript have been of great value; Dr. Horace G. Smith, president of Garrett Biblical Institute, who made possible a leave of absence without which this book could not have been written; Eunice Beatrice Baab, my wife, for her invaluable assistance in reading the proofs and preparing the indexes; and Mr. and Mrs. H. P. Burger of Tucson, Arizona, in whose friendly guest house on the edge of the desert most of this book was written.   OTTO J. BAAB

Contents

1. The Study of Old Testament Theology[1]

ONE of the most striking and influential developments in the modern study of religion has been the rise and wide acceptance of the critical method of Bible study. This movement began with the Renaissance and the Reformation, when the revival of classical learning and the breakdown of medieval authoritarianism stimulated a new interest in biblical languages and permitted a new freedom for the study of the biblical documents. The results of this movement in terms of knowledge are decidedly impressive. The discovery of new manuscripts, research in the texts of ancient versions of the Bible, such as the Septuagint and the Vulgate, and the diligent study of the grammar of the biblical languages made it possible to prepare better and more reliable texts and translations of the entire Bible.

The study of history, especially that of the ancient Near East, of which Palestine is the center, helped greatly in understanding the Bible, in particular its social and cultural background. Thus these writings have taken on new meaning; their relevance to their own times and their relationship to literatures and cultures outside of Palestine have been more fully realized. All of this has been accomplished by skilled specialists using the tools of the scientific method.

So satisfactory have been results of this research that it has met with general approval, except in particular geographical areas and religious groups in America. There appears to be a general assumption that continued historical, textual, and literary study of the Old Testament will restore to men living in an age of science the biblical faith of their fathers, or at least a reasonable facsimile thereof. Yet a certain anxiety is beginning to be felt by the biblical critics themselves. Some of their number note the disturbing fact that at the very time that the conclusions and discoveries of biblical criticism have been most widely disseminated—through preaching, teaching, and the press—a general biblical illiteracy prevails. This illiteracy is coupled with a general in-

[1] The material in this chapter is in part adapted from my contribution, "Old Testament Theology: Its Possibility and Methodology," to *The Study of the Bible Today and Tomorrow* (ed. Harold W. Willoughby; Chicago: The University of Chicago Press, 1947) and is used by permission of the publishers.

difference to the teachings and faith of the Bible, an indifference which increases in proportion to the increase in educational opportunities for learning about the Bible. Certainly those who use the Bible with the greatest unction and fervor are not those who hold academic degrees, as a rule.

THE PROBLEM OF INTEGRATION

This situation confronts modern man with a dilemma: as a creature of an age of science he must accept the scientific method; as a man of faith which has been engendered by a biblical culture he needs the assurance that his faith is true, and that its divine object is the very heart of reality. To accept the one, he must evidently reject the other. The biblical critic, for all his devotion to the truth, has accentuated this dilemma by furthering a process whereby the ultimate truth of the Bible has become more and more difficult to find. He pushes his investigation zealously in an effort to explore and analyze every facet of fact and hypothesis. He sees the Old Testament as the record of Israel's life and history, which has similarities to documents depicting the life of neighboring peoples of the Semitic world.

The reader of this literature, under the guidance of the critic, encounters a series of documents recording the various stages in the evolution of the Hebrew religion. He learns that there are many books, many sources within sources, many authors and editors, many ideas and diverse viewpoints on many subjects. In this multiplicity of facts to which biblical science has given him access he seeks in vain for a single object of worship or a commanding ideal for conduct. We may well inquire if the very accumulation of information does not prove to be religiously barren as far as faith is concerned.

This is not a situation peculiar to the field of biblical science, of course; the study of physics, chemistry, and even sociology frequently produces detailed, fragmentary knowledge of facts in a given area without imparting a sense of the meaning of these facts in their wider setting of human need and ultimate truth. But these sciences do not directly deal with subject matter purporting to affect the issues of life and death for man, while biblical study does. The motives of the Reformers which influenced the rise of biblical criticism were deeply religious motives; and the development of this science since the Reformation has continuously been inspired by the genuine piety of devout men, in both the Jewish and the Christian traditions. They searched the Scriptures in order to find the Word of God as well as to comprehend the historical and literary character of these books. The degree to which biblical studies in our generation have adversely affected the growth of biblical piety measures the failure of these studies to secure the results intended by the founders of modern biblical criticism.

As a result of this situation, which is marked by a virtual abandonment of the Bible as the authoritative basis for religious faith, biblical scholars are beginning to evaluate their work, not simply on the basis of the advancement of technical knowledge, but likewise in the light of its religious consequences. Books are beginning to appear in larger numbers on the theme of the relevance of the Bible for modern life and the value of its great ideas and religious teachings.[2] Concurrently, considerable debate has arisen among Old Testament scholars as to the possibility and nature of biblical theology.[3] There are those who assert that the formulation of theological doctrines is the task of the theologian, and that the Old Testament critic should be content to provide him with his raw materials—facts as to the historical character and major ideas of the biblical books with which he deals. At the best a theology of the Old Testament can only describe the religious phenomena found in the historical documents. Others maintain that a theology which is simply descriptive is hardly worthy of the name. The complete presentation of what is contained in the Old Testament includes the questions of validity and authority. To justify the approach and purpose of this book, these two views should be examined.

DOGMATIC THEOLOGY

Old Testament theology has usually been described either dogmatically or historically. In the first instance, the presuppositions of the author determine a priori what is found in the biblical sources. By logical deduction from these premises the data are determined and systematized into a coherent pattern whose unifying principle is, not the living experience of the men of the Bible, but the creed which the biblical theologian brings to his task. The earliest Christian attempts to use the Old Testament theologically probably took the form of collections of passages from the prophets which suggested a messianic teaching. This messianic material was detected by looking for evidence of early Christian conceptions of the life and career of Jesus. In a more formal fashion the church fathers applied this method to the Old Testament and discovered therein ideas of judgment, sacrifice, and sin which they

[2] R. B. Y. Scott, *The Relevance of the Prophets* (1944) ; G. E. Wright, *The Challenge of Israel's Faith* (1944) ; W. C. Bower, *The Living Bible* (rev. ed., 1944) ; H. H. Rowley, *The Relevance of the Bible* (1944), *The Re-discovery of the Old Testament* (1946).

[3] W. A. Smart, "The Death and Birth of Old Testament Theology," *Journal of Religion,* Vol. 23 (1943), Nos. 1, 2; W. A. Irwin, "The Reviving Theology of the Old Testament," *Journal of Religion,* Vol. 25 (1945), No. 4.

had held before undertaking their study. Consequently Old Testament theology was Christian theology of one kind or another, not only because it was written by Christian scholars, but because its aim was to validate doctrines derived from the New Testament by reference to the Old.

This Christian dogmatism dominating Old Testament interpretation until the modern period may not be dismissed or be treated too lightly. It is true that it was not scientific or inductive; it is also true that proof-text exegesis gave a distorted view of the teachings of the Old Testament, with the result that its authors were made to say what they never intended to say. Nonetheless dogmatism in its insistence upon the continuity of historical revelation rendered a valuable service by affirming an important truth. Even though its zeal for documenting its Christian faith by drawing upon Hebrew sources caused it to overlook or minimize the historical situations conditioning the biblical text, this zeal was motivated by a true insight that history cannot be atomistically conceived. On the contrary, its temporal events possess a relationship of meaning derived from a supreme reality whose name is God. This is particularly true of that phase of human history worked out in Palestine and recorded in the Bible. Here the first man Adam and the last man Christ stand at the two ends of a history revealing the complete and final truth about God and man.

Yet the dogmatic method of writing Old Testament theology is handicapped by its lack of interest in the historical method and in the disciplines which it demands. Unless all the ground gained since the Revival of Learning by the human mind and spirit is to be surrendered, uncritical dogmatism cannot be yielded to. Freedom of inquiry, tolerance of ideas which are not approved, factual observation, analysis of sources, classification and evaluation of data, continuous verification of conclusions, and the unremitting search for new knowledge have achieved priceless results in emancipating the mind of man from ignorance and gross superstition. For this reason the liberal biblical critic must cherish his heritage of intellectual freedom and use it thoroughly in his research.

HISTORICAL THEOLOGY

It is the liberal biblical scholar who has produced what may be called historical theology in contrast with the dogmatic type just discussed. By this is meant theology which is written in the spirit of scientific and historical criticism. This requires identification and comparison of the documents and a study of their historical background, authorship, and the relationship of their teachings to the contemporary culture. With these and similar questions the historical student occupies himself. If he tries to formulate a theology of the Old Testament—provided he admits the possibility of such a venture—these are the questions he will ask. An examination of books whose subject is the theology of the Old Testament shows that those of the critical school are composed from this historical viewpoint.[4] Each writer is conscious of the development of religious ideas through the several periods of Israel's history; each treats the sources critically; and each is inductive rather than deductive in his treatment of the biblical text. Minor differences in emphasis, organization of material, and a preference for either a topical or a chronological approach do not obscure the fact that there is general agreement as to the nature of the task—an accurate description of the religious teachings of Israel in the light of the appropriate historical setting.

The books in this category are similar to Old Testament works which have no reference to theology in their titles.[5] These deal admittedly with the historical study of Israel's religious ideas and practices. The Old Testament, for these writers, is the record of a definite historical religious culture whose main features may be identified with the same precision as the excavation of an ancient artefact by an archaeologist. Israel's religion is the product of a historical culture, and an exact description of that culture and the religion which it produced is the goal of the Old Testament theologian and of the historian of Hebrew religion.

If such literary efforts may be called Old Testament theology, their value seems to lie in their unbiased objectivity. Any critical scholar, whether conservative or liberal, Protestant or Catholic or Jew, could formulate a historical theology of the Old Testament which would be essentially the same as that produced by others using the same materials and methods. Fundamental differences would be the measure of failure to make a full use of the critical methodology and resources. Ideally, therefore, there can be only one theology of the Old Testament —as there can be only one biology or astronomy—when all is said and done. Such a theology can theoretically win the acceptance of all students, no matter what their religious connections, provided all subscribe to the principles of the historical method. This will indeed be a

---

[4] A. B. Davidson, *The Theology of the Old Testament* (1904); E. Sellin, *Theologie des Alten Testaments* (1933); L. H. Köhler, *Theologie des Alten Testaments* (1936); W. Eichrodt, *Theologie des Alten Testaments,* Vols. I-III (1933-1939); M. Burrows, *An Outline of Biblical Theology* (1946).

[5] A. C. Knudson, *Religious Teachings of the Old Testament* (1918); H. W. Robinson, *Religious Ideas of the Old Testament* (1913); W. O. E. Oesterley and T. H. Robinson, *Hebrew Religion* (2nd ed., 1937); I. G. Mathews, *Israel's Religious Pilgrimage* (1947).

scientific theology of the Old Testament, verifiable, communicable, and universal in its appeal to intelligent human beings.

Such a theology has the advantage of social concreteness, for it be-longs to a particular community of people, the Hebrews, living with other communities in a period of history whose tensions and temper can be described with great vividness by the competent scholar. As the theologian extracts from their social-historical context the characteristic religious ideas of the Hebrew Scriptures and presents them systematically, he can consult historical records to clarify and confirm his conclusions. He can test his results pragmatically by reference to the historical experience of a people whose faith was hammered out upon the anvil of adversity and social conflict. The result is a grass-roots theology capable of empirical confirmation and social application. Originating in the market town of Bethel, in the suburb of Anathoth, in the city of Jerusalem, and in the foreign land of Babylonia at a time when life was torn by economic, social, and international struggle, this theology was the verbal expression of spiritual realities the acceptance of which was deemed by its proponents to be essential to national security and peace.

Hebrew history may be viewed as a demonstration of faith with positive and negative sides. Hebrew historians consciously interpreted the history of their people in terms of the creative and ethical activity of the living God. In national disaster they saw his judgment, in victory his lovingkindness and mercy. At all times events confirmed his nature and will for men. Thus historical biblical study brings to light the very circumstances and situations which had theological significance to the writers of the Old Testament. It is not difficult, therefore—assuming the continuity of the historical process—to find stimulus in this literature for the study of the theological meaning of world events in our own time, a period in which conflict, social cleavages, and religious confusion provide points of resemblance to the ancient biblical world.

In spite of these values inhering in the historical-critical approach, its application to the faith of the Hebrews raises a serious difficulty. Under its influence the student finds that the biblical writings contain several distinct and apparently contradictory viewpoints or theologies. He learns that Israel's religion unfolded through definite stages—such as animism, polydaemonism, polytheism, henotheism, and monotheism —according to a principle which is consistently illustrated in all religions. The Bible's chronological strata show a variety of religious patterns, each one of which is relative and conditioned upon the culture producing and sustaining it. There is not only variety but disparity between these patterns. Thus the task of presenting a single theology of the Old Testament seems to be a hopeless one.

Critical research may still produce a biblical theology, if its purpose is a "purely historic discipline, aiming at the accurate presentation of historic fact and recorded thought in an impartial objective way, without meantime taking into account the bearing of that on permanent normative religious truth." [6] Obviously this must be the aim of the biblical theologian if the Bible is regarded as mainly a depository of interesting but loosely related ideas and customs. When he has given a faithful account of these, his work is done. Yet the question remains, Can the term "theology" be applied to this type of research? The answer is Yes only if this definition is held to be valid. What if the "accurate presentation of historic fact" produces a miscellaneous assortment of religious data whose chief relationship is provided by the accident of preservation in a common literary corpus? Can such a collation of facts be called a theology by the furthest stretch of the imagination? This brings us back where we started: with the historian of religion whose work is essential to the furtherance of knowledge—and relatively meaningless for meeting the issues of life.

THE QUESTION OF VALIDITY

The above definition—representing that of many critical scholars in the biblical field—declares that biblical theology cannot take into consideration the matter of ultimate meaning and validity. As the term theology is commonly used, however, it suggests the orderly formulation of religious ideas held to be true representations of ultimate reality as that reality affects the life and destiny of men. Theology always claims, according to its adherents, to be in some sense exclusive and final in its pronouncements. It may do this without dogmatism; still its claims imply finality and truth for the beliefs which it affirms. It is not content to state propositions which are tentatively offered as being possibly true. On the contrary, it asserts vigorously and confidently what it believes to be valid regarding truths held to be indispensable to salvation. This suggests that a consideration of the question of validity is a legitimate task for the Old Testament theologian.

It may be objected that such an inquiry will bog down in the religious prejudices of the one who makes it. Will not his effort to find objectivity in Israel's religion be successful simply because his philosophical and religious presuppositions will be decisive and predetermine the outcome? It must be admitted that presuppositions are necessary to any

[6] D. S. Adams, "Theology (Biblical)," in Hastings, *Encyclopaedia of Religion and Ethics.*

kind of scientific investigation and must be used consciously while under rigorous scrutiny and control. The real question deals with the origin and nature of the presuppositions used. We may note, for example, the common assumption in the study of religion that beliefs or customs which are comparatively late are superior to those that are earlier. This time fallacy has affected many books written on the subject of biblical religion in recent years. Another presupposition underlying studies in biblical religion and history derives from the philosophy of scientific naturalism. This conception of reality is preoccupied with the phenomenal world of sense experience and tends to reduce everything to terms amenable to measurement and quantitative analysis. Under these circumstances the supersensuous and spiritual levels of experience in the Bible can hardly receive much attention from the critic.

These are assumptions drawn from modern philosophy, especially from a modification of the Hegelian concept of development, which takes the form of unilinear evolution. We may well question the validity both of the philosophy of history from which these assumptions are taken and of their use in the study of the Old Testament. Would it not be wiser to draw our assumptions from biblical philosophy instead of contemporary philosophy by thoroughly absorbing the spirit and viewpoint of the biblical records themselves? Thus the objective facts and the *biblical* meaning of these facts will guide the critical investigator. The suitability of attempting to formulate an Old Testament theology which involves both description and evaluation is suggested by the need of modern men and by the fact that validity is continuously claimed by the Old Testament itself for the major beliefs which it records. When Old Testament research is pushed to the limit and not restricted by assumptions derived from the student's philosophical position, this claim and the religious experiences from which it grew can be given the same weight as that attached to matters of text and historical event.

Such an attitude is in full accord with the scientific techniques peculiar to objective research. This means that the biblical documents must be read in the light of extrabiblical inscriptions of Canaanite, Babylonian, and Assyrian origin, as these exhibit the homogeneous culture of the Near East in biblical times. Every aspect of the life which gave rise to the Old Testament requires intensive investigation. The history of the Israelites, their moral standards, social customs, and religious beliefs must be included in this study. Yet in addition to these and other legitimate subjects of research there exists a relatively unexplored area of biblical experience which is of supreme importance in arriving at an Old Testament theology—the religious consciousness of the people who were responsible for this literature. A quest for all the facts cannot ignore this conspicuous fact standing out in every book and page of Scripture—that its authors were poignantly aware of an influence from without which they declared to be the power and activity of God.

THE RELIGIOUS EXPERIENCE OF ISRAEL

The Old Testament's "Thus saith the Lord," or "The word of the Lord is like a burning fire in my bones," and scores of similar statements demonstrate conclusively the orientation of the prophets and saints toward the God who spoke to and through them. The critic may argue that these men were mistaken and confused a personal ethical urge with divine revelation, but he must admit the existence of these passages and offer a suitable explanation of their prominence. The literary evidence of this pervasive religious consciousness cannot be lightly dismissed as scribal glosses or corruption of the text—a device not unknown to scholars into whose theories the biblical text does not fit—since such evidence permeates the language and thought of the entire canon.

Apart from this fact of the sharp awareness of God which runs through the Old Testament, any real understanding of this literature is impossible. The expert may use his skill in extricating from the records of the life of biblical man information respecting the historical situation or the biography of an individual author; yet the dead past remains dead, because the quickening power of religious faith which once animated it eludes him. Thus the background and teachings of Amos may be identified, while the passion for the righteousness of God which was the meaning of his life may be overlooked. Or the priestly writer of Gen. 1 may be viewed as the literary craftsman who skillfully revised an old Babylonian myth, and not as a man caught in the grip of a mighty truth about God and his world. The key to the understanding of biblical religion and history is the biblical faith by which biblical men lived.

Any effort to explain away this experience of God or the supernatural in the Old Testament, or to minimize its importance, betrays an unscientific bias which is incompatible with the critical method and purpose. For example, an interpretation of the familiar phrase "The word of the Lord came to . . ." as signifying simply the figurative language of the Hebrew prophets or editors whereby they tried to show the importance of what they had to say reveals a serious misunderstanding of prophetic psychology and religion. Such an interpretation is a polite way of reducing the prophet's God to a figure of speech. Surely the language the prophets themselves used nowhere justifies this attitude. Their words and their deeds reveal their intense realization of the divine will working in them and in their community. Their courageous defiance of the *status quo* and stern criticism of powerful rulers in the name of God is inexplicable apart from their personal experience of a living God, who was far more than the verbal symbols used to describe him.

Critical and constructive research begins, then, with the central and controlling experience of the men of Israel—the experience of God —and goes on from that point to identify the major concepts of religious experience to the extent that these are amenable to formulation and systematization. This is the starting point for the writing of a biblical theology which seeks to represent the spirit and perspective of the Bible itself. It is exceedingly significant that the belief in God as revealed in the pages of the Old Testament proves to be indispensable to the critic's work of analyzing and co-ordinating the vast amount of material dealing with other religious concepts of Israel's faith. Obviously God was the central reality for this people and is therefore basic to our entire study. An understanding of the idea of God becomes the clue to knowledge on such matters as sin and salvation. In fact, the pervasiveness of this idea and its intimate association with all other phases of Old Testament belief create difficulties for the student who tries to isolate it for purposes of study.

It is perfectly apparent that no complete theology as such can be found in the Old Testament. This literature deals with other matters, although it is full of theological material. The theological student must isolate this material, organize it, and give it meaningful expression. To organize the ideas which he finds, he is bound to apply logical principles derived from his own scientific training. The dynamic, activistic religion of Israel does not easily yield to this treatment. In view of this problem, one can only try to preserve the vital, organic quality of the biblical ideas by constantly viewing them in their historical setting and by seeking to describe them from the point of view of the men who held them, with the hope of permitting the Old Testament itself to state its faith to the modern reader.

2. *The Meaning of God*

THE most profound and exciting quest of the ages is the search for the ultimate meaning of the universe. Not many men are philosophers as they engage in this quest; but all pursue it, either with sharp awareness or with but a dim realization of their goal. Esthetic and social activity as well as theological or philosophical inquiry are significant indications of the universality and earnestness of this seeking after the final meaning of the world which supports the life of men. Whether the result takes the form of sensuous pleasure, an ethical code, a metaphysical system, or a religious creed, the assumption is that a formula for living has been found which corresponds in some sense to what the universe finally means. Usually the clearest expression of this formula employs the vocabulary of religion, and particularly the word "God." This is certainly true for the vast majority of men. Hence the content and value of this idea in the Old Testament has great importance, since this literature together with the New Testament provides by far the greatest portion of the Western world's religious vocabulary.

In the Old Testament itself the single concept which is overwhelmingly emphasized is the concept of God. Many terms are used to express this idea, depending upon the preferences of the various biblical authors and the period of history and culture in which they lived. Such words as Yahweh, Elohim, El, El Shaddai, Yahweh Sebaoth, Eloah, Elyon, and the like may be noted. It would be of interest to show the characteristics of Israel's God set forth in the written records chronologically arranged, as these vary in emphasis from century to century. Through much of this variety and historical change, however, one concept of God stands out conspicuously. This concept has marked and clearly defined elements which fully justify a treatment of the meaning of God rather than a survey of the history by which the noblest idea of God in the Old Testament finally emerged.

The material used in the following discussion is selected without regard to the principle of chronological development, since it is believed that much if not all of this literature bears the mark of a fairly consistent theistic position. Such a position may not have characterized the documents at the time of their original composition, but it was inevitably imposed upon them sooner or later in the history of their transmission and use by the religious community. This is not to say that primitive ideas of God do not appear in the Old Testament. On the contrary, for these writings have had a long history of oral and written transmission, a history covering nearly twelve centuries. During this time, especially prior to 400 B.C., the documents took shape as the growing deposit of community experience, as they were constantly adapted to changing needs. Thus in more primitive communities the conceptual content of the books would reflect the intellectual and spiritual level of those who wrote them.

However, it is precarious to assert real primitivity for the Old Testament. Except for fragmentary war songs, folk poems, and ancient laws (Judg. 5; Gen. 4:23-24; 9:25-27; Exod. 23:19) there are probably no greater number of examples of animism in the Old Testament than there are in the beliefs and practices of modern man. For example, the J narrative, which may be dated in the ninth century B.C., contains along with traces of magic and primitive beliefs a profoundly searching analysis of human nature and divine mercy in the story of the Garden of Eden. We may grant that this story is vividly pictorial and anthropomorphic without dismissing it as the product of an age unable to distinguish between dreams and reality. The early date of a source by no means guarantees the primitivity of its religious teachings. Truth occasionally breaks into history in apparent defiance of cultural antecedents. It would not have been easy for a contemporary to predict the epochal contribution of a Yahwist, an Amos, a Socrates, or a Buddha. Consequently, while we fully appreciate the immeasurable value of historical research, our use of the Old Testament in an attempt to formulate its fundamental theological truths must also take into account the limitations of this approach.

THE LIVING GOD

Perhaps the most typical word for identifying the God of the Old Testament is the word "living." The living God is the peculiar God of these writings. This signifies the God who acts in history, who performs mighty deeds of deliverance, and who manifests his power among men. He demonstrates that he is a living God by disposing of Israel's enemies: "Joshua said, 'By this you shall know that the living God is in your midst, and that he is surely going to drive out of your way the Canaanites'" (Josh. 3:10). When a saint of old becomes deeply despondent, he finds consolation in the realization that his God is a living God who can assuage his spiritual thirst: "My whole being thirsts for God, for the living God" (Ps. 42:2). How great is the exultation of the psalmist who cries out:

> How lovely is thy dwelling-place, O Lord of hosts!
> My spirit longs and pines
> for the courts of the Lord.
> My heart and my flesh give a shout of joy
> for the living God! (84:1-2.)

David experiences a renewal of his strength as he faces Goliath and recalls that his God is the living God (I Sam. 17:26, 36).

The meaning of the term "living" when applied to God is clearly shown in a passage from Jeremiah:

> But the Lord God is the true God,
> He is the living God, the everlasting King. (10:10.)

The context of this verse deserves attention (cf. 23:36). It is because God is the living God that his wrath causes the earth and the nations to tremble in fear. He, the living God, has made the earth and created the heavens by his power. In contrast to this living God the gods that are made by the hands of men are shameful frauds which will be utterly impotent when called upon to help their worshipers. This passage definitely declares that the living God is one who has power to save, whereas idols, which cannot save, really have no life.

The adjective meaning "alive, living" occurs at least sixty times in the formal oath which contains the name of the Hebrew God. The usual translation reads, "As Yahweh lives" (See Judg. 8:19; Ruth 3:13; I Sam. 19:6; 20:21; etc.). The inclusion of the word for "living"—appearing as a verb in our translation—in the oath formula has the purpose of guaranteeing the divine support of the act, or refusal to act, stipulated in the oath which is made. By calling upon the living God, whose power to punish an oath violator is connoted by the word "living," the will of the oath taker is reinforced and the performance of the terms of the oath is assured. In addition to this interpretation, it is likely that the invocation of the divine name in the oath was believed magically to effect the actual materialization of the Deity himself. This, however, is incidental to the purpose of showing how the formula includes a central reference to the living, functioning God of Israel.

Experienced Power

This is God, not simply an idea, therefore; he is an experienced power, acting upon and through human life and the natural order which sustains it. He delivers, redeems, saves, helps, and blesses. Verbs rather than abstract nouns are needed to characterize him. Apart from the limitations of the Hebrew language in dealing with abstractions such as are involved in a philosophical approach to theism, the nature of the God idea itself as found in the records of Israel calls for dynamic, functional terms expressing creative power. Since God is a living God, he is unavoidably involved in all of the complexities and uncertainties of life. His life interacts with that of his people. He operates through and in the historical process. In his activity the phenomena of change, growth, destruction, deliverance, defeat, victory, and all other manifestations of life are present. It is impossible to confine this God to a verbal definition or an abstract concept, because he is a living God who delivers Israel.

Idols and God

Over against this view may be placed the *non-Hebraic concept of God,* particularly the idolatry denounced in the Bible so vehemently. Practically all of the Old Testament books in their defense of the faith lash out at the contemporary forms of idolatry. In this attack the biblical writers make clear their own conception of foreign gods. Idols represent gods which have no life. They may not be dead, but they may as well be, so obvious is their weakness and helplessness. Men who seek their aid do not receive it. These weak gods cannot even save themselves in a crisis:

> Bel crouches, Nebo cowers;
> Their idols are consigned to beasts,
> They are laid as a load upon weary cattle.
> They cower, they crouch together;
> They cannot rescue the load,
> But themselves go into captivity. (Isa. 46:1-2.)

To show the weakness and inadequacy of idols the prophets bitterly and caustically satirize them and hold up to ridicule the process whereby they are manufactured. They are made from wood overlaid with gold from Ophir, worked by skillful craftsmen (Jer. 10:8-9). From the tree which constitutes the core of the idol the worker takes wood and makes a fire with which to warm himself or to cook his food. A portion of the tree which *the Lord himself had planted and watered* the technician uses for the construction of an idol (Isa. 44:14-17). No wonder such an object is the personification of utter impotence and

26

folly! In striking contrast the God of Israel is a powerful, living God abundantly able to tear down and to build up, to save and to destroy.

By reducing to ridiculous impotence the idols or so-called gods of their day, the Hebrew writers achieved the basis for a genuine monotheism, which was the result of practical instead of speculative considerations. These men were not interested in the question of monotheism as such. They were concerned to deepen and extend their conviction as to the saving power of their God in the lives of the members of the community of Israel. They found in God alone the means of help. He had guided the nation from its very beginning. He had delivered it from bondage in Egypt; he had brought it through all manner of calamities into the Promised Land, where he had helped it achieve its true destiny as the servant of Yahweh. No other god had done this; no other god had demonstrated such power and strength. By the test of actual experience he had proved to be the only living God, capable of demanding and receiving the loyalty of men. This logic of incontestable experience could finally produce only one result— the designation of God as the only God, at least for Israel.

It is this aspect of God's nature as presented in the Old Testament which accounts for the strong emphasis upon God as a *God of history*. In a remarkable degree the Old Testament is conscious of history, although there is no fully developed and consciously matured philosophy of history within its pages. Its interest in history is simply its interest in God as a powerful, living force in the historical process. We may note that history, as organized human experience, derives its meaning and organization for the Hebrew writers from the purpose of the living God, who controls the process according to his will and nature.

After creating man, he selected the founder of the nation and presided over the inauguration of the Israelitish community. At each crisis in that community's history God made his presence felt through rebuke, punishment, or, more rarely, victory over the enemy. When the monarchy was established, he admonished and dethroned kings if they departed from his instruction, or he encouraged and prospered them if they obeyed. Whenever a king "did that which was evil in the sight of the Lord" (I Kings 15:26, 34; 16:25; II Kings 15:18, etc.), his reign was marked as a failure. On the rare occasions when a good king appeared, he was acclaimed as one who "did that which was right in the sight of the Lord" (II Kings 15:34). It was the living God whose great purposes would be realized in the grand finale of history—the coming of the divine kingdom. Only because the drama

of history was directed by the living God could this magnificent fulfillment be conceived as a genuine possibility or even a predetermined
certainty.

THE PERSONAL GOD

The God of Israel is personal. His life is a personal life which goes
far beyond mere movement or consciousness. This personal quality
may be better understood in comparison with the kind of life manifested by the popular gods of Palestine called the baals. These were
gods of fertility who supervised the processes of agriculture and reproduction. They were often localized and worshiped at particular
shrines. Thus there were the Baals of Tyre (I Kings 16:31-32),
Peor (Num. 25:3), Hazor (II Sam. 13:23), Hermon (Judg. 3:3),
Shalishah (II Kings 4:42), Gad (Josh. 11: 17), and Perazim (II
Sam. 5:20). Although worshiped in different places, these baals shared
the same general character and function. Occasionally one assumed
a position of special prominence because of the political strength of
the city-state supporting his cult. It is probable that the Baal of Tyre
was rather widely recognized and was invoked in business as well as
purely religious transactions in the region of northern Palestine and
Phoenicia. Ahab's marriage to Jezebel of Tyre undoubtedly influenced
the religion of Israel and the violent reactions of the grim and fierce
prophet Elijah.

In spite of the popularity and prevalence of baal worship, even by
the Israelites, the baals may be regarded as mere projections of the
fertility principle and therefore as impersonal beings possessing little
or no self-direction or individuality, if we can believe their chief and
most caustic opponents—the prophets of Yahweh. The fact that magical
means were utilized to secure the favorable action of the baal illustrates
this point. The ritual of the sacred dance (I Kings 18:26-28), the
planting of the sacred garden (Hos. 10:12), the preparation of the
vineyard of the Loved one (Isa. 5:1-4), and similar practices indicate
the magical and impersonal nature of baal religion and its gods.

The personal nature of the God of the Old Testament is readily
shown by reference to nearly any portion of this literature. We may
note, for example, the allusions to the so-called anthropomorphic functions of God. God resolves, walks, talks, hates, rebukes, angers, is
jealous, and loves those whom he chooses. He has breath, a back, a
face, and hands. The instances are too numerous for any attempt at
specific and complete citation to be made. It is clear that God is viewed
as having personal and even manlike traits whereby he may communi-

cate or otherwise relate himself to others. Yet these evidences of personal being are extremely superficial and inconclusive. They obviously fail to distinguish God from men; neither do they identify the deeper meaning of personality.

There is no word for personal or personality in the Old Testament, just as there are no words for many other abstract ideas which have come into our language from classical rather than Hebraic sources. But this does not mean that the idea symbolized by the term "personal" is inappropriate for Old Testament thought. As a matter of fact, the basic ingredients of the concept are to be found in the many indications of the self-determination, the ethical freedom, and the affective character of the divine life. There is abundant evidence on each of these points, and its accumulation readily leads to the conclusion that the God exhibited in the Old Testament is personal in the deepest and most significant sense.

Let us consider first the matter of *rational self-determination.* While this is not usually emphasized in Old Testament theology, it has more weight than is often attached to it. The tendency among biblical scholars and theologians to associate the principle of reason with Greek philosophy and the principle of righteousness with Hebrew thought is justified, but it creates a false impression. It cannot be denied that the logos and nous of Greek thought point to reason as an absolute which is pre-existent and eternally an aspect of ultimate Being. This is not the Hebrew way of thinking about God. According to biblical thinking God is a self-determining and self-directing center of consciousness conceiving purposes and working for their realization in the processes of history as well as beyond. This assumes the power of thought and reflection as well as memory and volition.

God, however, is more than a rational principle, even though he works in a rational manner. The divine power to project a purpose which is selected from a number of alternatives presupposes a high degree of intellectual activity. Yet the choice of a purpose which may occasionally run directly counter to what men may regard as reasonable suggests the presence of elements in the divine nature which are other than rational. Men faced by the fact of an inescapable commission which threatened to reshape the pattern of their lives rebelled vigorously, although they finally obeyed the heavenly vision. Moses thought it highly unreasonable that God should select him to liberate the Hebrew slaves in Egypt. Jeremiah believed that his qualifications for the task of prophesying to the nations in a day of doom were nonexistent. It was often necessary for God to declare to men that his ways were not their ways, and his thoughts were not their thoughts, before they could comprehend the strange commands laid upon them. If these commands were rational, their rationality derived from a divine logic which was often in conflict with human reason.

The self-direction of God is seen in every document of the Old Testament. In the two accounts of the Creation it is clear that God determined his acts through no considerations brought to bear upon him from without. His decision to create was reached as a result of the interplay of forces within himself. "God said, 'Let there be light!'" (Gen. 1:3.) This utterance requires a preconceived purpose which receives fulfillment in the very pronunciation of the words quoted. The creation of man, the curse of Cain, the sending of the flood, the selection of Abraham as the father of the nation, the lives of Jacob and his sons, the servitude in Egypt, the exodus and the conquest of Canaan, the rise of the monarchy, the fall of the nation, the exile and the restoration—these were not chance occurrences or even primarily the result of political, geographical, or cultural forces; they were in fact the consequence of the divine purpose conceived in the mind of God and carried out by the exercise of his will.

To the Old Testament historian perhaps the most remarkable phenomenon is the frequent presentation of Israel's God as the supreme obstacle in the nation's self-chosen path. With bitter fury the God of the nation attacks his people's hopes and purposes. He lashes out at its leaders, excoriating and condemning them in unequivocal language. Jeremiah addresses one of the kings of Judah thus:

> But your eyes and your thoughts
> Are set on nought but your ill-gotten gain,
> On the shedding of innocent blood,
> And the practice of outrage and violence. (22:17.)

And Micah does not mince words when he speaks, on behalf of God:

> Hear this, now, you heads of the house of Jacob,
> And rulers of the house of Israel,
> Who abhor justice,
> And distort everything that is right;
> Who build Zion with blood,
> And Jerusalem with guilt. (3:9-10.)

These examples could be multiplied with ease. They serve to show the severe conflict which exists between the plans and purposes of the nation and those of God. In truth, the very idea of the nation as a monarchy is viewed by the Elohistic writer as repugnant to God, for it seems to set up in the person and office of the king a rival to God: "they have rejected me from being king over them" (I Sam. 8:7-18).

So powerful and tenaciously held are the purposes of God that they are used to override the will of an entire nation, if that will is out of line. If this means the downfall of the nation, God's purposes must nevertheless be sustained. Here is a supreme mind thinking and planning for the consummation of self-conceived ends and undergirding thought with the power to express it concretely in history. The Being able to do this is not a god but God. In all cultures parallel to the Hebrew the gods are largely acquiescent and readily swayed by the wishes of their devotees. All that is required are gifts and the performance of the ritual which accompanies their presentation. This is the case because of the nature of the non-Hebraic deities. They have no minds of their own, save as tradition and priestly conservatism have accumulated records of modes of behavior ascribed to them but really drawn from popular thought and belief. On the other hand, the God of Israel listens to no man in making his decisions. The mind of God is his own, even though men often make the mistake of identifying their thoughts and plans with his. This high degree of rational self-determination, so pronounced in the Old Testament, serves to accent the personal nature of God.

Another mark of personal being is the possession of *ethical freedom* and autonomy. In the character of God this ethical quality may be said to have reached its highest embodiment. God is continuously seeking to secure justice among men. The legal codes—even the most primitive—the prophetic books, the psalms, and the wisdom literature reveal this desire to a marked degree. It is true that the concept of justice has a strong social and juridical character in the Old Testament. No student of the concept can fail to note how a desert economy of a seminomadic community has colored it. Simple tribal democracy carried over into the life of the Hebrew people in Palestine and affected their thinking about God. As the prophets engaged in their intense struggle against the economic and religious baalism prevailing in their time and viewed as utterly antithetical to all that they cherished, they reaffirmed this idea of justice and found that it symbolized to them an important aspect of God's nature.

The social context of this concept, however, should not prevent our recognition of its very great theological significance. Those who find in the nature of man's social experience the data for ethical consciousness and the essential content of all moral experience are compelled to recognize that theirs is a modern and not a Hebraic viewpoint. The Hebrews, whatever the modern explanation, saw in God the source of all good, including ethical values. In him was absolute good, not a relative, conditioned good. The justice of God was not always the justice of men. With what vehemence God shattered the complacency of the so-called righteous men of Israel (Isa. 5:7; Amos 5:15, 24).

> "Of what use is the multitude of your sacrifices to me,"
>   says the Lord;
> "I am sated with burnt-offerings of rams
>   and the fat of fed beasts;
>
> . . . .
>
> Bring no more worthless offering!
> Foul smoke it is to me.
>
> . . . .
>
> Your hands are full of bloodshed—
>   wash yourselves clean;
> Put away the evil of your doings
>   from before my eyes;
> Cease to do evil, learn to do good;
> Seek justice, restrain the oppressor;
> Uphold the rights of the fatherless, defend the cause of the
>   widow." (Isa. 1:11-17.)

These people had faithfully performed all of their religious obligations—so they thought—and their consciences were clear. They had forgotten their little notions of goodness and piety needed to be evaluated in the light of the goodness and justice of God. Only then could the dimness of their moral vision appear.

The transcendent good found in the being of God, while not the result of anything that man had done, constituted constantly a demand upon men for strenuous moral effort. This divine good created unrest and anxiety among those who faced it, for they saw it, not as loveliness to be enjoyed, but as will to be obeyed. That is to say, the divine goodness was conceived as functional in the world. It always manifested itself in relation to the power and purpose of God, not as a thing in itself. The living God, who had conceived in his mind a purpose for his people, demanded that they do justly and love mercy. The awareness of the justice of God always took the form of the requirement of ethical obedience and its resulting social and personal readjustment. This requirement appeared as an absolute one which demanded full acceptance and unhesitating performance, or deliberate and defiant rejection. There was no middle ground on which to compromise. God's ethical demands were reinforced by the entire being of the Almighty—in all of its majesty and power. The ethical phase of this being must therefore be understood in connection with all other elements in the divine nature. A discussion of any one of them is artificial and inadequate when separated from the whole, since God was conceived by the Israelites as a living reality and not as an intellectual proposition.

The Hebrew posits ethical freedom for God. He is held to be greater than the ethical ideals of men and free to operate in his world according to his own sometimes inscrutable plans. There is no justification for identifying God with justice or eternal goodness in a moralistic effort to accommodate Hebrew thought to a different viewpoint. God is not the apotheosis of justice, even though he frequently uses his power to realize justice in the world of human beings. This means that God acts according to a higher principle than that which motivates the ethical conduct of men, and that he often baffles them by moving in mysterious ways to perform his righteous and wonderful deeds. The student cannot identify the true and essential being of God by concentrating upon his moral attributes. He is not bound by the ethical criteria formulated by men. His freedom lies in the fact that not only is he righteous—he is also holy. To this last concept it is now necessary to turn attention.

THE HOLY GOD

The more primitive form of the idea of holiness may be treated very briefly. Originally holiness was exclusively a magical concept which designated persons, objects, or places to which a quasi-physical quality of nonhuman origin was attached. This quality, or more properly, attenuated substance in animistic religions has such names as mana or orenda, signifying impersonal superhuman power or contagion connected with the god or gods of the community. Among the Israelites this power was called *kodesh,* a word derived from a root meaning "apartness, sacredness." The idea of separation or withdrawal is emphasized. In this sense the ark was set aside as a sacred object to which holiness had been imparted because of its use in the worhip of Yahweh. Likewise the sacred female prostitute of ancient Palestine was called a *kedeshah,* since she was set aside, consecrated, to the service of her god. The community of Israel was also holy for the same reason (Lev. 11:45). This power of holiness had dreadful potency in cases of accidental contact with it. The well-known incident of the death of Uzzah, who put out his hand to steady the ark as it was being hauled to Jerusalem by oxen and met his death, may be cited (II Sam. 6:6-9). But enough has been stated to show the early view of holiness which was by no means abandoned by later Judaism.

Even in this earlier meaning was resident the thought of that which was uniquely and distinctively sacred and removed in kind from the secular aspects of life. There appeared as an accompaniment of certain types of religious experience dreadful and awe-inspiring overtones, giving rise to both fear and fascination. This is the *mysterium tremendum et fascinosum* identified by Rudolf Otto in his influential work on the subject of the holy element in religion.[1] Man became vividly aware of an Other, not necessarily as personal, but always as differentiated from himself and fatefully related to his own destiny. The differentiation between man and this superhuman world of the sacred and taboo was sharp and clear. In Hebrew religion the boundaries between them were indicated by specific rules and prohibitions regulating the conduct of the holy community, and protecting its members from the consequences of overstepping the bounds of the secular and trespassing upon the realm of the holy.

When the pattern of the God idea emerged more distinctly in Israel, and its peculiar features became increasingly apparent, the idea of holiness assumed greater importance, for it served to call attention to what was exclusively divine. God was holy and the source of all holiness, because God was *himself* and not man. The "godness" of God is high-lighted by the word "holy" when it is used in connection with him. When this term is used to describe God, any thought of a man-created God is impossible.

The idolatrous creation of God in man's own image is forever precluded by this insistence upon God's absolute holiness. Immanentism and pantheism are incompatible with this concept. The one stresses the presence of the Divine in the world, and the other the identity of the Divine with the world, whereas holiness signifies transcendence with respect both to the world and to man. God's presence in the world is maintained by Hebrew writers; how otherwise could his will and redemptive activity be made known to man? Yet the qualifying factor of holiness effectually prevents this immanence from resulting in his complete humanization and the loss of his identity as God.

It may help to illustrate this reasoning by direct reference to certain illuminating biblical passages. A psalmist rhapsodizes over the greatness of God and notes that his power exceeds that of any other deity and is revealed "among the peoples" because his "way is in holiness"

[1] *The Idea of the Holy* (tr. F. W. Harvey, 1923).

34

(Ps. 77:13-14). All of the nations dwelling in the ends of the earth are to observe with wonder a remarkable demonstration of the power of God, who "has made bare his holy arm" (Isa. 52:10). "His holy arm" stands for his great power as against the puniness of the strength of all the nations. This holiness of God provides the basis for his trustworthiness, since it stands for the superhuman power of God to deliver those who trust in him. Without this power or holiness the fathers' confidence in God would have been ill-founded (Ps. 22:3-4). God is greater than all nations and all peoples.

> The Lord is great in Zion,
> And high is he over all the peoples.
> Let them praise thy great and terrible name!
> Holy is he and strong! (99:2-3).

The name of God is holy and terrible (111:9). His holiness is manifested in the destructive display of power against his enemies, the strongest of whom must yield before his might. Even the dreadful Chaldeans, who laugh at their enemies' futile attempts at resistance, are to be punished by him, whose holiness is of old (Hab. 1:10-12).

The glory and transcendent majesty of God are brought out by the writer of the ancient poem celebrating the defeat of the Egyptians at the Sea of Reeds. Here God magnificently displayed his power so that the poet was moved to cry:

> Who is there like thee among the gods, O Lord?
> Who is there like thee, so glorious in holiness,
> So awe-inspiring in reknown, such a wonder worker? (Exod. 15:11.)

His holiness is both glorious and supremely powerful. When God wishes to give the most solemn assurance of the inevitable fulfillment of his word, he may swear by his holiness, as when the doom of the voluptuous women of Samaria is pronounced (Amos 4:2). When God's decrees are at stake, none of the limitations which hinder and frustrate men in carrying out their purposes are at work. His holiness means the might of his pure godhead which will permit no human defiance to stand in his way.

In the book of Isaiah the title "Holy One of Israel" is used twenty-four times. This term underscores the meaning under discussion. The Holy One of Israel has a purpose which is challenged by evildoers (Isa. 5:19, 24); he is the object of the loyalty of the faithful (10:20); he is mighty in the midst of his people (12:6); he will be sought in the day of dreadful judgment (17:7); the poor will exult in him (29:19); calm confidence in him is the way of salvation (30:15); he is more effective than Egyptian armies (31:1). The situation is much the same in the poems of the Second Isaiah, as the following suggestions show: He is Redeemer of Israel (41:14; 43:14; 47:4; 48:17; 49:7); his people will glory in him, because he will make the desert a delightful habitation for the poor and the needy (41:16-20). He is the savior (43:3), the creator of the world (45:11), and the bestower of dignity upon an enslaved people (55:5; cf. 60:9, 14). In all of these references God's holiness is not only a metaphysical abstraction but also the ground for redemptive action in the historical scene. While it therefore takes the form of an activating principle in the Old Testament, its use in that literature implies a reality which is beyond history and the human scene. So it may again be affirmed that holiness is that essential character of deity which places the God concept in a completely exclusive category, sharply distinguishable from the human and the naturalistic.

Compelling evidence for this conclusion may be noted in that classical account of religious experience found in the sixth chapter of Isaiah. In the year of King Uzziah's death the young prophet was meditating in the temple, absorbed in the thought of the king's death as it might affect the life of the nation. The confused and frightening international situation was also possibly in his mind. This is the probable background for Isaiah's vision. Its content is highly significant. In a setting of swirling smoke, seraphic voices, and flowing robes there came to his consciousness a vivid picture of a holy God whose holiness filled the whole earth. In response to this manifestation of God's holiness the very foundations of the thresholds shook, and the house of God was filled with smoke, we are told. These incidental accompaniments of the theophany need not divert us from the central elements in the prophet's experience, however. Confronted by this vision of the blinding glory of God, whose holiness was well-nigh unendurable, Isaiah was overwhelmed by the sharp realization of his own utter unworthiness. A new and disconcerting self-awareness was aroused by this vision of God. No wonder he cried out, "Ah me! I am lost." The holiness of God, which he now perceived as never before, revealed to him the terrifyingly deep and wide chasm which existed between God and man.

The fact already demonstrated—that God's holiness did not take the form of sheer, paralyzing power—is evident here also. This holiness was made known for *redemptive* purposes, in that it provided genuine self-knowledge based upon God's own nature and will. In the climactic moment when he actually knew God, Isaiah experienced his deepest knowledge of himself. This knowledge paradoxically evoked from him profound contrition and, also, previously unrealized resources which enabled him effectively to respond to God and declare, "Here am I! send me." Such an ethical and personal reaction to this amazing vision of the holy God of Israel would hardly have occurred had the holiness involved in the divine nature appeared simply as undifferentiated supernatural power. In harmony with the true nature of holiness—as the fundamentally redemptive power of God, possessed by him alone—an ethical reaction did occur, and Isaiah found himself in the possession of powers and capabilities whose existence he had not before realized. On the other hand, if the vision had been based upon a God who was good but not holy in the biblical sense, and who was a kind of projection of certain social values highly regarded by the community, the radical nature of Isaiah's experience would be incomprehensible. It was the holiness of God which was responsible for the soul-shaking nature of the "call" of this prophet. Because God was truly God, this man yielded his life to him.

It has been the custom to describe the moralization of the idea of holiness in the Old Testament and to make a distinction between ritualistic and ethical holiness. This approach to the problem is misleading. In fact, it can be maintained that both the priestly writers and the prophets interpreted the meaning of holiness in the same way. For the priests the community was holy because of its intimate association with its holy God. It was set apart from the world of nations by this association, for something of the separateness and uniqueness of God was imparted to the people through this relationship. The requirements of the ritual were designed to preserve this apartness and distinctiveness, this godlikeness. Since holiness is not essentially ethical, man's experience of it through communion with God is not necessarily ethical; it is rather the preservation of a withdrawn, sacred community, through the observance of divinely authorized regulations and laws.

The prophets also viewed holiness as identifying the ultimate and essential nature of God. It was loyalty to him and knowledge of him in all of his holiness which would preserve the community and enable it to fulfill its destiny in the world. Men were called upon to obey his will, not because they had arrived at the conviction that it was a righteous will, but because it was *his* will, the will of the holy God of Israel. God himself was the source of life and hope, not particular statutes or instructions emanating from him in the form of ethical or ritualistic demands. This is the only conclusion that can be drawn from a reading of the priestly and the prophetic literature when we seek to discover the assumptions of its authors.

To the extent that this holy God as set forth in the Old Testament was always thought to have will and purpose for his people, it can be argued that holiness was never amoral or immoral and hence never required a process of moralization. The basic idea of holiness never changes in Hebrew thought, unless the argument for a counterconclusion is allowed to rest upon fragmentary textual evidence extracted from its wider context. The idea always suggests transcendence, divine power, the awful otherness of God, which nonetheless makes possible the nearness of his redemption. Even though the priests regarded the protection of the people's holiness as largely a matter of sacraments and ceremonial rites or taboos, and the prophets pointed to personal devotion and ethical obedience as the means of preserving the nation's integrity, both groups were concerned to glorify the holy God by creating a holy community. It must be repeated that the problem of moralizing the divine holiness was not an issue for any of the biblical writers. We may then inquire, In what way is the righteousness of God related to his holiness, if there really is any connection between the two? This is another way of asking, In what way is the righteousness of God related to his essential nature?

The point has already been made that the so-called attributes of God demanding discussion in any theological treatise—and this includes the idea of divine goodness—are at the best arbitrary and highly artificial symbols of the reality called God. They furnish helpful clues to this reality and should never be treated as complete and final representations of his nature. This holds for the ethical aspects alleged to belong to the divine Being. It is understandable that men, when caught up by the wonder and truth of love and justice, should regard these principles highly and associate them with the nature of God. The Bible, however, never deifies such ethical principles, although particular groups and individual writers saw more clearly than did others the social and ethical meaning of Israel's God. Justice receives its greatest effectiveness in the teachings of the prophets largely because they believed it to be supported by the living, holy, and transcendent God, whose power rules the world. It is toward this God that the nation must direct its loyalty and devotion; it is to him that they must look for salvation. They are to "let justice roll down like waters" because *he* demands it, not because of any intrinsic worth which the quality of justice exhibits in its own right. "Seek the Lord, that you may live," the prophet urges (Amos 5:6). Merely to turn to the doing of good without radically seeking the God who gives goodness and righteousness positive value is held to be futile.

Thus holiness brings us closer to the heart of the meaning of God in the Old Testament than does righteousness. It is the biblical word which most clearly distinguishes the God concept from all other concepts of human thought. Yet it cannot be understood in complete isolation from all other ideas associated with God. The holy God is a living God at work in the world with righteous and intelligent purpose. He is a personal Being calling men to seek and serve him. His holiness stamps his life and personal character with the quality of deity. It declares to the world that he is God.

[margin note: Holiness Summary]

THE SPIRITUAL GOD

This God who is a living, personal, and holy being, redemptively related to the life of men is also spiritual. Although a fuller treatment of the concept of spirit will be given in the chapter dealing with the nature of man, a brief analysis is required here to show the background of the meaning of God as spirit. The word most commonly translated "spirit" in the Old Testament is *ruach,* although a word (*neshamah*) used less often appears to have a similar meaning. *Ruach* means variously "breath, wind, temper, disposition, spirit of living beings, the spirit of God." The wicked are said to perish through the "breath of God" (Job 4:9). The forceful language of the poem in Exodus includes this word also:

By the blast of thy nostrils the waters were piled up;
. . . .
Thou didst blow with thy breath, the sea covered them. (15:8, 10.)

Ruach is imparted as a prophetic spirit according to a number of documents. In so far as this spirit is believed to come from God, this usage is important for our purpose. Moses was instructed to lay his hands upon Joshua, "a man of spirit" (Num. 27:18). In this manner Joshua was commissioned to be a leader of the Israelites, the spirit giving him the qualifications which he needed for that position. The spirit of Elijah was transferred to Elisha when the former departed "by a whirlwind to heaven" (II Kings 2:11-15). When Saul was anointed king by Samuel, the latter promised him that he would prophesy after receiving the spirit of the Lord (I Sam. 10:6). Upon the arrival at Naioth in Ramah of the messengers of Saul, when they beheld a group of prophets under Samuel prophesying there, they too received the spirit of God and began to prophesy (I Sam. 19:20-22). In the experience of the prophet Ezekiel the spirit of prophecy is conceived to be so potent that it exerts physical pressure and actually moves him from one place to another: "A spirit lifted me up and carried me away" (3:14).[2] The spirit of God bestows upon those who receive it the power to prophesy.

In the critical days of the coming of Cyrus, when many Jews were living in exile in Babylonia, the prophet called Second Isaiah seized the opportunity afforded by the startling victories of this Persian leader to proclaim the greatness of his God as the determiner of history. It was his God who had called Cyrus and given him success.

> I brought him, and made his way prosperous.
>
> . . . .
>
> And now I the Lord God have sent him,
> endowed with my spirit. (48:15, 16.)

The spirit has equipped Cyrus to function as God's agent in redeeming his people. These citations prove that the power to prophesy and to serve even as a military leader for God was conferred by the spirit.

When we inquire more precisely into the nature of God's spirit, we observe that it may refer to the mind or purpose of God. Speaking for Yahweh, the prophet Isaiah denounces Israel (see also Prov. 1:23):

> Ah, you rebellious children, . . .
> Who carry out a purpose that comes not from me,
> And who form an alliance that is not according to my mind [ruach]—
> Adding sin to sin. (Isa. 30:1.)

The word also means prophetic and ethical power. Micah declares:

> I am full of power,
> The spirit of the Lord, justice, and strength,
> To declare to Jacob his crimes,
> And to Israel his sins. (3:8.)

Here the spirit of God gives purpose and courage to the prophet so that he can face the nation with burning condemnation and judgment, in the name of the God whose spirit is in him.

The belief that the spirit of life which man possesses is a gift of God suggests also that this spirit in man belongs to God; otherwise he

---

[2] Note the interesting but farfetched attempt of the article "Ezekiel's Abnormal Personality," by Edwin C. Broome, Jr., in the *Journal of Biblical Literature* (Sept., 1946) to make a Freudian interpretation of this prophet's experience.

cannot dispense it as a gift. The spirit of God then means a principle of life which can be given, or withheld, or even withdrawn (Zech. 12:1; Job 27:3; Ps. 104:29-30). From the naïve standpoint of certain biblical narratives, the spirit may even be involved in frenzied deeds performed by men, which are believed to be inspired by an "evil spirit from God" (I Sam. 16:15, 16; 18:10—all are J). These are incidental references, however, occurring only a few times in the entire Old Testament. They suggest an animistic psychology in which strong emotion or abnormal conduct is readily referred to spirit possession.

A principle of life.

An interesting account is found in the priestly story of Creation (Gen. 1:2). This story contains the expression *ruach elohim,* literally translated as "the spirit of God." Here, if the more literal meaning is taken, may be seen the creative principle of life acting upon primeval chaos and darkness to produce life and order. God's spirit symbolizes this life and order which cannot appear without its activity. In view of the ancient Semitic myth lying behind this biblical story, wherein Marduk produces order by slaying Tiamat—*tehom* (the deep)—and utilizing her body to make the earth and the heavens, the use of the literal Hebrew is preferable. The spirit of God is substituted for Marduk, the Babylonian god, and this spirit is the creative power used by the Hebrew writer to destroy chaos to bring order into the universe.

The use of the concept of spirit to represent the presence of God among his people may also be noted. "Be strong, . . . and work; for I am with you . . . , and my spirit is standing in the midst of you; fear not," the Lord encouraged Israel (Hag. 2:4-5). God in days of old had led Israel from Egypt and through the hardships of the desert by his holy spirit, although they had "grieved his holy spirit" by their rebellion (Isa. 63:10-14). For the individual worshiper as well as for the entire holy community God's spirit was a present, cleansing, strengthening reality, the departure of which would be a tragic loss.

Evidence of Spirit of God

(3)

Represents presence of God Amoung His people.

> Create for me a clean heart, O God,
> And renew a steadfast spirit within me.
> Cast me not away from thy presence,
> And take not thy holy spirit from me. (Ps. 51:10-11.)

The soul could rely upon the guidance of the holy spirit to learn God's will and to discover the right way of life.

> Teach me to do thy will,
> For thou art my God;
> Let thy good spirit guide me in a straight path. (Ps. 143:10.)

Evidently the spirit was considered to be present, guiding the faithful in the way of life.

A saint of Israel has given us a remarkable account of the intimate association of his soul with God. Psalm 139, which he composed, reveals the deep wonder and the exquisite delight of his contemplation of God's dealings with him. While probably a very late psalm, it brings to a kind of spiritual climax the pietistic utterances found in earlier parts of the Bible. The psalmist testifies to the intimate knowledge of his daily life and innermost thoughts which God possesses. God is so completely present that he enfolds him "behind and before" and puts his hand upon him. To describe this nearness the word "spirit" is used.

> Whither shall I go from thy spirit?
> And whither shall I flee from thy presence? (139:7.)

In imagination this saint considers where he might go to depart from this presence and finds that the highest and the lowest places in the universe and the places of deepest darkness can be no obstacle to God's spirit. *In any place* his spirit will protect and comfort the psalmist's soul. The spirit is, in fact, the seal and sign of God's presence in the soul of the saint.

Our study of the evidence as to the spirit of God shows how spirit is contrasted with flesh as God is contrasted with man. This is clearly stated by Isaiah.

> Now the Egyptians are men, and not God;
> And their horses are flesh, and not spirit. (31:3.)

This spirit is not that associated with ghosts and shades from the underworld; it is rather the symbol of the power, purpose, and presence of the living God active in the world of men. This power and purpose may be experienced by men of faith who commit their lives to him and are thus enabled to receive his spirit as prophets, saints, and wise men. The spirit signifies all that God is and all that he may mean to men in righteousness, redemption, and personal peace. It also means much that man is, since man has been made in the image of God and accordingly has received his spirit.

THE CREATOR GOD

It is now possible to direct our attention to the idea of God as creator. This is not the earliest aspect of God's nature to be stressed in the Old Testament. Although an undeveloped form of the concept of

42

W

Creation appears in the Yahwistic story in Genesis 2, this idea is not
well worked out until the priestly story appears as it is now preserved
in the first chapter of Genesis. Nonetheless the thought of God as
creator is an indispensable feature of biblical theology. The occurrences
in the records of important allusions to this idea and then an interpretation of the phenomena, which may be integrated with the general
view of God as presented in this chapter, should now be considered.

In Genesis there are two accounts of the creation of the earth and of
various forms of life. The earliest, that of the Yahwist (J), written
about 850 B.C., simply assumes that Yahweh made the earth and the *Simple*
heavens and then made man out of the ground and gave him life by
breathing into his nostrils the breath of life. God made also a garden
containing trees, two of which were singled out by special names, and
he made beasts and birds as well. The cultural milieu of the narrator is
reflected in this story by the absence of any reference to fish. The author
of the original version of this story evidently was familiar with life on
the edge of the desert. In the other account—it cannot be called a story
—a far more sophisticated version is apparent. The whole process of
Creation is sketched in sweeping, breathtaking stages. From the primeval
chaos to the rise of civilized man celebrating faithfully the Sabbath as a *Grandeur*
day of rest, the whole drama of the emergence of oceans and continents,
the appearance of the sun-controlled day and the moon-ruled night,
cereals and fruit trees upon the earth, creatures of the deep and of the
dry land, and finally the man and the woman whom he created is magnificently outlined. Here is seen in action the God of order, cosmic power, intelligent purpose, and holy personality. He is a transcendent God,
operating not within the process but outside of it, securing his preconceived ends by decree and simple utterance. "God said, 'Let there be
light!' And there was light!" (Gen. 1:3-4.)

The writer of Isa. 40–55 was strongly influenced by the Babylonian
thought prevailing in the land of the Exile. From the literature of
this land he must have gathered quantities of material dealing with
the creative function of Marduk and other Babylonian deities. This
served his purpose exceedingly well when he desired to urge upon his
people the infinite superiority of Yahweh over other so-called deities.
This superiority was particularly noteworthy when the question of the
deity's relation to the natural and social order was considered. The
prophet of the Exile triumphantly announced the supreme power of
his God as seen in his acts of Creation:

Do you not know? do you not hear?
Has it not been told you from the beginning?

Have you not understood since the foundation of the earth?
It is he who sits enthroned above the circle of the earth,
So high that its inhabitants are like grasshoppers;
Who stretches out the heavens like a curtain,
And spreads them like a tent to dwell in. (Isa. 40:21-22.)

Or again,

Lift up your eyes on high,
And see! who created these [heavenly bodies],
Leading out their host by number,
And calling them all by name—
Through the greatness of his might,
And the strength of his power,
Not one is missing? (40:26.)

Note the skill in debate shown by this writer as he subtly alludes to the astrological deities—the heavenly bodies—and states that his God made them, so they come at his beck and call.

This chapter in Isaiah is worth further attention, because it shows an important *religious value* in the concept of Creation. The author of this material does not recite the creative deeds of his God in order to satisfy a logical need for a complete discussion of the concept of God. His main interest is religious. The God who creates and has created continues to work among men in the re-creation and renewal of their lives. "The Creator of the ends of the earth" never gets weary or faint. On the contrary, he gives power to those who need it, even to the young men who grow tired and give up the struggle.

They that wait on the Lord shall renew their strength,
They shall put forth wings like eagles,
They shall run and not be weary,
They shall walk and not faint. (40:31.)

The power to create the universe is also the power that can renew the spirits of disheartened men. This truth may be seen again and again in the Old Testament, but particularly in the book of Isaiah. The Lord, who is creator of the heavens and the earth, who gave and gives life to its inhabitants, continues his creative work by selecting his servant to open the eyes of the blind, to liberate those who are in prison, and to be a light to the nations. (42:5-7).

The purpose of God's creation of Israel is indicated in still another chapter in Second Isaiah. The nation which he loves will be protected

44

and guarded in the future as in the past. And at long last God will restore his exiled people from every part of the earth to the land of Palestine.

> I will say to the north, "Give up!"
> And to the south, "Hold not back!
> Bring my sons from afar,
> And my daughters from the end of the earth—
> Every one who is called by my name,
> Whom I have created and formed
> And made for my glory." (43:6-7.)

Creation — for the glory of God.

The creation of his people has been brought about for the sake of the glory of God. It was not by chance but the result of a divine purpose which envisioned the selection of a holy people from the sons of Creation. This people was to become a living witness to the saving power of God. This is the explicitly expressed religious meaning of Creation to the writer of Isa. 40–55 and the implied meaning of many other biblical writers who deal with the concept at all.

In the book of Job the use of the idea of Creation varies with the purpose of the author as he presents different interpretations of his central problem through his dramatis personae. Job himself is made to dwell much upon God's creative power as he searches for a God who can help him. He may ask how a man can be right with God, who

> removes mountains, they know not how,
> Who overturns them in his anger;
> Who shakes the earth from its place,
> And its pillars are shattered;
> Who speaks to the sun, and it does not rise. (9:5-7.)

⑤ Creator controls natural order

Only the creator God could so impressively control the natural order. Job continues his complaint and says that even though he were innocent, how could mortal man speak to this kind of a God? His friend Bildad tells him that God's power over nature is so great that mere man should not attempt to understand it. The mighty power observed by man as he looks upon the natural order is only a partial indication of the Creator's amazing activity.

> Behold these are the outskirts of his way;
> And how slight a whisper do we hear of him!
> But the thunder of his power, who could comprehend? (25:14.)

God's power as creator and controller of nature is incomprehensible, so that man cannot fully understand. Under these circumstances he might as well admit his intellectual limitations. The plain purpose of the Yahweh speeches in the last part of the book is to impress Job—and all men—with his utter inability to fathom the ways of God in nature. God is made, in these speeches, to hurl at this poor man a veritable bombardment of unanswerable questions regarding the foundations of the earth; the boundaries of the seas, the mystery of light and dawn; the nature of snow, hail, and rain; the movements of the constellations; and the strange habits of wild beasts; some of which still stump the modern scientist. No wonder Job finally replies,

> Behold, I am insignificant; what can I answer thee?
> I put my hand over my mouth. (40:4.)

In the teaching of the prophets, except where allusions to nature are used metaphorically in order to make a point, they frequently serve to show the terrible and righteous anger of God upon Israel. The pride of man is to be brought low in the Day of the Lord, as will everything else that is haughty and high, including the cedars of Lebanon, the oaks of Bashan, the high mountains, the hills, and the ships of Tarshish (Isa. 2:11-16). In the Song of the Vineyard it is said that God will remove its hedge and will command the clouds not to rain upon it (5:5-6). Because of Israel's pollution of her land through shameless intimacy with sacred prostitutes, the showers have been withheld and the spring rain has not been allowed to fall, we read in Jeremiah (3:2-3). In fact, the whole earth is envisioned as a chaos by the prophet as he meditates upon the nation's evil conduct. The earth is a chaos, the mountains are quaking; the birds have disappeared, and the cities are desolate (4:23-26). For Amos the moral order and the natural order are one. The righteousness of God may cause drought and famine to come upon certain areas (4:6-11), and rain and abundance of food to be experienced elsewhere. The Creator makes use of nature, not just to sustain life, but to vindicate his righteousness.

This is also the purpose of the divine control of nature in the apocalyptic sections of the Old Testament. The awful drama of a world upheaval is characteristic of this type of writing. In Isa. 24 it is related that on the day of the Lord the earth will crack and break asunder; it will reel like a drunkard; and the sun and moon will hide their light. The apocalypse in Zechariah says that nature will be transformed: "It shall come to pass, in that day, that there shall be neither heat, nor cold, nor frost. And there shall be continuous day . . . ; there shall be light

46

at night-time." (14:6-7.) Before this change occurs, the Mount of Olives will be split in two (14:4). The well-known description in Joel needs no elaboration. Portents in heaven and on earth are mentioned; there will be blood and fire and smoke. The sun will become dark and the moon will look like blood (2:30-31). These cosmic accompaniments to the coming of salvation must be understood as the dramatic setting for the appearance of the God of judgment, who is also the God of creation and the ruler over nature.

The method of creation had little or no importance to the biblical writers. Such matters as *creatio ex nihilo,* creation by fiat, or creation through an evolutionary process, were of no interest to these men. Even though they had possessed the appropriate vocabulary and thought forms, such matters would have seemed irrelevant. Their interest lay in those areas of experience in which divine help for the Israelitish community could become available. God's choice of the nation, the establishment of the covenant, the people's violation of this covenant, the punishment which ensued, as well as the hope for a glorious future preoccupied them. The concept of Creation deepened their sense of dependence upon God, quickened their conscience as they realized that sin was sin against the Creator of all, and gave them hope that the power of the Creator could redeem them from evil. There was also the idea—to be discussed in Chapter 3—that the Creator in his creation of man had granted the latter a measure of his own spirit, thus making both moral obedience and worship possible.

The cited biblical passages make it possible to come to definite conclusions as to the nature of God as creator. The material is largely self-explanatory. Man and the universe are contingent upon the fact of God. They derive their existence from him. They are consequently not self-sufficient or self-contained. They have meaning and value—if we follow this reasoning—only in the light of their relation to him. Nature cannot be explained except by positing the prior existence of God. It expresses his power and his purposes, among which are the provision of a home for man and a means of promoting his ethical-spiritual maturity. Thus the concept of Creation is largely religious in its import; cosmological considerations are definitely subordinated to this interest.

This idea of the creator God, as is true also of the holy and personal God, has meaning only in relation to the total concept of God and to the other individual aspects of the divine nature. We have discussed the concept of God as reflecting a Being who is living, personal, holy, spiritual, as well as creative. These several ways of viewing God may be integrated into a religiously meaningful and logical whole by present-

47

ing this Being's creative capacity as the historical means whereby he projected himself into the world of nature and men for the purpose of expressing his entire self. The living God is, of course, a creating and a creative God. Life on all levels tries to perpetuate and propagate itself. The divine life sets the example and provides the impulse for this process by the activity involved in Creation. Creation is the extension of the life of God, and it takes its highest form when it makes possible the life of persons. If God is personal, then his most distinctive act of Creation is the creation of man, who is like him in sharing his personal nature. The holy God is creative. Holiness in association with personal and spiritual traits denotes the transcendent power which enables God to act as God, and not as man, in creating both the world and human beings. While men may act creatively, they can never rival God and form a universe of matter, energy, and ethical values. In this area theirs is the task of discovery and application rather than creation. God, not man, is the creator in the ultimate sense. The power and majesty which guarantee this may be indicated by the word holiness.

THE ONE GOD

The final concept here submitted in the study of the meaning of God is that of unity. We must reject the easy evolutionism which sorts out the records, arranges them in neat piles on the basis of decisions as to dates, and finds a convincing illustration of development from animism to absolute monotheism, with all the stages from polydaemonism to henotheism in between. Aside from the difficulty of dating many of the documents—and for some of them the problem is becoming increasingly complicated—many of the books present a bewildering juxtaposition of highly advanced and relatively undeveloped ideas in the same general context. Of course this is due in part to the intense scribal and editorial activity to which all of the canonical books were subjected over longer or shorter periods of time. This confusing admixture of material is also explicable on the basis of the biblical writers' comparative indifference to the principle of logical consistency. For our purpose the prominent emphases in each book have been selected, in the belief that this method will give a fair picture of the situation as it prevailed in Israel's religious consciousness throughout much of its history.

The concept of the oneness of God was not reached primarily through logical analysis by Hebrew thinkers; their approach was pragmatically religious and experience centered. The life and *social experience* of the community, with its inner tensions and its relations to other

48

groups, made up the historical ground for the achievement of monotheism. The great doctrine of modern Judaism as of biblical Judaism, drawn from Deuteronomy—"Listen, O Israel; the Lord is our God, the Lord alone" (6:4)—was not formulated except as the result of prolonged and decisive acquaintance with this particular Deity. Undoubtedly the leadership of Moses, the work of the great prophets, and the faith of the many anonymous believers in ancient Israel helped to shape this doctrine. Loyalty to this God and the observable and desirable consequences of this loyalty, in the form of prosperity, long life, inner strength, victory in battle, social stability, and the like, strengthened the position of Israel's God in the community and tended to make his worship increasingly exclusive.

In much of the Old Testament Israel's primary dependence upon the one God, whose personal name was Yahweh, is either directly stated or clearly implied. Whether we examine the early Yahwist narrative, the other documents of the Pentateuch, the prophetic books, or the later literature, we may readily detect the importance to Israel of this God. Traces of less advanced beliefs and practices—of relative unconcern for a picture of Yahweh worship—may be discerned in the early poems, law codes, legends, and other literary fragments found in the corpus Genesis–Kings. For example, the teraphim upon which Rachel sat in order to hide these household gods from her father (Gen. 31:34) and the ephod and teraphim in the shrine of Micah the Ephraimite (Judg. 17:4-5) show that polytheism was present as far as these accounts are concerned.

Various writers try to explain how Israel came to worship their God and to call him by his name Yahweh. The appearance in the book of Exodus of two such explanations, found in the Elohistic (3:13-15) and the priestly (6:3) sources, precludes any assumption that Israel had always adhered to the God Yahweh. But there is no need to press the point as to the existence of a precedent polytheism any further. The conspicuous fact remains that the biblical records predominantly testify to the centrality of Yahweh as the God of Israel. This God, as defined and depicted in the Old Testament, exhibits a unity of nature in many of the documents, behind which obviously lies a history of interest to both the historian and the critical theologian. Let us note not so much the history as the forces determining it.

One of the factors leading to the idea of the unity of the divine nature may be called the religious, using this term in a broad social-cultural sense. Elmer A. Leslie in his book *Old Testament Religion* develops the thesis that this religion at its best came about as the result of the

49

conflict between prophetic Yahwism and Canaanite *baalism,* the former receiving sharper and clear definition through pressure from the latter. While this interpretation of Israel's religion betrays a tendency toward oversimplification, it nonetheless does emphasize an important means of understanding the unity of God. The creative impact of baalism upon the worship of Israel's God deserves further exploration.

To identify the nature of this impact, a short description of baalism will be in order. The term baalism comes from the word "baal," the name of the numerous gods of fertility widely worshiped in Palestine before the Hebrews arrived and after they had established themselves in that land. The baals symbolized the entire agricultural-commercial economy and may even be regarded as the symbol of a strongly material-istic and naturalistic world view. They were therefore not simply gods whose idols received adoration, sacrifices, and petitions for crops and children. They really stood for a powerful culture firmly entrenched in Palestine and widely supported by powerful financial and political in-terests. The fact that baalism catered to man's sensual and lustful na-ture by its appeal to sex did not weaken its popularity by any means. It is not surprising that this religious culture made serious inroads upon the worship of Yahweh.

In opposition to baalism stood the culture and religion of Yahweh worship, centering in a God of the simple, desert-dwelling, seminomadic community, who was probably first encountered by the early Hebrews in the land of Midian. Yahweh represented tribal justice and austerity in personal conduct. Life in the desert nurtured frugality and self-denial and a religion that was simple and stern. When this religion was trans-lated by the prophets into the language of Israel's experience in the settled life of Palestine, it retained much of its original character, es-pecially its conceptions of justice and freedom. But exposed as it con-stantly was to the voluptuous and seductive baalism, with all of the latter's economic and sensual allurements, the religion of Yahweh was threatened with corruption and even with the loss of its true identity. Thus it was that baalism was bitterly attacked by Yahweh's champions —the prophets—and fiercely repudiated. In this process it was inevitable that the conception of God should be affected.

First of all, the God of Israel took over certain of the functions of the baals. Hosea makes the revolutionary pronouncement:

> She [Israel] did not know
> That is was I [Yahweh] who gave her
> The grain and the wine and the oil. (2:8.)

Here, without fanfare or elaborate introduction, Hosea calmly announces that Yahweh, not the baals, is the giver of agricultural abundance. So the God of the desert becomes the God able to meet the needs of men in an agricultural community and economy. The process of assimilation is not confined to this one function, it should be noted. The political power of the baals, which at times were consulted by the heads of the state, was gradually transferred to the God who had come from the desert. Whenever the kings and diplomats consulted the priests of the baals, they were ill advised in matters of foreign policy, the prophets declare. Thus

> Ephraim has become like a silly dove, without sense;
> They call to Egypt, they go to Assyria. (Hos. 7:11.)

The results are disastrous. Only through firm trust in the God Yahweh can the nation be saved from military and political defeat. But, declares Isaiah,

> If you do not believe [in Yahweh's power],
> Surely you shall not be established. (7:9.)

The very process of denunciation directed against the baals was also a process of stabilization and unification as far as the nature of Israel's God was concerned. This denunciation, often bitingly satirical, turned the Israelites whom it convinced from the baals and from the baalized worship of Yahweh. Their faith was purged of baalism, and the God of their fathers was seen in a truer light as the possessor of every necessary quality for saving his people. The baals were called "broken cisterns" (Jer. 2:13), "a stock" or "a stone" (2:27); their worshipers were denounced as "pampered horses, lusty stallions" (5:8), "a wild ass . . . sniffing the wind in her passion" (2:24). These so-called gods "are altogether stupid and senseless" (10:8). A baal is a "fat bull" (Hos. 4:17).

> Samaria's calf [made of wood]
> Shall become splinters! (8:6.)

The men of Israel made molten images and then sacrificed to them— "men kissing calves" (13:2).

The corollary of this ridicule of the baals is the glorification of Yahweh, who thus becomes the great and only God of Israel. In the passage in which he scoffs at the baals as stupid, Jeremiah hails the incomparable God:

There is none like thee, O Lord!
Thou art great, and thy name is great in might.
Who would not reverence thee, O King of the nations? (10:6-7.)

The degree of the ridicule of other gods marks the intensity of the writer's faith in Yahweh. Only as the soul of the champion of this God is caught up by a sense of the greatness and grandeur of the Being he worships does he have a strong desire to overthrow other gods. The deeply devout man is the most ardent opponent of baalistic paganism. Love makes exclusive demands. The object of supreme love is one and not many. The redeemer is the Holy *One* of Israel (Isa. 41:14). The first commandment is religiously and psychologically necessary, for God as the supreme object of love and worship must be a single being; there can be no competitors for this exalted position (Exod. 20:3).

In addition to the religious factor which influenced the determination of the unity of Israel's God the *ethical factor* is also a decisive one. Righteousness is uniquely an attribute of God. It is known that other gods in the history of religion are acclaimed as righteous, but the term in such instances has a different meaning. It may merely suggest victory or triumph measured by popular expectation and hope. In Israel the meaning is radically different. God as an ethical being has an independent will against which men and nations may be broken if they see fit to defy it. This will is not subject to the whims and vagaries of mortal men, because it belongs to the Creator of the whole earth, whose holiness guarantees the accomplishment of his purposes in human history and even beyond history. These purposes are self-consistent in their unification around a common center—the divine selection of Israel for the redemption of the world. This selection is ethical in that it demands reciprocity on the part of Israel, and the redemption is also ethical through the use of judgment and repentance. What we have, then, is actually a single purpose, a single will, a single ethical being, and a God who is one. In this way the moral experience of men as they reacted to the righteous God and were made aware of the authority and the rigor of his ethical demands led to a realization that he was transcendently good and the sole source of life's highest values.

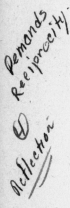

Israel's ethical and religious experience could not have produced the idea of one God apart from more or less self-conscious *reflection* upon the problem of monotheism. Although such reflection is not prominent in the literature of Israel, except in the wisdom writings, it is certainly not entirely absent. It is definitely a third factor in the appearance of an articulate monotheism. As he reflects upon the meaning of critical events in contemporary history, the prophet of the Exile, Second Isaiah, observes the military successes of Cyrus the Persian and draws certain theological conclusions therefrom. Clamorous voices were publishing the news of this event and hailing various gods as its instigators. The prophet was compelled to scrutinize the premises of his own theism and to weigh in the balances of his reason the conflicting claims of the followers of these deities. Which god was in fact the Lord of history? Was it not reasonable to suppose that the mighty Marduk, lord of Babylonia, had brought to pass this world-shaking event? Were not the mythologies current in Babylonia logical interpretations of the nature and function of the gods, among whom Yahweh was not included? Had not the inadequacy and indeed the inferiority of the prophet's God received a terrible and humiliating demonstration in the recent defeat of Judah and fall of Jerusalem?

This reasoning as to the meaning of events resulted in the Old Testament's most unqualified assertions as to the uniqueness and the unity of the God of Israel.

He is the true God—

.   .   .   .

"I am the Lord,
and there is no other. (Isa. 45:18.)

Was it not I the Lord—

.   .   .   .

none apart from me?

.   .   .   .

For I am God, and there is no other." (45:21-22.)

There is but one God in the whole universe, and he is the Lord, God of Israel. Other gods have no real existence whatsoever. This positive statement accurately conveys the conclusion reached by a critical mind preoccupied with world events and his people's predicament. The truth which it proclaims fittingly concludes our discussion of the belief in a *List* God who is living and personal, spiritual and holy, righteous and *Summary* unique. For characteristics of God which are closely related to his function as savior the reader may turn to Chapter 5, "Salvation in the Old Testament," where such concepts as grace, kindness, love, and forgiveness are discussed. While they might have been included in this chapter, they appear in their most meaningful light when presented as indications of God's part in the work of salvation. Such a division of the material dealing with the nature of God can be justified on the ground that it is closer to the empirical nature of Israel's religious thinking.

3. The Nature of Man

IN 1942 there appeared the book *The Bible Is Human,* by Louis Wallis, a sociologist, who in previous volumes had attempted to interpret the Old Testament from the standpoint of socio-economic theory. Surprisingly enough the aim of this book is to identify the reality of God in the history of Israel. The same title might serve to cover the content of this part of the discussion on the nature of man in the Old Testament. Certainly the Old Testament *is* human. Its pages pulsate with the throbbing life of its colorful characters. Their robust deeds and virile, uninhibited conduct, so frankly recounted, amply demonstrate that man is very much alive in this literature. In books regarded as sacred by many millions of people and revered as the revealed word of God is to be found also the word of man. Man in the Bible is not the man of conventional Christian art—dressed in spotless garments with an expressionless face, and usually posing in a lifeless manner in the foreground of a somewhat dreary landscape. On the contrary, man is sketched with vivid realism and absolute honesty. Possibly this realism of the Bible, which projects with cogency and power both the nature of the highest that can be known about the universe and the unvarnished truth about man, is the reason for its effectiveness in confronting men with themselves and with God.

In this collection of ancient writings is the march of time—time replete with dramatic history. This history is highly personal, for it devotes its attention to many individuals of both sexes, who occupied positions of importance in the nation, or who responded to an inner call and followed the vision of God. The procession of humanity is epitomized in this story. Kings and commoners, saints and sinners, politicians and priests, prophets and prostitutes, patriots and traitors, great and small appear in this moving panorama. Here we find Adam, who in yielding to his wife disobeyed God and was cursed with toil and death; the wife herself, who found it impossible to resist the temptation with its triple enticement—was not the fruit of the forbidden tree palatable, attractive in color, and the likely source of new experiences?—and Cain, who in a fit of jealous anger killed his brother. Here too is Jacob, the conniver and lover, whose love of a good bargain was redeemed by his patient love of Rachel; and Rachel herself, who comically sat upon the teraphim which she had stolen from her father and excused herself for not dismounting, and thus disclosing the gods beneath, on the plea that "the ailment common to women" was upon her.

In this procession of humanity belong Joseph, who foolishly divulged his adolescent dreams of superseding his older brothers and was sold into slavery for his pains, only to rise to a position of authority which permitted him to rescue his family from famine; and Moses, self-conscious about his lack of fluency in speech, but a man of murderous anger when he witnessed the mistreatment of one of his countrymen at the hands of an Egyptian. Stupid, swashbuckling Samson, the border ruffian of the clan of Dan, who excelled equally in his bouts with women and with Philistine warriors, but who rose to heroic heights in his self-inflicted death, which destroyed many Philistines and ruined their temple, comes alive on the pages of the Bible; as do Deborah, arousing the laggard Hebrew tribes and leading them to a great victory over the Canaanites; and Jephthah, fulfilling his vow to the God who had given him victory by sacrificing his own daughter. The young Moabite widow who would not forsake her mother-in-law, and whose story gives the lie to all mother-in-law stories by manifesting a memorable love and loyalty, belongs here too; as does Hannah, who prayed at Shiloh for a son; and Michal, of a later period, who scorned her royal husband because he stripped himself and danced in public before the ark of the Lord.

It is a long procession, and we cannot ignore the young men David and Jonathan, whose mutual love caused the untimely death of the latter to wring these words from the lips of David, "O Jonathan! by your death am I mortally wounded" (II Sam. 1:25); or the youthful folly of the young ruler Rehoboam, who refused to heed the plea of the elders of the northern tribes that he adopt a democratic policy for his reign. The figures of Jezebel, the queen of Israel, and Elijah, the raging prophet who hated her, are also visible. The latter's precipitous flight to Mount Horeb after a successful showdown with the priests of Baal at Mount Carmel betrays the ebbing of his courage; and Jezebel's death upon the paving stones of the court at Jezreel marks the gruesome end of her proud career. There in the drama is Micaiah ben Imlah, the only man of God among hundreds brave enough to tell the undesired truth to the king. We see Amos, the shepherd, thundering out against King Jeroboam his word of judgment; and Hosea, daring to marry a prostitute to make his religious message convincing.

It becomes clear that this procession never ends, for it is the procession of humanity. It is a procession which will not end until history ceases. This is man as he is—and as all men are. It is not a touched-up and posed portrait; it is a candid-camera shot, taken when biblical man was too busy fulfilling his mission to be concerned about the imperfections of the record.

MAN IN RELATION TO HIS GROUP

As we study biblical man from a closer vantage point, we may more precisely analyze his nature and discover its distinctive features. First of all, man as we find him in the Bible exists not so much in his own right and by his own decisions as in his relation to his group and through its traditions and customs. His whole being is inextricably bound up with the life of the entire community. Hence man appears as a corporate personality rather than as an individual. Such social entities as family, clan, tribe, and nation must be examined if man is to be understood. It is significant that Adam is both the name of the chief human actor in the story of the Garden of Eden and the Hebrew word for mankind. Pure individuality is not found in the Old Testament; what looms large in biblical thinking is the social entity wherein each man may find the only kind of self-realization—if that term may be used—of which he has any knowledge, namely, *the welfare of the community* to which he belongs.

The patriarchal narratives in Genesis provide an example of this emphasis upon the value of the community for interpreting man. While scholars are not in entire agreement, many are on record as asserting the probability that each patriarch is actually a tribe or clan, and that the personal form of the stories is the result of literary adaptations of the material to the interests of the storyteller. This view gains support from the hints or even flat statements in the Bible itself. We may note the words "Esau (that is, Edom)" in the story of Jacob and Esau (Gen. 36:1). Although the words "that is, Edom" are probably an explanatory gloss inserted to identify Esau as a nation, they nevertheless show an accepted practice of specifying a nation by naming its supposed ancestor. The language of another passage (Gen. 10) strengthens this view. Here the so-called individual descendants of Noah are given names which are used elsewhere for nations. For instance, "the descendants of Ham were Cush, Egypt, Put, and Canaan. . . . The sons of Shem were Elam, Assyria." (10:6, 22.) Every member of a clan group shares the consequences of the conduct of its individual members. This is particularly seen when a sin has been committed. Guilt and punishment are not confined to the actual perpetrators. The ties of blood and corporate personality which unite them require them all to suffer. As an illustration of the application of this principle the sin of the four men of the Korahite group may be noted (Num. 16:1-35). Their leader Korah and three of his followers dared to defy Moses and to challenge his authority as Israel's leader. As a consequence of this act of rebellion God caused the earth to open and to swallow up all the men of Korah, including their households. In the modern sense it is obvious that not all of those punished were guilty. In the biblical sense, on the other hand, they all were guilty through the effect of the concept of collective personality. A modern parallel may be found in the law's treatment of a corporation as a personality. In the story of Korah's fate the collective punishment administered was extended to the members of the families of the guilty parties.

This horizontal extension of guilt and punishment may be compared with its vertical extension in the case of Saul's family (II Sam. 21:1-9). As was customary, the coming of a famine became the occasion for consulting God to determine its cause. When David made inquiry of God, perhaps through an oracle, he received this answer, "It is for Saul and his bloody house, because he put to death the Gibeonites" (21:1). So it became incumbent upon David to make amends for the deed of his predecessor, Saul. He called for a conference certain Gibeonites, who made haste to say that they would not be satisfied with a gift of money, neither could they inflict the appropriate penalty—the shedding of blood—without the consent of David. If the king permitted it, however, they would be appeased by the surrender to them of the seven surviving sons of Saul. This was done; the sons were hanged, and presumably the famine was ended. Here the sins of their father were visited upon the next generation, which, according to Oriental notions, had inherited their father's guilt and must suffer the consequences.

There was both a positive and a negative side to the vertical solidarity of the community as understood by the writers of the Old Testament. The community was blessed as well as cursed by reason of the behavior of its members, generation after generation. Anthropologists readily find in this literature numerous parallels to the customs of other ethnic communities. Conformity with tribal mores is so deeply imbedded in the nervous systems of the members of the group that violations are looked upon with horror. The shock caused by the realization that a violation has been committed has been known to cause death. In Israel, God is regarded as the defender and preserver of the

57

community's solidarity and is both judge and executioner when a transgression occurs. He is also the giver of prosperity and well-being when conformity with traditional standards and mores prevails. In the Deuteronomic version of the Decalogue this God announces that this is his function: "for I, the Lord your God, am a jealous God, punishing children for the sins of their fathers, to the third or fourth generation of those who hate me, but showing grace to the thousandth generation of those who love me and keep my commands." (Deut. 5:9-10.) In this case the results are determined, not primarily by conformity to custom, rather by a particular kind of attitude toward God. No matter which of the two attitudes is adopted, the results are far-reaching.

Having dealt thus far largely with the effect of the idea of corporate personality upon the welfare of the community, we may now observe its relation to man's *religious life*. In the worship of God and in the experience of his presence the Hebrew individual and the community respond and react as a single entity in situations frequently occurring in the Old Testament. So thoroughly has the individual's life been conditioned by the fact of a powerful community consciousness in which personal desire and individual ambition are subordinated that his search for the highest takes forms dictated by community patterns. This is true, even though specially gifted individuals may break with one community on religious and ethical grounds and proceed to create another. The prophet who attacks rampant secularism and hurls his invectives even at kings is surely an unconventional nonconformist, openly repudiating his group and all that it represents. In a sense this is true; yet we should look for such a prophet's motive. It appears to lie in his desire to revive what he holds to be an ancient way of life permeated with the spirit of justice and devotion to God. This is the genuine pattern for constituting the true community of God, which he conceives as having existed in the past and as being a possibility for the future.

> When Israel was a child, I came to love him,
> And from Egypt I called him. (Hos. 11:1.)
>
> You only have I known,
> Of all the families of the earth. (Amos 3:2.)
>
> But do you return to your God,
> Practice kindness and justice,
> And wait for your God constantly. (Hos. 12:6.)

The nation is urged to *return* to God and once again to be just and kind, as though this had been a previous condition of its life. The prophet denounces one type of community while working within the framework of another which is present by faith only. As a matter of plain fact, he is never completely detached from the physical group with which he lives. Its history, its hopes, its thought forms, and its destiny are largely his, no matter how radical his social criticism or how indignant his denunciation.

The problem of the authorship of the individual psalms is relevant to this question of man's corporate experience of religion. Should each psalm be associated with an individual author, or is the religious community to be named as its author? When the heart cry of Ps. 51 reaches our ears, do we hear Israel pleading with God,[1] or are we listening to the petition of a stricken soul deeply conscious of personal sin?

> Have pity on me, O God, in accordance with thy grace;
> In thine abundant mercy, wipe out my transgressions.
> Wash me thoroughly from my guilt,
> And cleanse me from my sin. (51:1-2.)

It can be maintained that years of national adversity, suffering, and spiritual hunger for Zion caused the emergence in exiled Israel of this poem, which expresses the heart hunger and spiritual sensitivity of a chastened and purified community. Under these conditions the first-person pronoun can be interpreted to mean the religious community, and not a particular person writing as an individual.

This psalm and other examples of devotional poetry in the Old Testament may be taken to reflect the spiritual experience of the worshiping community, developing through several generations, or even centuries in the case of the oldest psalms, and bearing the mark of intense struggle, debasing sin, and noble aspiration. In the use of this literature the individual became one with his group and shared the spirit which moved it, whether the mood of the moment was contrition, trust, or glad thanksgiving. He found himself, and he also found the God of his soul's desire through his unreserved participation in the acts of communal worship, whereby the rich resources and inspiring traditions of his people's history were made available to him.

The means devised by the Hebrews for the *preservation* of the group from disintegrating processes will suffice to show the importance

[1] For brief discussions of the collective authorship of this great penitential psalm consult: W. O. E. Oesterley, *The Psalms*, Vol. I, (1939); C. A. Briggs, *The Psalms*, Vol. I (International Critical Commentary, 1906); R. H. Pfeiffer, *Introduction to the Old Testament* (1941).

of the idea of collective or corporate man in the Old Testament. Their discussion will also help us to understand how difficult and slow was the process whereby the individual finally did emerge and achieve full self-awareness. The marriage pattern in ancient Israel was one of the means developed to promote the solidarity of the group. The bulk of the evidence points to the patriarchal form of family life. The father was the autocratic head of the family group. He had the power of life and death over his household. It is noteworthy that young Isaac did not demur when Abraham tied him to an altar and raised the sacrificial knife (Gen. 22). If he did raise objections, there is no record of them. The dignity of the father-ruler was violated when a son of Noah saw his drunken father's nakedness and communicated the fact to his two brothers (9:22). It isn't the drunken father, so thoroughly intoxicated that he shamelessly exposed himself, who is cursed, let it be noted. Canaan, whose father, Ham, saw Noah in the cave, is the object of the curse.

The father or head of the clan group has the power to enforce its regulations and to transmit his blessing to his sons. The basis of the contest between the twin brothers Jacob and Esau is the struggle to secure the blessing of the first-born from Isaac, their aged father. When such a blessing is given, it is irrevocable (27:37). By deception Jacob receives this blessing and becomes the founder of a great nation. Jacob's last will and testament as recited orally from his deathbed to his sons is a similar demonstration of the power of the patriarchal father (Gen. 49). In this scene the dying patriarch pronounces the fate and fortune of all of his sons. In spite of the uncomplimentary character of some of his remarks, such as his accusation that Reuben committed incest, the poem is followed by a notation that "he blessed them."

Marriage was endogamous rather than exogamous. Great pains were taken to insure marriage with members of the Hebrew group. When Abraham was old, he sent his most trusted slave to his own land to secure a wife for his son Isaac. He made this servant swear not to marry his son to a "daughter of the Canaanites" (24:3). In the same manner Isaac instructed his son Jacob to marry a cousin, a daughter of his uncle Laban (28:2). Profiting from the example of his brother Esau, who had married two Hittite women, Isaac doubtless sought to prevent similar conduct on the part of his other son. Marriage within the family or clan was thus the rule and not the exception. By this practice purity of blood could be maintained. Furthermore, and doubtless of even greater importance, traditional social patterns and religious practices could be preserved and perpetuated. Danger of group disintegration was greatly minimized. Patriarchal control of the group and marriage to blood kin only combined to create effective resistance to hostile attacks from without and from within.

Since it is the subject of rather extensive treatment in Chapter 5, the matter of the covenant experience of Israel will not be stressed here. It is, however, one means of holding the community together. Pervading the Old Testament is the belief that Israel sustained a special relationship to God which had been inaugurated by a bilateral covenant or agreement freely made on the basis of mutual understanding. This covenant was concrete evidence of God's promise to bless the nation which he had chosen. The assurance of the fulfillment of this promise was contained in the legal requirements which God had laid down. Performance of these guaranteed the favor of God. From the anthropological standpoint their performance also assured the survival of the community's culture and customs, for these were bound up with religion. Beyond this, the survival of the group itself was made possible.

By constant reference to this covenant and its ethico-legal demands, Israel fixed its attention upon a common history, a common practice, and a common hope. The history was dominated by the event of Israel's election; the practice centered in obedience to God, which involved all the interests and relationships of life; and the hope was for the realization of the divine promises. By this fixation of attention the community became conscious of itself, its peculiar relationship to God, and its special destiny. This made it all the more compact and closely integrated. Under these circumstances it was inevitable that biblical man should, for all practical purposes, be co-extensive with the biblical community. It would be absurd to deny him personal consciousness and thoughts, desires, fears belonging to him alone. It is claimed that these find their biblical expression through group media which are so effective that apart from them the individual must remain largely unknown.

"MAN AS A CREATURE"

We have seen biblical man as peculiarly involved in, and identified with, his group. Another prominent indication of his nature is his creatureliness. Man is a creature sharing the weakness and limitations of all creatures. He is flesh and so is subject to sickness and death.

> Man, that is born of woman,
> Is of few days and full of trouble.

Like a blossom he comes forth and is withered,
And he flees like the shadow and does not endure.

(Job 14:1-2.)

A man's days are like the grass.
Like a flower of the field, so he blossoms;
For the wind passes over it, and it is not.

(Ps. 103:15-16.)

"My spirit must not remain in man forever, inasmuch as he is flesh." (Gen. 6:3.) Being flesh, mankind is weak, and God is powerful. If a man trusts in God, he need not fear men, who are but flesh (Ps. 56:4). God shows his mercy by pardoning guilt when he remembers that men are flesh and therefore weak and helpless (78:38-39). Men are flesh in contrast with God, who is spirit (Isa. 31:3). For this reason reliance upon man is futile. All flesh is like withering grass, a fading flower, which is destroyed when the wind of the desert blows upon it, but the word of God endures forever (40:6-8). In this last passage the poet seems to rejoice in the frailty of human flesh in order to glorify the everlasting God.

The weakness of man in comparison with the power of God is again brought out in the Chronicler's history of Sennacherib's invasion of Judah. King Hezekiah reassures the people and tells them to be strong and of good courage, for they have on their side a greater power than the Assyrian. "With him is an arm of flesh, but with us is the Lord our God to help us and to fight our battles." (II Chr. 32:8.) Jeremiah accepts this concept of flesh when he cries,

Cursed is the man who trusts in man,
And makes flesh his arm of strength,
His mind being turned from the Lord! (17:5.)

Man is thus undependable, not because of sinfulness, but because in him is weakness inherent in his nature as creature participating in the frailty of all created beings.

Man's relation to animals dooms him to inescapable limitations and to frequent disappointments in his attempt to transcend them. The fact of the relation is indisputable. Fish, sea monsters, birds, reptiles, wild and domestic beasts, and man were alike created by God. In the first Creation story the process of Creation is evidently the same. God molded man from the dust of the earth, and then he made beasts and birds from the ground (Gen. 2:7, 19). "When the Lord saw that the wickedness of man on the earth was great, . . . [he] said, "I will blot the men that I have created off the face of the ground, both men and animals, reptiles, and birds of the air; for I regret that I ever made them." (6:5-7.) Men and animals are included in the same condemnation and judgment. After the flood is over, the establishment of the covenant of the rainbow is attended by a statement that God will remember his covenant, which he has made with man and with "every living creature of every sort" (9:15). The flood will never occur again. Obviously, the similarity of the fate of man and animals, who perished together in the flood, is connoted by these passages. Man and beast are equally perishable.

This view is emphasized in Ps. 49, whose author in a melancholy vein comments on the sad fate of all men, both the wise and the foolish. Even though a man accumulates wealth and possessions, he dies and leaves them to others. He suffers the same fate as an ox, which hasn't sense enough to know that it is mortal or to be troubled by the thought. Man is "like the beasts that perish" (49:12). The "gentle cynic" who, old and weary of soul, belatedly tries to solve the mystery of life concludes that the human family is subjected by God to the afflictions and monotonies of life that he may uncover man's beastlike nature. "It is that God may test them and see that they are beasts." (Eccl. 3:18.) He finds that man and beast suffer the same fate because they share the same breath of life. Both die. "All go to one place; all are from the dust, and all return to the dust." Who can prove the contrary, as some vainly try to do—that man's spirit goes upward and the beast's goes downward? When all is said and done, one is compelled to conclude that it is better to be a living dog than a dead lion (9:4). In this, man has a dubious advantage over the animals; for he at least, if living, knows that he will die. Beasts and dead men do not have this knowledge.

The close connection between man and animals makes them both children of nature. Man breathes the air which surrounds him; he reproduces his kind as do the animals; he partakes of food; he sleeps for the renewal of his strength; he wears clothing—perhaps the skins of animals—to protect his body; and he lives with his own kind for survival and companionship. In none of these activities does he differ greatly from the beasts of the field. A complete study of man might develop these points fully and outline how man for survival purposes created social, political, and technical instruments for the furtherance of his life. As a conscious organism struggling for existence, he should be depicted as one who makes all of the complicated adjustments demanded by his basic drives, which brought his civilization into existence. These are proper questions for investigation by the anthropologist and the historian, and the Old Testament is not devoid of interest in them.[2] To avoid an undue prolongation of this phase of the discussion, however, this most interesting avenue will not be explored.

MAN AS A THINKING BEING

Turning now to the next part of the outline, let us proceed to make an analysis of the psychology of biblical man. There are several Hebrew words that may be made the basis for a study somewhat akin to that made by modern psychologists when dealing with human beings today. These words are: *ruach* (spirit), *nephesh* (soul), *lev* or *levav* (heart, mind), and *basar* (body). It should be noted that the first of these words has received extensive treatment in Chapter 2. It is now examined to determine its bearing upon our understanding of biblical psychology.

When used of men, *ruach* has a wide range of meanings, from "breath" to "the spirit of prophecy." It may connote wind, air, gas, temper, disposition, vivacity, vigor, courage, anger, patience or impatience, spirit (bitterness of spirit), and the spirit of prophecy.[3] It is imparted by God (Zech. 12:1); it is the principle of life within man (Job. 27:3); it is preserved by God (10:12); it is the life of all human beings, which God holds in his hand (12:10); it is given by God to all people upon the earth (Isa. 42:5); God is the "God of the spirits [*ruach*] of all mankind" (Num. 16:22; 27:16); God "weighs the motives [*ruach,* plural]" of each man (Prov. 16:2). At death the *ruach* departs from man (Pss. 31:5; 78:39; 146:4; Job 17:1; 34:14; Eccl. 3:21; 12:7). In its departure it does not always return to the God who gave it. Occasionally it seems to be simply equivalent to the coming of death.

The writer of the late book of Ecclesiastes is puzzled by the mystery of the creation of the individual in the womb. He accepts the general belief that the spirit comes to man from God—perhaps his belief is influenced by Hellenistic philosophy—and, realizing the fact of conception and the growth of the fetus in the womb, informs his readers of their ignorance,

[2] See W. C. Graham, *The Prophets and Israel's Culture* (1935); C. C. McCown, *The Genesis of the Social Gospel* (1929); D. Jacobson, *The Social Background of the Old Testament* (1943).
[3] Brown, Driver, and Briggs, *Hebrew and English Lexicon of the Old Testament* (1907), pp. 924-26.

THE NATURE OF MAN

> You know not what is the way of the spirit
> Into the bones [4] in the pregnant womb. (11:5.)

Man has the spirit, but how he received it no one knows. Elsewhere (Isa. 57:16) it is stated that it is somehow through the activity of God that the spirit enters the bodies of men. The precise method of its entry remains unexplained. These writers were wrestling with the mind-body problem, which is of perennial philosophical and religious interest. Evidently they had as little success as modern writers with more impressive tools of research.

Without listing the rather numerous occurrences of the word *ruach* where it means a positive and powerful disposition expressing itself in a variety of ways, let us sum up with the statement that *ruach* is that element in human nature which is most closely connected with the nature of God. It is the endowment of man with the energy and the capacity for religious activity. Through its possession man may lift his face from the clod and turn to the eternal verities of truth, beauty, and goodness. The spirit in man enables him to hold communion with the spirit of God. This term suggests more than any other the content and meaning of the phrase "in the image of God" (Gen. 1:27).

Ruach, although God-given, is not mechanically implanted in the body of man. The biblical words which tell about the coming and the departure of the *ruach* are necessarily figurative, as must be any language that deals with supersensuous experience. Biblical psychology is not as close to the early modern faculty psychology as it is to the functional psychology of more recent date. When the concept of spirit appears, it appears in action, as the functioning of the total organism directed toward the display of courage, the manifestation of anger or self-control, the indication of bitterness of heart or of a jealous disposition (Josh. 5:1; Prov. 18:14; Ps. 76:12; Isa. 19:3; [5] also Judg. 8:3; Exod. 6:9; Gen. 26:34; Num. 5:14). It is called into use to denote the deeper emotional drives which move the self to act or to refrain from acting. In spite of this behavioristic emphasis the biblical sources are in agreement that *ruach* or spirit is a divine creation. It is never conceived as simply one of the ways in which the human organism functions in the presence of particular stimuli, as is the case with behavioristic thought.

The second psychological term is *nephesh,* variously translated as "soul, living being, life, self, person, desire, appetite, emotion, passion."

---

[4] Here and elsewhere regarded as the seat of life.
[5] Mostly negative examples of spirit as the seat of courage.

It is sometimes used to distinguish man's inner being from his body or flesh (Isa. 10:18; Deut. 12:23; Ps. 31:10; Job 14:22). At death the *nephesh* departs; when life is restored, it returns. So in the case of Rachel we read, "Just as her spirit [*nephesh*] left her (for she died), she called his name Benoni, but his father called him Benjamin" (Gen. 35:18; cf. Jer. 15:9; Job 11:20). In the book of Psalms (16:10; 30:3; 49:15; 86:13) and in Job (18:22, 28, 30; 33:18) a strong desire is expressed that the *nephesh* be delivered from Sheol, the place of death. These passages probably mean that their authors were seeking the postponement of death, not a recall of the soul from the underworld. In a large number of cases—seventy, to be exact—the word means man himself as a living being. It may also designate the emotions and desires of men, such as gloom, discontent, grief, rejoicing, and good cheer. This meaning, judging from the frequency of its use, is second only in importance to the meaning of life itself.

Again, it should be pointed out, the word under discussion does not refer to a thing in itself, a faculty of the mind subject to exact description. Instead it is a convenient symbol for the identification of the whole life of a man, more particularly in its affective and nonbodily form. This life is the self, distinguished not so much by having memory, reflection, or moral integrity as by having the principle of vitality, which disappears at death. The term means both biological and psychic life. The latter level is included, for the *nephesh* is the seat of the emotions and personal desires. It is not "soul" in the metaphysical Greek sense, where a sharp dichotomy is required. The *nephesh* is not ultimately separable from the living bodily organism, whereas the soul of classical Greek philosophy is thought to be.

The word translated commonly in the King James Version of the Bible as "heart" is another significant psychological term. This word, in Hebrew, is *lev* or *levav,* and its literal meaning is "heart." From the fact that the context often demands a translation meaning the seat of thought or of will, the translation "mind" is frequently more appropriate. The Hebrews, along with other peoples, thought of the psyche as residing, not in the brain, but in the heart, kidneys, liver, or bones. There was no hard and fast differentiation between the functions of these organs. In any case, *lev* was by far the most important. The familiar phrase "with all thy heart and with all thy soul"—in the American Translation one finds the reading "with all your mind and heart"—is a favorite of the Deuteronomists (Deut. 4:29; 6:5; 10:12; 11:13; 13:3; 26:16; 30:2, 6, 10; Josh. 22:5; I Kings 2:4; etc.). Here *levav* and *nephesh* are combined. In rendering these words in modern English, the translator has accurately caught the connotation of the Hebrew. *Levav* as the seat of thought and volition is compared with *nephesh* as the seat of emotional drives and of the affections.

Specific citations support the choice of the word "mind" as the best meaning for *levav*. The first comes from the pen of Isaiah, who as a spokesman for Yahweh speaks of Assyria as the rod of his wrath (10:5). This nation is executing the purposes of the Hebrew God without knowing it. It will spoil Israel and plunder the land in keeping with the divine will. Assyria is an unwitting instrument in the hands of the Almighty:

> But not so does he think,
> And not so does he plan;
> For destruction is in his mind,
> And to cut off nations not a few. (10:7.)

In his *levav*—used twice here—he has other plans, those of an imperialistic nation intent upon conquest and plunder. After reflection and careful planning on the part of its leaders this nation embarks upon a campaign which involves consideration of military personnel, food and equipment, invasion routes, the disposition of the enemy, and overall strategy. The psychological instrument of this thorough planning is the *levav* of individual Assyrians.

In David's prayer on behalf of his people he mentions the "thoughts of the heart" of his subjects (I Chr. 29:18). A psalmist speaks of the "imaginations of the heart" (73:7). Elsewhere the meaning of *lev* as indicating mental processes and purpose is confirmed. To Solomon, as a result of his humble prayer, God promises to give a "wise and discerning mind" (I Kings 3:12)—a wise heart, literally—the special purpose of which was judicial discernment as the judge-king tried the cases brought before him. An interesting reading is found in the story of Jacob's cleverness in getting away from Laban with a larger flock of sheep than the latter had counted on (Gen. 31:20). We are told, "Jacob outwitted Laban." A literal translation reads, "Jacob stole the mind [*lev*] of Laban." In other words, Jacob planned so cunningly that Laban was unable to circumvent him. In the book of Proverbs the intelligent man is called "the wise in heart" (16:21; cf. 18:15— both K.J.V.). God is said to have closed the *lev* of evil men against reason—that is, he gave them closed minds—in Job's bitter lament against God (17:4). These references, while not exhaustive, will demonstrate the meaning of *lev* as mind. Wherever this term appears, however, it also bears the meaning of volition and judgment. It is never the symbol for rational power alone.

Our study thus far permits the conclusion that biblical man, from the standpoint of a psychological approach to his nature, is a *unitary* being. He is body, spirit, self, feeling, mind, and heart. He is all of these, yet none of these in particular if one tries to identify him with any single category. He is all of these only as they are recognized as the varied evidences of his single nature. When they are viewed as mutually interdependent and as having little meaning in isolation from each other, they assume their true character. Man has reality in the Bible because he *is,* not because he is a spiritual being, a bodily organism, or a thinking-feeling center of consciousness. Israel's thinkers did not minimize man's power to conceive ends and to will them into being; neither did they glorify the body and its natural functions as ends in themselves. They achieved a balance between body and mind in their thinking about man which enabled them to avoid certain intellectual problems, and which confronted them with others just as difficult. They had no problem as to the sinfulness of matter, so that asceticism never arose as an influential movement in Israel. They did create the problem as to man's ultimate destiny beyond history, since body and soul must share the same fate in the absence of a real dualism as to human nature.

MAN AS AN ETHICAL BEING

No picture of biblical man can fail to incorporate a delineation of his ethical nature. Man is an ethical person, that is, a being capable of making moral choices in the light of alternatives, and of acting thereon. It is also possible for man to refuse to make choices considered by the community or conscience to be desirable, or to make wrong choices. Two typically biblical limitations upon this discussion of man as ethical come to mind. One is the fact of man's existence as a collective personality, and the other is the positive theistic focus of all biblical ethics. This means that our survey of the pertinent materials must be oriented toward these two propositions, if we are to avoid the criticism of modernization.

When man is observed as a corporate or collective personality, ethical consciousness and social consciousness are closely allied. Appeals to adhere to some ethical ideal are usually presented to the nation rather than to the individual, or possibly to particular groups within the nation. Amos addresses the wealthy women of Samaria, for example, and rebukes them for injustice. For him injustice and justice have real and serious social implications. A solitary good man is inconceivable, although Yahweh does call upon Jeremiah to look around in the streets of Jerusalem:

> Search her squares,
>> if you can find a man,
> One who does justice, and aims at honesty. (5:1.)

This language is rhetoric rather than ethical theory, however.

In the Old Testament the belief prevails that man is ethical. He *may* do justice and love mercy; he *may* repent and let righteousness flow down like a mighty stream; he *may* wash his hands of the blood of violence and cruelty and succor the widow and orphan; and he *may* substitute justice for bloodshed and righteousness for the cry of the afflicted. This conduct is within his reach. The very fact that Israel's ethical leaders—the prophets, the wise men, and the lawgivers—urge upon the people the doing of good shows their belief in its possibility. The stubborn resistance of power-holding groups in the nation to the summons to live righteously should not blind us to the reality of the ethical ideal advocated by these teachers of morality with such passionate insistence and devotion. In examining the nature of this ideal, we shall come closer to the man of the Bible, for and by whom it was conceived.

The practice of justice in the sanctuary, the gate, and the market place is man's ethical obligation. Amos, Hosea, Isaiah, Micah, and Jeremiah, as well as later prophets exhort men to do justly in their social and institutional life. Their writings are full of such exhortations. Even where denunciation takes the place of exhortation, as it often does, the same purpose of exalting the claims of justice and securing its embodiment in the national, urban, and rural community is apparent.

> They have sold the innocent for silver,
> And the needy for the sake of a pair of shoes.
> And they buffet the heads of the poor. (Amos 2:6-7.)

> Hear this word, you cows of Bashan,
> . . . .
> Who oppress the weak, who crush the needy. (4:1.)

> You trample upon the weak,
> And take from him the increase of his wheat. (5:11.)

> You who oppress the innocent, take bribes,
> And put aside the needy in the courts. (5:12.)

> Making the measure small and the price great,
> And changing false scales. (8:5.)

The system of land control and tenure should be brought under the control of justice also, because unrestrained greed is breaking up the holdings of the small farmer. Hear the cry of Micah:

> Woe to them who devise wrong,
> And work out wickedness upon their beds.
> In the morning light they do it,
> Because it is in their power.
> They covet fields and seize them,
> And houses, and carry them off.
> So they crush a yeoman and his house,
> A man and his possessions. (2:1-2.)

> For the sake of a mere trifle,
> You take a heavy mortgage. (2:10.)

> Her [Israel's] chiefs pronounce judgment for a bribe,
> And her priests declare oracles for hire,
> And her prophets divine for cash. (3:11.)

The entire social order is marked and corrupted by gross venality and avarice.

Isaiah joins with Amos and Micah in his negative and inferential support of the social ideal based upon justice. He too is interested in the protection of the small farmer, and lashes out against the unprincipled and ruthless foreclosure of mortgages:

> Ah! you who join house to house,
> And lay field to field,
> Till there is no more room,
> And you are left to dwell alone
>   in the midst of the land! (5:8.)

Note also the sarcasm in the following:

> Ah! the heroes at drinking wine,
> And the warriors at blending liquor;

> Who acquit the guilty for a bribe,
> And wrest the rights of the innocent from him!
> (5:22-23.)

Licentiousness assists greed in corrupting the local courts in Isaiah's day. Jeremiah's famous temple address strikes this note of strong ethical concern also. After telling the multitude how great was the folly of trusting in the temple for salvation in time of national peril the prophet continues:

> For only if you amend your ways and your doings—if you practice strict justice one toward another, if you keep from oppressing the resident alien, the orphan, and the widow, from shedding innocent blood in this place, and from following other gods to your own hurt—will I establish your home in this place. (7:5-7.)

In a positive vein these men challenge the nation, and especially leaders, to turn to justice as their goal and practice.

Seek good and not evil that you may live. (Amos 5:14.)

> Hate evil, and love good
> And establish justice in the court. (5:15.)

> Sow for yourselves righteousness;
> Reap the fruit of piety. (Hos. 10:12.)

> Do you return to your God,
> Practice kindness and justice,
> And wait for your God constantly. (12:6.)

> Cease to do evil, learn to do good;
> Seek justice, restrain the oppressor;
> Uphold the rights of the fatherless, defend the cause of
> the widow! (Isa. 1:17.)

In all of these poignant prophetic cries is a glimpse of a magnificent social vision. In them is foreshadowed the coming of justice for the innocent and the helpless poor, of personal decency and social responsibility for the wealthy, of honor and good faith among the judges, of honesty among merchants, and of a sense of integrity among realtors. When justice comes, men who have the power given by wealth and position will use it with a high feeling of obligation to the common good. Religious leaders, be they prophets or priests or teachers, will use their ecclesiastical office in an unselfish desire to advance God's good purposes in the world and will avoid maneuvering for personal advantage or gain. And laymen will not use the formulas and formal observances of religion as a substitute for ethical obedience to the moral law. All of this means that man, the source and center of this ethical transformation, will be true to that ethical self which is a part of his being. Further evidence of this ethical-social ideal may be found in Deut. 15:1-8; 16:18-20; 20:5-9; 24:17-22; Lev. 19:9-18.

Momentous changes came into Israel's thought with the experiences of the Exile. Among these was the new importance of the *individual*. This does not contradict what has been argued above relative to the idea of collective personality as the typical concept of the Old Testament. Along with the newer emphasis found in Jeremiah, Ezekiel, and the wisdom literature in particular, the older concept retained its importance and effectiveness. The breakdown of the nation as a political entity required a process of adjustment which finally resulted in the appearance of the spiritual community of Israel to replace the former national community. The influence of the ethical and spiritual teachings of the prophets, together with the personal suffering of the Exile, inspired a search for new foundations for living. This created a new consciousness of the value of the individual, whose personal suffering and faith necessarily moved to the foreground with the recession of the idea of the political community as the unit of salvation.

A soul gifted with unusual sensitivity to pain and spiritual values brooded over the ancient truism,

> The fathers have eaten sour grapes,
> And the children's teeth are set on edge,

and in deep protest declared this to be untrue. He declared that "everyone who eats the sour grapes shall have his own teeth set on edge." He went on from this declaration of individual responsibility to announce that the individual was really the true center of religion; upon him God would write his Law so that it would be imprinted upon the heart of each man who in deep personal faith would obey God and keep his commandments (Jer. 31:29-34). Ezekiel too seizes upon this idea of the centrality of the individual when he asserts on behalf of God, "I will give them a new heart, and will put a new spirit within them" (11:19), and more specifically when he follows Jeremiah in declaring the inadequacy of the old proverb and announces personal responsibility for sin: "He who sins shall die" (18:4).

The wisdom writings do not evince any interest in the older national religion as practiced before the Exile and revived in the restoration when the temple was rebuilt. Their interest is at the same time more universal and more individualistic. Hence their depiction of ethical man is colored by the idea of individualism. This interest does not exclude the biblical concern for justice and group welfare; it locates two focuses in the ellipse of ethical experience, instead of just the community. The community and the individual in their creative interaction exhibit the real nature of ethical man.

Turning then to the wisdom books of Job and Proverbs we find that the former contains a complete summary of the personal elements which make up the good life. In one notable passage Job is seen defending his character and wistfully recalling his happy state before the affliction from God came upon him (Job 29, 31). In the olden days he had the respect of old and young, a respect that had been won by his charitable conduct toward the poor and fatherless. Those on the point of death blessed him for his kindness, and his beneficent gifts made the widow glad. In righteousness and justice he served as eyes for the blind and feet to the lame. In defense of the needy he "broke the talons of the wicked."

In a remarkable apologia Job vindicates his character further as he reacts to the cutting jibes and unjust accusations of his "friends." [6] He has shunned the evil of adultery; he has acted democratically in his relations to his servants; when there was hunger, he satisfied it; nakedness, he provided clothing. Although he had great wealth, he trusted in righteousness rather than gold. He did not rejoice over the evil which overtook his enemy. In a word, this is a man fully incarnating, in so far as one individual can possibly do so, the lofty ethical ideal of the Hebrew prophets. He does this by acting with a sharply sensitive social conscience and with a strong feeling of personal integrity which motivates his ethical behavior without the necessity of external sanctions.

The ethical ideal in the book of Proverbs, while not as inspiring as the one set forth in the prophetic books and in Job, is helpful in rounding out the Old Testament teaching on this subject. The late introduction to the book gives an excellent though brief preview of what follows. It takes the form of a statement of purpose:

[6] This statement is correct only if a view of the book of Job which includes the speeches in these two chapters is held. There is a reasonable doubt that these speeches belonged to the first edition of the book.

That men may gain wisdom and instruction,
May understand words of intelligence;
That they may receive instruction in wise conduct,
In rectitude, justice, and honesty. (1:2-3.)

The good life is thus based upon the virtues of wisdom, uprightness, justice, and integrity. This is fully borne out by nearly every verse in the book of Proverbs. The good man abstains from association with bad men who traffic in ill-gotten gain, and who exploit their fellow men. He gives aid to the needy and provokes no quarrels. He refuses to be seduced by the wife of another, remaining content with the wife of his youth. He is industrious, restrained in speech, amenable to instruction, honest in his business dealings, kind of heart, capable of keeping a confidence, generous toward others, thoughtful of the members of his household, self-controlled when provoked, and intent on planning for the good of others. By his industry and honesty he accumulates wealth, in the possession of which he is modestly self-effacing. He is a good though stern father, cautious in giving his confidence to others, tranquil of mind, gentle and generous in speech, a good listener, a faithful friend, and a loving son to his parents. In a word, he pursues justice and mercy in the spirit of wisdom, and thus enjoys long life, prosperity and honor.

In the biblical record ethical theory is never viewed humanistically or as rooted in human nature and the social order. The source of human good lies in the *nature of God,* not ultimately in the nature of man. Man's very life is contingent upon this other reality; his ethics and his ethical nature are derived from it. Consequently righteousness and justice, mercy and lovingkindness, when applied to human conduct, are never named as generalizations apart from the context of the will of God. Man is required to act ethically and to establish justice in society by a command from without, not by an impulse from within. The numerous scriptural citations which have been made in this section of the chapter have all been found to contain—usually explicitly—undeniable allusions to the divine source of ethical values. This is vividly clear in the prophetic books and always implicit in the wisdom literature. In the latter the origin of ethical insight and knowledge is said to be religious faith—the fear of the Lord is the beginning of wisdom (Job 28:28; Prov. 9:10).

This is the reason justice has such potency in the Old Testament. It is divinely originated and validated. Human conscience is tested and searched by the mind of God. What this conscience approves after the divine scrutiny ceases to be social custom or an inner urge

74

toward goodness; it has become an irrefutable command of the ever-lasting God, absolute and unconditioned by human shortcomings and ignorance or cowardice. For this reason the prophets were not content to be teachers of morals. By the nature of the case they were compelled to expound their ethical insights and ideas as the revealed will of God. These, they firmly believed, had come to them with such power and clarity from God himself that they were compelled to proclaim them, no matter what the cost. So they were prophets primarily and teachers incidentally. Convinced that their message truly corresponded with the will of God, they uttered lofty moral truths with passion and unfor-gettable vividness. The word of Micah, delivered by him in the latter part of the eighth century, was recalled over a century later, when the defenders of Jeremiah remembered the earlier prophet's ethical condemnation of Israel and the fulfillment of his prophecy by the fall of that country. The forcefulness of the prophets and the depth of their religious conviction made the ethical phases of their message unusually impressive.

MAN AS A FREE BEING

The freedom of man in the Hebrew Scriptures is a corollary of his ethical nature. In the nation which freely chose the God Yahweh at the instigation of Moses and thus began an ethical relationship with him, and in the individual who turned his face from the darkness of idolatry to the light of God, this freedom may be seen in operation. In the realm of everyday decisions in the Old Testament there is never any question about the autonomy of the individual. The sons of Lamech launch the adventure of human civilization by founding cities, inventing the art of metalworking, and inaugurating the use of musical instruments. Presumably they do this of their own volition. Men marry and are given in marriage; they pioneer in new lands and adjust them-selves to strange customs and peoples; they buy land, gather wealth, and lose it—all through the exercise of freedom. And in weightier matters human freedom is recognized, whether these have to do with moral conduct or obedience to God.

We are informed that God desired to test Abraham, for example, and instructed him to take his only son, whom he loved much, to the land of Moriah, where he must offer him as a burnt offering to God (Gen. 22). The narrative reveals that upon receipt of these instructions the father promptly complied—"So next morning Abraham rose early." It is the consummate skill of the narrator rather than the in-sensitivity of Abraham which occasions the omission of any reference to his travail of soul as he faced the alternatives and struggled freely to make a decision. Obedience was avoidable, but nonetheless Abraham chose it. The decision of Joseph's brothers to sell the young dreamer into slavery was accompanied by a delicate balance of personal feelings and individual desires. One brother wanted to kill him, another counseled moderation; circumstances beyond their control brought a caravan in sight; so they sold him (Gen. 37). An indefinite multiplication of such intances would be possible. It is obvious that the Hebrews viewed freedom in the common-sense fashion of modern man. For all practical purposes man was free. Biblical man went his own way, acting as though he were free, and raising few questions about the contingencies of nature, heredity, social and cultural environment, and economic necessity, which hemmed him in and limited his action.

The greatness of God's power over the life of his people and over nature would seem to shrink man's freedom, or even to eliminate it entirely. In holiness and majesty God ruled the life of men; how could they avoid a divine dictatorship determining their every thought and deed? This presentation of the problem would hardly be recognizable by the men of the Bible; they knew the experience of refusing the demands of God and stubbornly seeking their own ends. So they were keenly conscious of their own will, which could be exerted to oppose even the will of God. This empirical fact far outweighed any speculative considerations respecting freedom and determinism. Men knew that they were free because they actually were able to defy or to ignore the demands of God. Whether this defiance proved to be successful in the long run is another matter.

The commission of *sin* by Israel is a demonstration of the existence of freedom. Rebellion against God is frequent. Forceful injunctions are laid upon the nation to listen to the words of the law, to honor parents, to abstain from murder, adultery, theft, and lust, to remember past sins and past mercies, to love the Lord their God, to observe all his commandments. Before this nation is set a blessing and a curse, hinging upon obedience or disobedience (Deut. 11:26-28). "I have put life and death before you, the blessing and the curse; therefore choose life, that you as well as your descendants may live." (30:19.) The very presence of the Law presupposes lawlessness and sin—and moral freedom. Commands to comply with a particular code, such as the Decalogue, call for a redirection of the human will, whose reality and freedom are thus affirmed.

At this point the prophets may again be called in as witnesses. In the dramatic contest between Yahweh and Baal on Mount Carmel, the account of which is clearly a condensation of a long historical struggle between two opposing cultures,[7] the prophet Elijah confronts the spectators with the necessity of making a clean-cut and unequivocal decision. They have straddled the fence long enough. "How long are you going to limp upon two diverse opinions? If the Lord be God, follow him, but if the Baal, follow him." (I Kings 18:21.) He challenges them to make up their minds and proceeds to assist them by presiding over a remarkable demonstration of the power of Yahweh. The oracles of the great literary prophets abound in imperatives summoning the nation to action based on sincerity of purpose and a new devotion to the God of justice. In Isaiah we find, "Hear the word of the Lord; . . . give ear; . . . put away the evil of your doings; . . . cease to do evil; . . . seek justice; . . . restrain; . . . uphold; . . . come now; . . . hear now; . . . go now; . . . return; . . . quake with fear; . . . draw near to listen; . . . behold!" Amos says, "Proclaim; . . . hear and testify; . . . come to Bethel; . . . prepare to meet your God; . . . hear this word; . . . seek me; . . . seek the Lord; . . . seek good; . . . take away from me the noise of your viols; . . . go; . . . prophesy; . . . hear this; . . . behold!"

In the view of the prophets the men of Israel and Judah had the power to respond to the word of the Lord, even though that word was a radical one eliciting from human beings the most strenuous moral and spiritual effort of which a man is capable. That word of God is a deadly attack upon the egotism and passions of men, upon their complacency and self-will. When it is answered, it is answered by an act of faith which permits the substitution of God's will for that of men. This means nothing less than a voluntary, wholehearted committal to the demands of God, and a love for him which absorbs the heart and mind and soul. This love is freely given: man may love other gods and withhold his love from his Creator. That this possibility became an actuality may be seen in the biblical emphasis upon the sin of idolatry.

Our survey has disclosed the presence of three principal types of freedom in the Old Testament. There is practical freedom, which permits a satisfactory amount of self-expression in making life's routine decisions. This is the freedom which all men share without raising profound philosophical questions as to whether they really have it. Unperturbed by the implications for the problem of freedom of God's power over his life and thought, biblical man goes blithely on his way, announcing, "I will; I propose; I intend;" as though he really were

[7] See p. 50.

free. The second kind of freedom is ethical freedom, in the exercise of which man may eat of the tree of the knowledge of good and evil, or he may refuse to eat. As a free, moral person he may elect what is good and reject what is evil, or do just the opposite—and suffer the consequences. From his very creation he was made aware of this possibility, and in his continuing social experience this fact was driven home to him by the admonitions of his moral leaders and by the disturbance of his own conscience. Finally there is religious freedom. Through its possession man may turn to God with his whole heart; and through it he may defy his Maker and remain content with lower loyalties. These are the three freedoms of biblical men as they knew them.

MAN A RELIGIOUS PERSON

Without doubt the Old Testament's description of man as a religious person is its most conspicuous testimony about man. This does not mean that man in the biblical record is remarkable for his piety. Even a hasty reading of the literature will correct that misapprehension. Israel's spiritual guides encountered an overwhelming weight of indifference and spiritual inertia when they tried to lead the people in the way of faith. Complacent, content with their own resources, blind to ethical values, given to trust in physical power and military might, they constituted the immovable object against which the irresistible force of prophetic denunciation was hurled with no visible result. The testimony does mean that the attention of the Bible is focused upon man chiefly as a religious person, capable of entering into a relationship with God. Man's very spiritual blindness or indifference is of interest to biblical writers because these conditions bear upon that relationship. In fact, man's total activity, no matter what its nature, is considered important for this reason. This interest ranges in the Old Testament from the meditations of the mystic to rules governing camp sanitation.

Man as a religious being is *dependent upon God,* from whom he received his life, and through whom he has hope of salvation. God is his creator and preserver, the giver and sustainer of life. Man as a corporate personality finds himself under the control of the God of history, without whom the nation could not have made its appearance. The nation, which is collective man, was originated by God's selection of Abraham and by the divine guidance of his sons and grandsons. God brought their descendants out of Egypt; he went before them in time of danger as they entered the land of Canaan; he advised and rebuked their leaders throughout the nation's history; and he revealed a new concept of national destiny when political disaster overtook it.

Religious man is able to feel deeply his dependence upon God. Associated with feelings of trust and gratitude, this feeling of dependence appears most prominently in Israel's book of worship, otherwise called Psalms. In the presence of foes man can lift up his head and trust in God (3:3).

> Thou alone, O Lord, makest me dwell in safety. (4:8.)

> All my foes shall be ashamed and sore terrified (6:10),
> For the Lord has heard the sound of my weeping. (6:8.)

> Arise, O Lord, in thine anger,
> Lift up thyself in wrath against my foes. (7:6.)

> How long, O Lord—wilt thou continually forget me? (13:1.)

> How long shall my enemy triumph over me? (13:2.)

Afflicted by his enemies the pious man turns to God, who is his refuge and strength, his rock and fortress (18:1-2). The Lord answers prayer in the time of trouble when enemies are near (20:1, 7); he is man's unfailing friend (23), his mountain-fort (31:2), his deliverer from sickness (31:10-16; 38:5-6, 21), and a well-proved help when need is great (46:1).

The heart of this religious man is made glad when the divine mercies are counted.

> O all peoples, clap your hands!
> Shout to God with a glad voice! (47:1.)

Human voices are not adequate to sing God's praises (34:1-2); orchestral music is needed to supplement these. The horn, the lyre and lute, the drum and strings and cymbals are to add their swelling rhythm of sound and harmony to man's mighty chorus of praise to God (81:1-2; 150). Man is capable of deep gratitude to his maker and redeemer, the Lord of history and of all life. He has created all things, snow and hoarfrost, wind and rain, the heavens, the earth and all creatures living thereon (104; 136; 146–148). He is the Lord of history, having through its vicissitudes delivered his people in a glorious manner (78; 81; 83; 105–106). Therefore the psalmist cries:

> Let all the people say, "Amen."
> Hallelujah! (106:48.)

Man cannot live without God. His whole being longs for the living God, even as a wild beast in the desert longs for water.

> As a deer longs for the water-courses,
> So my whole being longs for thee, O God.
> My whole being thirsts for God, for the living God.
> (42:1-2.)

There is no craving so absorbing and so intense as man's craving for God. The satisfaction of this longing by the gift of God's lovingkindness produces in the heart an immense gratitude and upon the lips continuous songs of praise and thanksgiving.

From this feeling of dependence, and related feelings, comes the *need of prayer*. Man prays because it is his nature to pray. As a created being whose very existence is derived from another, he is doomed to constant frustration and tragic incompleteness unless he turns to that Other. This turning to God to fulfill his life is prayer. The prayer of petition or intercession is only one part of this life with God. The longing for help and deliverance from foes or from desperate illness, and also the longing for God himself, is expressed in the Psalms. Disturbingly conscious of his needs and of his inability to meet them, the psalmist finds in God a source of unfailing strength and comfort. And when, stricken by the realization of his sin, he can obtain no help from men, he appeals to God, who gives himself as a means of help.

> O God, thou art my God; I seek for thee;
> My spirit thirsts for thee; my flesh yearns for thee. (63:1.)

> Thy grace is better than life. (63:3.)

Man's highest good is communion with God, declares the writer of Ps. 73, when the problem of the wicked perplexes him. He has no rational answer to this problem, but upon entering the sanctuary he receives the answer of faith:

> Yet I am always with thee;
> Thou holdest my right hand. (73:23.)

> And having thee, I wish nought else on earth.
> (73:25.)
> But as for me, the nearness of God is my good.
> (73:28.)

Man is made for God, and he can have no peace until he rests in him.

MAN AS THE IMAGE OF GOD

Man's dependence upon God rests upon the fact that he is a creature; his power to worship his Creator and his deep religious craving are rooted in the fact that he was made in the divine image. From God he came, and for God he is destined. Earlier in this chapter allusion was made to man's creaturely nature, which he shared with other creatures. Created from the dust of the ground, as were they, he shares their fate as a child of nature. He is weak and mortal, like the grass that withers in a day. From another standpoint man as a creature is different from other creatures in that his is a special creation. To his nature was added an element found in no other created beings—godlikeness.

Five times the priestly writer uses the Hebrew word *selem* to signify "image, likeness" (Gen. 1:26, 27, 27; 9:6; 5:3). The more precise connotation of the word is not so easily determined. If we use the context in which the term occurs in connection with the creation of man and consider not only the particular verse but also the surrounding material, tentative results may be secured. After his creation man is given instructions to reproduce, to subdue the earth, and to have authority over fish, birds, tame animals, and crawling things upon the earth. As God has supreme authority over his creation, so man has this limited power over certain living things. "In the image of God," then, may include this assumption of authority; certainly it is not an authority which any other creatures are said to possess and is therefore unique for man. However, it must be admitted that this is not certain, since direct textual evidence is lacking.

In Genesis (9:6) we read, "Whoever sheds the blood of man, by man shall his blood be shed; for God made man in his own image [*selem*]." This sentence is a part of the covenant made with Noah after the flood. Permission is vouchsafed to eat the flesh of animals, even as previously man had been allowed to eat green plants. While animals could be slain for food after the flood, in view of this covenant, the blood must first be properly removed. But the lives of human beings must be protected, "for God made man in his own image." Thus human life is distinguished from other animal life by the fact of its special relation to God. This gives it a sacredness or inviolability which no other form of life possesses. Perhaps there is special significance in the recurrence of the command which appears in the Creation account also—that man is to be fruitful and multiply in the earth—although the word "subdue" is not repeated. Both sacredness and dominance are suggested by the passage here discussed, and both seem to be connected with the phrase "in his own image."

THE THEOLOGY OF THE OLD TESTAMENT

The Yahwist's version of the events of Creation, while not containing the word *ṣelem,* includes data which might help in defining that term. In this story the serpent engages in a conversation with the woman in the garden and insinuates that God's real motive in prohibiting the eating of fruit from the tree in the middle of the garden is to prevent man from being like the gods. "God knows that the very day you eat of it, your eyes will be opened, and you will be like gods who know good from evil." (Gen. 3:5.) This idea is found also in a later verse in the same chapter, where God says, "See, the man has become like one of us, in knowing good from evil" (3:22). The next statement in this chapter suggests that eating of the other forbidden tree will be rewarded with the gift of everlasting life. Possibly this gift also was considered to be an exclusive possession of the gods. If man became immortal, he would become like one of the gods. If the serpent was right, not so much in the immediate context of the story, but in the general setting of the book of Genesis, then man's power to know good from evil was imparted in his creation—departing here from the serpent story—and should be incorporated in our definition of the phrase "image of God."

Such an interpretation allows us to explain in theological terms the striking anthropological portrayal of man which we have found in the Old Testament. Whence comes man's ability to "know good from evil"? Biblical man is an ethical being, and his conscience receives its sensitivity and maturity from God. Wisdom and ethical understanding stem from the "fear of the Lord." In creating man in his own image, God, who is righteous, made man with the potentiality for righteousness. *Imago dei* has the further meaning of spirituality, as may be recalled from our earlier exposition of spirit in man.[8] This spirit is the gift of God and is definitely a divine characteristic which would normally be shared by anyone made in his likeness. *Ruach* in man is his God-given capacity for communion with God and for living religiously. No biblical doctrine is clearer than this. From God, who as creative mind conceives his righteous purposes, man obtained his rational powers whereby he can do the divine will, carry out ethical demands for social justice, and organize his life around an ennobling faith.

Let us conclude, as a result of this investigation, that "image of God" means partaking of the divine nature with respect to power to rule over other living things, ethical discernment in distinguishing good from evil, and a special sacredness of personality unknown in animals. These characteristics and those whose description has been outlined in

[8] P. 65.

detail in this chapter constitute the biblical doctrine of man as far as the Old Testament is concerned.

When we gaze at the star-studded heavens on a clear, silent night, we may well be filled with the awe which inspired the psalmist of old to exclaim,

> When I see thy heavens, the work of thy fingers,
> The moon and the stars which thou hast formed;
> What is man that thou shouldst think of him,
> And the son of man that thou shouldst care for him? (8:3-4.)

We do not know that this poet considered deeply all of the varied activities and capabilities revealed by man in his life in Palestine. Probably he was fully aware of them, since his poem shows dependence upon the priestly story of Creation and must therefore be relatively late. When we contemplate nature with him, in the mood of adoration of the God of nature, and then observe man in his intellectual power, his scientific control of natural forces, his enormous industrial and technological achievements, and his promise of still greater mastery in the future, we may feel moved to continue with the psalmist and add our wonder to his,

> Yet thou hast made him but little lower than God,
> And dost crown him with glory and honor!
> Thou makest him ruler over the works of thy hands,
> Thou hast put all things under his feet. (8:5-6.)

4. *The Idea of Sin*

WHAT a religion affirms concerning the meaning of sin is a high-ly suggestive clue to its entire creed. A definition of this concept is crucial for penetrating to the basic postulates held to be essential to a religion of salvation. It offers an understanding of the nature of the power that is worshiped; it throws light on the structure of that human nature which needs the salvation, and which does the worshiping; and it establishes the basis for our knowledge of the process of salvation itself. All religions may be classified from the standpoint of their peculiar conception of sin. Rationalistic religions or theological systems within a single religion, if they use the word sin at all, view its content as essentially a matter pertaining to the lack of knowledge or enlightenment. Ethical-humanistic systems see in sin the absence or inadequacy of ethical ideals with strong social implications. Strongly theocentric religions may find in sin the impassable gulf which separates God and man, making the latter's prospects for salvation completely hopeless save for the unmerited grace of God. Thus a discussion of sin should help one more fully to comprehend the distinctive faith of the Old Testament in its entirety.

HEBREW WORDS FOR SIN

It is proposed, first of all, to offer typical examples of the use of Hebrew words for the general idea of sin. The limitations of precise word studies are too serious to be overlooked, and the theological student particularly is obligated to examine the occurrences of special words in their wider religious and logical context of meaning as well as of historical background. Yet words are the symbols of ideas and of action; as such they cannot be neglected. The Hebrew words to be presented here are as follow: *hata'* (miss, go wrong, sin) and its derivatives; *'awon* (iniquity); *pesha'* transgression); *ro'a* (badness, evil); *ma'en* (refuse—to obey God's commands); *ma'as* (reject); *marah* (be contentious, rebellious); *kashah* (hard, severe, stubborn); *rûm* (haughtiness); *gabah* (be exalted); *resha'* (wicked, criminal); *'avlah* (injustice); *shagah* (sin of error, inadvertence); *hamas* (violence, wrong); *halal* (profane, defile); *sûg* (backslide); *sarah* (turning aside, defection); *'asham* (offense, guilt). This is not a complete list, but it will serve to show the rather extensive use of terms which denote the idea of sin in its various ramifications.

The root *hata'* may simply signify to "miss the goal or way," as "he who misses me [wisdom] wrongs himself" (Prov. 8:36). It may also mean the commission of evil against another person, as "in case a man sin against his neighbor" (I Kings 8:31; cf. I Sam. 26:21; II Sam. 19:20; I Kings 18:9; II Kings 18:14). Since our interest lies primarily in this word's religious meaning, the following are cited: "When Pharaoh saw that the rain, hail, and thunder had ceased, he sinned again and became stubborn, both he and his courtiers" (Exod. 9:34); and " 'Rise!' the Lord said to Joshua. 'What use is it to fall on your face? Israel has sinned; they have violated the covenant with me, which I enjoined on them; they have taken some of the doomed things' " (Josh. 7:11). Resistance to God and violation of the covenant pertaining to the destruction of everything in a conquered city are here involved. The word may even be used to indicate unconscious sins (Lev. 4:2, 13, 22). It may mean blasphemy or attacks upon God: "Job did not sin; nor did he charge anything unseemly against God" (Job 1:22). It may mean inner sin—Job said,

> Perhaps my children have sinned,
> And cursed God in their thoughts. (1:5.)

In one of the psalms this root connotes unbelief:

> Notwithstanding all this, they sinned still more,
> And believed not in his wondrous works. (78:32.)

Elsewhere the idea of rebellion is central:

> Your first father sinned,
> And your prophets rebelled against me;
> Your princes also profaned my sanctuary.
> (Isa. 43:27-28.)

Note also along this same line:

> But behold! I am bringing an indictment against you,
> Because you say, "I have not sinned."
> Why do you change your course
> with so light a heart? (Jer. 2:35-36.)

85

The speaker declares that Israel will be disappointed in an alliance with Egypt as she was with Assyria. In other passages sin is viewed as universal (I Kings 8:46); it is characteristic of youth (Ps. 25:7); it is expressed by the mouth (59:12); or it is depicted as a lurking beast (Gen. 4:7).

'*Awon* (iniquity, guilt, punishment of iniquity) is used less often than *hata*'. Of Job it is said by Eliphaz, "Your guilt instructs your mouth" (15:5). Job himself declares that God plasters over his guilt in order to possess it perpetually (14:17). The prophet records that the men of Israel have returned to the sins of their forefathers in going after other gods (Jer. 11:10), and that their guilt is not hidden from God (16:17). The word parallels *hata*' at times.

> Ah! those who draw guilt on themselves with cords of ungodliness,
> And the penalty of their sin as with cart-ropes. (Isa. 5:18.)
>> You have burdened me with your sins,
>> You have wearied me with your iniquities. (43:24.)

It is also parallel to *pesha*':

> Fools, because of their wicked ways [*pesha*']
> And because of their guilty deeds, were afflicted.
>> (Ps. 107:17.)

This familiar verse also illustrates the point:

> He was pierced for our transgressions,
> He was crushed for our iniquities. (Isa. 53:5.)

The term *pesha*' is usually translated "transgression." The first chapter of Amos shows its use with respect to the perpetration of brutalities in time of war by a victorious army against a helpless foe. These brutalities are called transgressions against Yahweh. They include thrashing war captives with heavy sledges from the lower sides of which sharp stones or metal protrude, creating a whole nation of displaced persons, murdering pregnant women, defiling the body of an Edomite king, and exploiting the poor of Israel. These are violent deeds which really constitute rebellion against God himself. *Pesha*' therefore is a strong word. Doom is to fall upon those who commit it (Isa. 1:28). Men who shamelessly flaunt their disloyalty by seeking other gods are guilty of this kind of sin (Amos 2:4; Isa. 46:7-8). They are rank rebels deserving no mercy because they have deliberately chosen to transgress the commands of God and to reject his lovingkindness and salvation.

The next word, *ro'a,* has less the meaning of sin than of ethical evil, if a real distinction between religion and ethics can be made. The Lord will punish his people for their evildoing in forsaking him (Deut. 28:20); oppression of the underprivileged is evil (Isa. 1:16-17); Judah is to repent—circumcise her heart—because of her evil deeds (Jer. 4:4); Israel's rulers have been irresponsible in caring for the nation and have thus done evil (23:2); and God is planning to bring evil upon them because of their evil doings (26:3).

Two other terms require only brief mention here. One is *ma'en* (refuse—to obey the divine command). So Pharaoh refused to let Israel go (Exod. 4:23); in the Exodus Israel refused to follow God's instructions (16:28); Ephraim refused to walk in accordance with the law (Ps. 78:10); and the nation refused to pay attention to the demands of the prophets (Zech. 7:11-12). The other term is *ma'as* (reject) and is illustrated here in connection with the rejection by the people of God. Israel has spurned the Lord (Num. 11:20); in desiring a king, they rejected Yahweh as their king (I Sam. 8:7); Saul is to be king no longer, since he has rejected God's word (15:23); the evil nation has spurned the word of the Holy One of Israel. Both of these words, as used in the places noted, point up the aggressive and volitional nature of sin, willfully elected as a course of conduct by individual men or by the entire nation. These words convey also the idea of a contemptuous dismissal of God's claims upon men.

Another term with a strong connotation of willful evil and rebellion against God is *marah* (be contentious, refractory, rebellious), whose derived substantive form means "rebellion." Those who do wrong are vigorously denounced by one of the psalmists, who prays for divine guidance in the presence of his enemies, "Because of their many transgressions cast them out because they have rebelled against thee" (5:10). Another pious soul recalls a former generation, which he describes as stubborn and rebellious, lacking in loyalty to God (78:8). The mind of the nation is intent on wealth and power and is indifferent to the needs of the poor and the afflicted. Practicing fraud and all manner of wickedness, its leaders are knaves who rebelliously turn away from the God of the harvest and listen to the prophets who prophesy by false gods. Even Zion defies the Lord, listening to no correction or reproof, and tolerating in her streets princes, judges, prophets, and priests who do violence to the law and to decency (Jer. 5:23; Isa. 3:9; Zeph. 3:3-4). The rebellion of his chosen people has grieved God's holy spirit, which through his love and compassion had been working for their redemption (Isa. 63:10). Finally, we may note that the term in its substantive form appears fifteen times in the book of Ezekiel (2:5, 6, 7, 8; 3:9, 26, 27; 12:2, 2, 3, 9, 25; 17:12; 24:3; 44:6). Here is found the prophet's judgment that Israel is "a rebellious household." This rebelliousness is associated with the denial of the true God and the practice of perverted forms of religion, such as the Tammuz cult (8:14).

The unyielding stiffness of will whereby God's grace proves to be resistible is expressed by several Hebrew words, including some of the foregoing, but especially by the term *kashah* (hard, severe, stubborn). For example, the story of the making of the golden bull or calf contains evidence of the fury of God, who denounces Israel as "stiff-necked" (*kashah*—Exod. 32:10; 33:3, 5; 34:9) and announces his intention of consuming his people. For wantonly running after other gods, setting up images, and bowing down before them, Israel fully deserves such punishment. In the summary of the nation's religious history—consisting chiefly of a series of apostasies—which is found in the book of Judges, the subjection of Israel to a foreign power and its resulting cry for deliverance are sketched. When its deliverer died, we are informed, "they would relapse, and behave worse than their fathers, by running after alien gods to serve them and pay homage to them; they would not abandon any of their practices or stubborn ways" (2:19). The prophet-poet graphically describes the stubbornness of the house of Jacob, who call upon God's name, but "not in truth nor sincerity" (Isa. 48:1). God says,

> I knew that you were obstinate,
> That your neck was an iron band,
> And your forehead bronze. (48:4.)

Sinful arrogance and pride are spiritual attitudes which also belong in the religion of the Old Testament—*rûm* (height, haughtiness). Isaiah refers to "the haughty looks of man" (2:11) and to "the haughtiness of man" (2:17), which will be humbled. He also mentions the "arrogant boasting of the king of Assyria, and his vainglorious pride" (10:12). The wise man sententiously announces that six things are hated by the Lord, one of which is haughtiness (Prov. 6:17). Another term having a meaning similar to that of *rûm* is *gabah* (be high, exalted). It is used in the derogatory sense in Ezekiel (16:49-50). The Sodomites lived in "pride, plenty, and thoughtless ease." They grew haughty and committed evil in the sight of God. Because of her unbounded wealth Tyre was "puffed up with pride" (28:2, 5, 17). As a noun this root signifies "haughtiness" and is parallel to *rûm*. Jeremiah (48:29) uses this expression to designate the pride and insolence of

Moab, while the Chronicler tells us that Hezekiah averted disaster by replacing pride with humility (II Chr. 32:26).

When we devote our attention to a word which is much more common in the literature of the Old Testament, namely *resha'*, we discover that this is customarily used for those who are wicked or criminal. It is the antonym for *ṣadik* (righteous). In a court of justice where a suit is to be decided, the one who is acquitted is called the innocent party, and to the guilty individual is applied the word *resha'*. So a murderer under the death sentence is named in this way (Deut. 25:2; Num. 35:31). The word is extensively used to indicate hostility to God, often in the psalms, where occasionally a technical meaning may be detected. Possibly in Ps. 1 the wicked are the broadminded Jews of the late Hellenistic period, who are not concerned for the meticulous interpretations of the legalists, whereas the righteous are the sternly faithful to whom the exact wording of the Law is a delight forever. Whether sects or community groups are singled out or not, the word nonetheless applies to those who are thought to be hostile to God and to his will. This is generally the case throughout the literature under consideration. It is clear that "there is no peace . . . for the wicked" (Isa. 48:22).

> But the wicked are like the uptossed sea,
> For it cannot rest,
> But its waters toss up mire and filth.
> "There is no peace," says my God, "for the wicked."
> (57:20-21.)

The wicked are to be destroyed; they do not serve God; they pervert judgment persistently and deserve utter condemnation.

Among the remaining words in this glossary of terms suggesting the Hebrew idea of sin is the noun *'avlah* (injustice, unrighteousness). Doers of injustice are denounced; they work wickedness in the heart (Ps. 58:2-3); the tongue utters untruth (*'avlah*—Isa. 59:3); one never accuses God of injustice (Job 36:23); no wrong is found upon the lips of Levi (Mal. 2:6); everyone given to injustice or dishonesty is detested by the Lord (Deut. 25:16). Provision is made also in the Hebrew language for the performance of unwitting sins. The usual term for this is *shagah* (and *sheganah*). For example, if the Hebrews make a mistake and fail to observe all of the commands of God, provided this omission is really inadvertent, a bullock may be presented as a burnt offering for the whole community (Num. 15:22-26). Saul is said to have committed an error when he put his army under oath not to eat food until the evening of a day of battle (I Sam. 14:24). Places of refuge are designated for the homicide who tries to flee from the blood avenger, since the homicide is one who kills unintentionally (Josh. 20:3, 9).

Ḥamas (violence, wrongdoing) should be treated here also. It is found fifty-seven times in the Old Testament. Of the more notable passages, that contained in the flood story is of special interest. The priestly writer, in accounting for the great flood, states, "Now in God's sight, the earth was corrupt; the earth was full of wrong-doing" (Gen. 6:11). It specifies personal violence in Job, "Lo, I cry 'Murder,' but I am not answered" (19:7). Evildoers fill their masters' houses with violence and deceit (Zeph. 1:9); violence and robbery are stored up in the palaces of Samaria (Amos 3:10); in Jerusalem, a city of falsehood, sounds of violence and robbery are heard (Mic. 6:12; Jer. 6:7); he who misses wisdom commits wrongdoing against himself (Prov. 8:36). As to the word ḥalal, it is used in Leviticus with the meaning of profaning or defiling the name of the Lord, as may be readily seen in the following: "You must not dedicate any of your children to the service of Molech; you must not profane the name of your God, of me, the Lord" (18:21). Amos observes that the wealthy pervert justice by bribery and also consort with harlots, thus profaning God's holy name (2:6-8). God's name can be defiled by both cultic and ethical corruption.

Several words—sûg (backslide), sarah (apostasy, defection), and 'asham (offense, guilt)—remain on our list of significant terms appropriate to the treatment of the concept of sin. The first is not used often. The psalmist sees no exception to the general apostasy or backsliding. When God looked down from heaven, he found none seeking after him; "they had all gone astray and all of them had done wrong" (53:3). Sarah has a similar meaning—"turn aside" in its verbal form, and a defection as a noun. The sinful nation revolts again and again, according to the prophet Isaiah (1:4-5). By casting away the molten idols made with their hands the children of Israel will be able to return to the God, against whom they have sinfully revolted (31:6-7). Finally, the word 'asham, used principally to identify offense, incurred guilt, or the guilt offering itself, belongs here. This type of offense or guilt can be removed by a measurable offering. Exact fines can be calculated and imposed upon the offender against Israel's law. Thus the trespass offering ordinarily was a ram, to which the guilty party was compelled to add a verbal confession of his crime, full restitution for the economic loss incurred by his acts, and a bonus of twenty per cent beyond the amount restored (Lev. 6:1-7).

This has brought together a rather conglomerate mass of lexico-graphic material, with which the nonlinguistic student may find himself laboring under difficulties; therefore we must now look for order and workable meanings in the assembled data. Can these illustrations of biblical words related to the idea of sin be classified in a logical manner? If we cut across the lines of differentiation between these terms, whose definitions in any case have been seen to overlap, broad classifications may be recognized. These may be identified as social sin, ethical sin, cultic sin, spiritual sin, and personal sin. Other schemes of organization are conceivable, such as one concerned with the origin of sin and the consideration of sin as carnal, as spiritual, or as intellectual. When this study is finished, however, it will be seen that such an approach has by no means been excluded.

SOCIAL SIN

By social sin are denoted conduct, purposes, and attitudes which are actually or potentially disruptive of the stability and welfare of the community. It must be remembered that the viewpoint constantly held in mind is not that of the scientific sociologist, but that of the critical historical-theological student whose chief concern is accuracy in the description and care in the appraisal of a particular body of religious convictions appearing in the literature of the Hebrews. What must be called social sin in the biblical sense would be characterized simply as unsocial or antisocial conduct in the scientific sociological sense.[1] This is the case by reason of the peculiar character of the Hebrew community and of its social patterns. It was a community of a covenant people, drawing its vitality and creative goals from faith in its special election by Yahweh, the just and merciful God from Sinai. The desire to conform to his will—and the disinclination to do so—was operative even before this nation's inception and continued to be in effect through the critical periods of its history, when its social institutions were undergoing development and adaptation to changing environmental conditions. Israel's economic and political instruments for maintaining life and for social control were subject to the influence of this desire and the faith lying behind it.

The old desert economy, based on Bedouin tribalism and relatively simple seminomadic folkways, became in the process of transformation a commercial-agricultural system dependent upon trade, the conservation of economic surpluses, and capital investments. Life in Palestine on

[1] See L. Wallis, *Sociological Study of the Bible* (1912); Jacobson, *op. cit.;* and L. Finkelstein, *The Pharisees* (1938), for excellent studies of the Hebrew community.

the trade routes of the Near East brought this about. Politically the patriarchal and tribal control of the community had to be supplanted by a more powerful centralized government, capable of integrating intertribal relations, of transacting business with other groups, and of exercising other functions of government. This adjustment of Israel's social life as seen by the sociologist deals exclusively with factors susceptible to identification and description by the scientist. Yet it fails completely to grasp a salient factor in Israel's social experience—the positive and concrete results of this people's awareness of its divine destiny. This awareness had vast social significance. It contributed to the manner in which the national community reacted to its social surroundings; it provided a critique for social change; and it established a homogeneity and group consciousness which had amazing survival value. In this process the idea and effect of social sin played a great part.

It is no accident that Israel's legal codes are both secular and religious in nature. Prohibitions against serving other gods are mingled with commands to abstain from murder and adultery. The reader of these codes is never left in doubt as to the authority which validates all of their regulations—it is God, the God who brought the people out of Egypt and led them into the land of Canaan. The seduction of another man's wife (Deut. 22:24), the wearing by a man of a woman's garment (22:5), the possession of a refractory son, and the cutting down of the fruit trees of a conquered city (20:19)—all are forbidden, since they violate the nature of the Lord's community. Sin is any act—whether it be sexual, economic, military, hygienic, or political—which threatens the destruction of the community. This includes acts of violence and social cruelty. Land-grabbers, who are eager to own large estates and have no scruples about using the law to this end and no conscience concerning the human effect of their seizure of a poor man's home, injure the entire community, whose welfare depends upon the fair administration of justice for the welfare of all. That this conduct is believed to be offensive to God does not deprive it of social significance. Greed for land endangers the nation's economy also, for land ownership by the masses is viewed as the basis of prosperity.

Other forms of antisocial conduct receive attention in the Old Testament. The onslaught of power and wealth upon the rights of members of the lower classes is here included. This occurred in the courts and in the markets of the land. Powerful men were denounced for their bribery of judges, with whose connivance they were able to exact unjust fines from their victims. Such men may have earned their money by successful dishonesty in business dealings. They bought up surplus grain from the small farmers in the environs of the city in which they had their headquarters and sold it for a huge profit in the market by mixing it with chaff, or by falsifying the scales with which the grain was weighed. With the increasing prominence of the commercial motive went a debasement of human values. Actual as well as economic enslavement of human beings was the result. Overweening lust for power and position animated those who were in positions of leadership and responsibility. The social order became top-heavy, dominated by wealthy groups whose misdeeds made them grow stronger and stronger. Conversely this social sin was also felt at the bottom of the social pyramid. The lower class of tenant farmers was in constant danger of being thrust into the lowest class—that of the serfs and slaves. This instability was vividly portrayed by the prophets, not only as inimical to the welfare of the community, but as evil in the sight of God; and they denounced the deeds which provoked it as unjust, iniquitous, wicked, and rebellious.

Aside from its other implications rank sensuality belongs in the category of social sin also. The prophets especially are outraged by the uninhibited displays of lust and appetite made by those who had money and leisure to pursue their unbridled desires. They excoriate the men and women who, unaware of the fate of Jerusalem or Samaria, gorge upon the best of the meat and the finest of the wine, who loll upon soft couches decorated with Damascene ivories in an effort to find strength for the next debauch. "Daughters of Zion" grow proud; they walk along self-consciously, making eyes at any man in sight, displaying their charms of person and costume as they parade through the streets (Isa. 3:16). Men, proud of their wittiness and wisdom, having no standard of conduct save that imposed by their self-righteousness, lack the moral courage or insight to fight against social evil or personal temptation. They are

> heroes at drinking wine,
> And the warriors at blending liquor. (5:22.)

But they condone or participate in bribery and exploit the innocent. Theirs is a sham courage and a mock heroism. Absorbed in the pursuit of personal indulgence and in self-glorification, "they are not heartsick over the ruin of Joseph" (Amos 6:6—1935 ed.), a ruin which is to come because of the social evil which they do.

The *political* character of social sin is emphasized particularly during the period of Israel's declining days when her final overthrow was adumbrated in the futile gestures she made to secure help from other nations, and in the frenzied abandonment of moral controls by her population. The term "Israel" has been generally used in this volume to identify the entire Hebrew people; it is now used in a narrower sense for the northern kingdom to distinguish it from Judah to the south. In both kingdoms overtures were made by their rulers to foreign powers in a desperate effort to avert disaster. In Israel, the northern kingdom, there were political cliques aiming at an Egyptian alliance, or an Assyrian one, or at national independence. The folly of all of this was tragically confirmed by the last days of this nation. Hoshea, its last king, after paying heavy tribute to Assyria, decided to terminate this drain upon the national treasury, whereupon his capital was besieged and finally captured. The story is not greatly different for Judah. Revolt against Babylonia, Assyria's successor in winning world control, occasioned the fall of the southern nation. In these crises Judah and Israel committed sin which was disastrous to national life, actually accelerating the process of deterioration and final defeat.

This sin is stressed by all the great prophets and other writers as well. It is denounced as rebellion against God and as utter folly as far as its avowed purpose is concerned. We may listen to Isaiah:

Ah, you rebellious children, . . .
Who carry out a purpose that comes not from me,
And who form an alliance that is not according to my mind—
Adding sin to sin—
Who set out on the way to Egypt. (30:1-2.)

Or Hosea:

When Ephraim saw his sickness,
And Judah his wound,
Then Ephraim went to Assyria,
And sent to the great king. (5:13.)

For Ephraim has become like a silly dove, without sense;
They call to Egypt, they go to Assyria.
As they go, I will spread my net over them;
Like birds of the heavens, I will bring them down.
I will bind them on account of their wickedness. (7:11-12.)

These words suggest a political shrewdness which their authors may not have possessed; or they may be understood as revealing the prophet's religious belief that reliance upon foreign nations was idolatrous, in as much as it looked to a nation rather than to God as its savior.

While the latter view is probably the correct one, we are not obliged to eliminate the political and patriotic aspects of the prophets' concern for Israel's predicament. They were seriously disturbed by the unintelligent and uninformed opportunist attitude of the nation's leaders in their dealings with other nations. They believed deeply that the obvious vacillation in this area betrayed a deep-seated weakness and corruption at the nation's very heart, the removal of which was the only hope of success against potential enemies and of eventual deliverance from evil. Hence they repudiated abortive alliances with heart and soul as being thoroughly bad and contrary to the best interests of the nation. In the theological terminology of their typically religious way of looking at national affairs, they called these alliances sin against God.

ETHICAL SIN

The classification of sin as ethical is doubtless more in accord with the thinking of modern students than is any other method of viewing sin. To them it seems obvious that anything contrary to the ethically right is sin. Sin is evil, and evil is opposed to the good. If sin is to be retained as a modern religious concept, its retention is evidently tied up with the possibility of its ethical interpretation. However this may be, what the Old Testament submits as the meaning of sin is what concerns us at present.

A proper perspective for understanding the biblical idea of sin demands a modification of the common conception of ethics as a product of man's moral consciousness. Although this subject received some attention in Chapter 3, the biblical method of explaining goodness deserves re-affirmation. Regardless of the conditioning human factors —such as the biological, psychological, and sociological—the one supremely determining factor in the creation of a structure of ethical principles whereby men may govern their lives is the fact of a creative, personal, and righteous God. He is responsible for the spiritual and ethical quality of human life, as he is the source of the physical nature which supports and reveals that quality in terms of sense experience. Therefore ethical demands are divine demands, and resistance to these demands in the commission of unethical acts is rebellion against God. With this setting for Hebrew ethics in mind we may proceed to a more direct examination of our subject—the ethical character of the Hebrew idea of sin.

Sin may be defined as missing the goal established by righteousness and, as a result thereof, the direction of human energy toward the accomplishment of ends which are not in harmony with this goal. The goal is an absolute one, determined by the ultimate nature of the divine goodness and power. Thus justice makes imperious demands upon its advocates. They are to let its cleansing power sweep through the nation like a mighty stream, removing uncleanness and renovating every area with its purifying and restoring power. Justice and righteousness are efficacious in realizing the good life, provided these mighty postulates are accepted by the minds and wills of men. When they are rejected, as is sometimes bound to happen in a universe built upon moral freedom, sin enters in. Consequently injustice and unrighteousness appear as ethical sin.

The concrete forms which this sin assumes have already received recognition. The ethical life and the unethical or sinful life cannot be equated with these concrete expressions of sinfulness or evil; they are merely the observable projections in time and space of the ethical quality of man's being which is their source. Corruption in the court, sanctuary, or market place is the outward sign of ethical sin within a man. That this is true the biblical appeal to men—who sin by doing deeds that are unjust—to quit their sinning and to re-orient their loyalties clearly shows. Ethical wrongdoing, which may be called sin, is not atomistically or legalistically conceived. Although Israel's moralists are realistic enough to specify the precise object of their ethical condemnations, they are never so superficial in their view of sin as to equate it with any particular social practice which is externalized or institutionalized in the community, and is beyond the reach of the heart and conscience. The accumulation of social behavior patterns or of individual deeds which are classed as evil may become the basis for a bill of particulars against a community or any of its members; it can hardly take the form of an ethical indictment. The former presupposes a community controlled by tradition or law; the latter presupposes an ethical personality capable of defying or complying with the moral law.

We have been attempting to show that sin from the ethical standpoint must be distinguished from the crimes of a law-possessing society or the overt individual misdeeds of a legalistic morality. While it might serve the best interests of the community to forbid marriage with foreigners and to set up a law enforcing this prohibition, it would not necessarily be sinful or unethical to engage in such a marriage. The ethical element would enter this situation when mixed marriage came to be regarded by mature persons in the light of their moral judgment and religious faith as altogether good and right, or as evil, or when the community as a whole—with the help of enlightened leaders—arrived at such a belief. This sort of a belief would be made the basis for ethical judgments as to sin and evil in this type of social situation. Likewise, an oath, an act of perjury, bribery of a judge, foreclosure of a mortgage against a poor man, the failure to marry the widow of one's deceased male relative, boiling a kid in its mother's milk, and other violations of community customs and standards are sinful in the ethical sense only if they involve the element of ethical judgment.

The practical wisdom in the book of Proverbs further illustrates the ethical nature of certain kinds of sin, largely in a negative way. It is difficult to detect the ethical quality of the following, although it may be found by diligent search:

> A foolish son is his father's ruin;
> And a quarrelsome wife is like a constant drip. (19:13.)

A woman's quarrelsomeness is a defect of character, no doubt, but not necessarily a mark of sinfulness. The originator of the proverb "a sensible wife is a gift from the Lord" (19:14) undoubtedly had ample reason to thank his Creator for a wife who knew her place and kept it, but he was hardly thinking of her ethical character. So with regard to the many other allusions to common-sense traits in the book of Proverbs it may be said that they suggest sensible ways of getting along with other people and with God, but that they do not show a profound and incisive ethical insight or strong ethical feeling. Indeed the dispassionate nature of the book's sayings is in marked contrast to the mood which pervades the Psalms and most of the prophetic books of the Old Testament. The proverbs exalt industry, patience, self-control, wisdom, child control, honesty, and law observance. Contrariwise, they deprecate foolishness, pride, avarice, greed, self-trust, penuriousness, intemperance, and even practical jokes (26:19.) There are ethical implications here, but they are sometimes buried deep. Practical good sense applauds these precepts, but they do not arouse ethical passion. To be sinful, human conduct must be able to evoke the protest of the enlightened conscience and the anger of the righteous God. Some of Proverbs' maxims do neither. Only when a deed has this power can it be called sinful.

CULTIC SIN

Sin against the cult represents the third of the classifications meriting our attention. Here belong failures to perform exactly the ritualistic requirements laid down by the cultus, voluntary or involuntary violation of dietary laws, infraction of rules governing the shedding of blood, and similar transgressions against the religious community. We may distinguish cultic from social sin by defining the nature of the religious community whose cultus is involved in this type of sin. When the community functions in relation to a distinct set of religious observances and forms, it is behaving as a religious community. Through public and private worship, observance of religious festivals, participation in ritualistic dramatizations of divine deeds, the offering of sacrifices and gifts to the deity, and compliance with taboos originating in the idea of the sacred, the cultic nature of the community's life is revealed. On the other hand, the community functions socially in maintaining itself, in developing control mechanisms to insure its survival, and in fostering institutions permitting the satisfaction of the social, sexual, economic, and political needs of the group. Clearly no absolute distinction can be made between the general social community and the community which functions religiously, in view of the well-known function of religion as a means of social control; yet there is a difference which can serve our purpose.

The sources for this study are in a large measure to be found in the priestly literature of the Old Testament. Along with this material other legal codes, the historical books, and the writings of the prophets are helpful to a lesser degree. Sin as cultic is outlined in considerable detail in the book of Leviticus. The full description of the sacrificial system in that book identifies sin as failure—for whatever reason—to observe the demands of this system scrupulously and in detail. Allowance is made for sin which is unintentional; and offerings for the removal of its effects are prescribed, as noted above. This kind of sin is referred to in general language in one passage,

"When any person sins inadvertently in the case of any of the things which the Lord has forbidden to be done, and does one of them, if it is the anointed priest who sins, thus bringing guilt on the people, he must offer to the Lord for the sin that he has committed a perfect young bullock as a sin-offering." (4:2-3; also 4:13-14, 22, 27.)

We may note here the effect of this sin upon the whole community and the implied urgency in taking steps to remove it. Obviously, also, this type of sin appears with respect to any of the ceremonial prohibitions imposed by the cult deity. In other words, the entire priestly code in its smallest details may become the occasion for sin.

Cases of sin are cited in Leviticus, where the performance of a forbidden act, such as touching an unclean thing or uttering a rash oath without awareness of its import, becomes sinful only when there is a

THE IDEA OF SIN

realization of the sinfulness of the deed performed (5:2, 15). The quickened consciousness of the individual affects the decision as to whether sin has been committed in these instances. On the other hand, unconsciousness of sin by no means absolves a person from guilt. He must bring a perfect ram as a guilt offering to the priest, who shall make atonement for him (5:17-18). The food taboos are intended to preserve the ritualistic purity of the community; and their nonobservance is not called sin, although certain of the purificatory rites for cleansing a woman who has given birth to a child, or a leper, include the use of a sin offering (12:6; 14:22). The eating of unclean food or the contraction of any kind of uncleanness is defiling in the sight of God and therefore sinful, we may reasonably conclude.

The so-called "Book of the Covenant" (Exod. 20-23) along with social and economic laws and prohibitions lays down commands along cultic lines, whose violation would make one guilty of sin. No sorceress must be allowed to live; God must not be reviled; three times a year a Festival of Unleavened Cakes is to be held, as well as the Harvest Festival, and the Feast of Ingathering at the end of the year. The first fruits of the soil are to be offered to God; a kid must not be boiled in its mother's milk. In Deuteronomy sin is also indirectly suggested by similar or additional prohibitions. Shaving the forehead for the dead is forbidden (14:1-2); no animal that has died a natural death is to be eaten (14:21); sorcery is strictly prohibited (18:9-14); an ox and an ass must not be yoked together (22:10); material blended of wool and linen must not be worn (22:11). In Malachi a later writer castigates the priests for despising God's name by bringing offerings for the sacrifice which are polluted and imperfect (1:7-14). Animals which are sick or defective are brought to the altar in place of the unblemished victims demanded by the Law. In this way the people treat the table of the Lord with contempt and sin grievously. Elsewhere Israel is called a rebellious people, who are habitually

> Offering sacrifice in gardens,
> And burning incense on tiles—
> Who sit in graves,
> And pass the night in caves,
> Who eat the flesh of swine. (Isa. 65:3-4.)

Cultic sins, directly named or merely implied in the sources, do not involve the exercise of moral judgment or reflective reason. They consist rather in deviations from the established patterns of religious behavior, sanctified by tradition and reinforced by the authority of Deity, operating through the sanctions of the community which worships him. The absence of ethical or social criticism which might pass judgment upon the cultus does not mean that this type of sin has no utility or validity. Its primary usefulness is in preserving the integrity of the holy community. After many of the priestly injunctions we note the words: "I, the Lord, am your God" (Lev. 20:7); "it is I, the Lord, who hallow you" (22:32); or "You must be holy; for I, the Lord your God, am holy" (19:2). So the concept of cultic sin acts as a deterrent to conduct endangering the solidarity and uniqueness of the holy community. Apparently irrational and meaningless restrictions when viewed in this light are seen to have considerable value. Israel, through divine election, was a community apart from the world, set aside by God to carry out a peculiar purpose—obedience to his will and the transmission of his word of redemption to the Gentiles. In the realization of this end, corruption and contamination from without and from within had to be resisted steadily, and this sense of the people's special status had to be stimulated continuously in the imagination of the entire community. Such a stimulus was provided by holding before the people cult objects and cult practices, and by enjoining them from acts which might defile their religion or adulterate their culture with pagan elements.

SPIRITUAL SIN

For the fourth classification into which certain phenomena pertaining to sin may be put, a definitive term is difficult to find. The word "spiritual" has been chosen, though its loose use in religious utterances is generally apparent. By this word in its present context is emphasized man's relationship to God as distinguished from his relation to the other objects of his attention in his total experience. It signifies the object to which he gives his highest devotion, and to which he looks for help. For the student of the Old Testament this denotes faith in God and the worship of him as compared with ethical relationships or attitudes. Spiritual sin—sin in the narrowly religious sense—involves the breaking of this relationship with God by means of the selection of a different object of worship in the available pantheon, or through the deification of personal desire and the attribution to it of divine status and power. These two processes may be identical, but both are sinful; they alike affect what a man thinks and does in relation to his God.

This is the particular conception of sin which is of absorbing interest to the writers of the Old Testament. Other meanings are peripheral; this is central. Sin as social and applicable to conduct tending to disturb social stability and peace, sin as ethical and in violation of the de-

mands of justice, and sin as cultic profanation of the holy community
—all derive their ultimate and real meaning from sin as rebellion
against God. It is God in his living relation to Israel who makes possible social security, the practice of goodness, and the ideal of the holy
community which the group struggles to embody. Loyalty to him is
decisive in determining the presence of sin. Disloyalty to him renders
Israel's social, ethical, and cultic efforts vain and useless. Every Hebrew
word defined in this discussion of sin relates sooner or later to the
crucial idea of the acknowledgement or sinful rejection of God as the
nation's Lord and Savior. *Hata'* conveys the thought of missing the
goal—set by God; *'awon* means iniquity, committed in spite of the
divine command; *pesha'* is transgression against the God of justice;
ro'a is often evil or wrongdoing condemned by this God; *ma'en* and
ma'as denote willful refusal to obey God and stubborn rebellion against
his will. Other terms for hardness, haughtiness, apostasy, and the like
may also be translated in numerous passages so as to bring out their
essential meaning with respect to the God-man relationship.

We may include in this category of spiritual sin the sin of idolatry.
This sin is so prominent that one is embarrassed by the wealth of
material. The eighth-century prophets were impressed by the prevalence
of idolatrous practices, although Amos paid little heed to what must
have been a flourishing cult of idol worship in his day. His special
interest lay in the social order and its internal manifestations of injustice. That he did not altogether ignore the worship of other gods
or the baalistic worship of the Hebrew God Yahweh may be inferred
from the following:

> A man and his father go to the same harlot,
> So that they profane my holy name.
> Upon garments taken in pledge they stretch themselves
> Beside every altar;
> And the wine of those who have been fined they drink
> In the houses of their gods. (2:7-8.)

And we may note the bitter irony of this:

> Come to Bethel, and—transgress!
> In Gilgal, multiply your transgressions!
> Bring your sacrifices every morning,
> And every three days, your tithes.
>
> . . . .
> For so you love to do, O Israelites. (4:4-5.)

These places named here were shrines in which so-called Yahweh worship had become baalized and perverted. The nation saw fit to replace Yahweh's worship with a form of ostentatious piety which gave full vent to religious feeling but made no place for the weightier matters of the moral law. So Amos was driven to say:

> For thus says the Lord to the house of Israel:
> "Seek me, that you may live;
> And seek not Bethel.
> You shall not go to Gilgal,
> Nor cross over to Beersheba." (5:4-5.)

With shrewd discernment the prophet realized that the nation, in resorting to the shrines at Bethel, Gilgal, and Beersheba, where Yahweh was probably worshiped in name at least, was engaging in the grossest kind of idolatry—self-glorification through the forms of an amoral religious system which sanctified ruinous national policies and personal greed.

The prophet Hosea is acutely conscious of the sin of idolatry. There are unsupported conjectures that he may have been a priest himself—witness his attacks upon members of the priestly class (4:4, 9; 5:1)—and had learned from sad experience of the unspeakable sexual perversions of the Yahweh-Baal shrines.[2] In his book the figure of idolatry as harlotry prevails. The nation in her faithlessness has rejected her God in favor of the baals, whose worship permits and even demands harlotry and "sacred" prostitution. Israel goes after her lovers, Hosea says; she plays the harlot; the wives of her sons commit adultery; the sons themselves

> go apart with harlots,
> And sacrifice with temple-prostitutes. (4:14.)

Fascinated by the licentious baals which they worshiped, the people actually changed so as to resemble the object of their affections: they "became an abhorrence like the thing which they loved" (9:10). After vehemently rebuking Israel for this abominable betrayal of the true God, who had brought them out of Egypt, the prophet turns to the nation and pleads with them:

> the Lord, the God of hosts,
> The Lord, is his name.
> But do you return to your God,

---

[2] It is quite likely that in popular thought these two gods were worshiped as one, and that their natures were not sharply differentiated.

Practice kindness and justice,
And wait for your God constantly. (12:5-6.)

In spite of everything God has done, and in spite of Hosea's exhortations, the corrupt nation continues to sin more and more, "in that they make for themselves molten images" (13:2).

Jeremiah fully comprehends the folly of idolatry when he announces on behalf of God:

> Has a nation changed its gods,
>   which are no Gods?
> Yet my people have changed their Glory
>   for that which is useless. (2:11.)

> They have forsaken me, the fountain of living water,
> To hew for themselves cisterns, broken cisterns,
> That can hold no water. (2:13.)

They have rejected Yahweh, their God, and turned to the baals. Israel is apostate and renegade in its shameless pursuit of gods which are not really gods. Such sin is shocking and incomprehensible in the light of the glorious majesty of the God they have forsaken, for

> the Lord God is the true God,
> He is the living God, the everlasting King. (Jer. 10:10.)

Only perverse sinfulness could account for such a performance.

In an earnest effort to bring the men of Judah to their senses and to teach them the lesson of obedience to the true God, Jeremiah invited the Rechabites to go to the temple and there to drink wine (chap. 35). When he set before them a bowl of wine with drinking cups, they refused to drink, appealing to the charge laid upon them by their ancestor, Jonadab, who required them to abstain from wine, from living in houses, and from agricultural practices, and to live in tents. To these faithful proponents of the simple life the prophet pointed when he sought to arouse the consciences of his hearers and to call forth a renewed loyalty to Yahweh. He announced the oracle of the Lord:

Though I spoke to you early and late, you have not listened to me; and though I sent all my servants the prophets to you early and late, saying, "Turn, I pray you, each from his evil way, and amend your doings, and follow not other gods, to serve them," . . . you have neither listened nor bent your ears to me. (35:14-15.)

The Rechabites were loyal to the ideals of their ancestor; but the men of Judah, although given every opportunity to do so, did not turn from their evil ways and forsake their false gods.

The militant attitude of the writers of the book of Deuteronomy toward the worship of idols is easily detected. The conception of God in this book is perhaps one way of accounting for this fact. Here God is a jealous God who insists upon absolute devotion and strict obedience; he is also a trustworthy God who keeps faith with his people. He and he alone brought the people of Israel into the promised land. This being the case, no other deity can possibly claim the nation's loyalty. Of particular importance, however, is the religious-political situation, under the influence of which the bulk of the book was written, in the latter part of the reign of Manasseh, king of Judah. This king was slavishly imitating Assyrian customs and religious practices in the hope that he might win the favor of the Assyrian government and its support in time of need.

Consequently Manasseh revived the baal religion, which had suffered a reverse in the time of Hezekiah, and built altars to astrological gods in the very temple at Jerusalem. He even offered his son as a human sacrifice and martyred the faithful, who were probably the ardent followers of Yahweh and included among their number many Yahweh prophets (II Kings 21). The book of Deuteronomy was published as a polemic against idolatrous baalism and the pro-Assyrianism of Manasseh. It is therefore exceedingly harsh toward idolaters, pronouncing upon them the death sentence (7:1-4; 13:6-16). A further reason for its hostility toward baalism and its drastic insistence upon the exclusiveness of God's demands may be found in the influence of the great prophets, whose teachings and admonitions had prepared the way for Deuteronomy's positive, even belligerent, statement of a religious monotheism.

The writers of that book well knew that the matter of survival itself was tied up with the question asked in the ninth century by Elijah, "How long are you going to limp upon two diverse opinions? If [Yahweh] be God, follow him" (I Kings 18:21). To the extent that they were the objects of Manasseh's persecution—and there is no reason to deny that some of them were—this question of survival was an unpleasant personal matter. And as they surveyed the state of the nation, whose lack of a constructive foreign and domestic policy was painfully reminiscent of the situation in Israel nearly one hundred years earlier, they saw no hope, save a revival of religion which would become a truly national movement, and which would center in the

God to whom the nation owed its origin. They inevitably associated with false religion or idolatry the entire national program set up by Manasseh. To them idolatry was the hideous symbol of an evil and ruinous way of life which led to death for the nation. This made it the sin of sins.

The Old Testament has a comprehension of spiritual or religious sin which exhibits considerable psychological insight into the mind and will of men. It understands that life on the personal level is not only reflective but volitional and emotional, even though these precise terms are not used. Man moves when he is moved by desire, and desire comes when a dominant idea receives the support of feeling or emotion. When this dominant idea symbolizes the highest which man and his community knows and is backed by the deepest feelings of which he is capable, then his conduct with respect to this idea becomes enormously effective. Therefore the correctness of the symbol used to depict to man's imagination the nature of this highest is all-important. If the symbol is Yahweh, it signifies justice, redemption through the historical process, and national survival. If the symbol is Baal, social corruption, rank materialism, and a suicidal national policy are thereby invoked. Idolatry is well understood in the Bible as differing from the pure worship of Israel's God in the fact of its personification and objectification of the human will in contrast with the superhuman transcendence of the true God. When an idol is worshiped, man is worshiping himself, his desires, his purposes, and his will.

This can be illustrated without difficulty from the available records. The idols are so described as to give the impression that they are devoid of a will or mind of their own. They have names and devotees, it is true, and even great wealth, as indicated by richly adorned edifices and the great landed estates owned or held in trust for their gods by the members of the priestly class in the case of gods supported by a powerful state. Notwithstanding this fact the idols are the work of men's hands, and the personal qualities they are alleged to possess are really ascribed to them by human beings by a magnificent process of self-deception. These idols are the glorified projections of the will of their human followers and supporters. In them the passion, sordidness, and grandeur of human beings are dramatically represented; in them the baser stuff of human nature comes to the foreground, thanks to the corrupting influence of a ritual and a cultus which knows no objective criterion for the criticism and evaluation of its pretensions. For this reason the idols are incapable of offering salvation to anyone; they cannot even save themselves (Isa. 46:1-2). In the very nature of the case the idols are impotent; they are after all only the visible, tangible expression—in stone, metal, or wood—of human desire and need. They are a tragically pathetic demonstration of the complete futility of all human effort to save humanity.

PERSONAL SIN

Closely related to the sin of idolatry is what may be called personal sin, in the perpetration of which the individual is conscious of no outstanding evil act, although he is deeply distressed by the realization of his estrangement from God. The overt sins of which he may have been guilty are less distressing than the aching sense of a spiritual void signifying that God has departed from him. This void has not been created arbitrarily by an unpredictable whim of God; its existence is due to the sin of the individual.[3] This is a type of sin which is neither social, ethical, cultic, nor religious in the sense of idolatrous. It resides in the innermost being of a man and implicates his real self, his own ego, in a radically personal manner. It is a consciousness of guilt and of personal alienation from God, rather than a transgression against any of the divine commands or a rebellion against his will. The man of God may cry out for pity and forgiveness because of his transgressions, and he may acknowledge his guilt in the divine presence, but this does not accurately portray the nature of his sin. Something has happened to sever his relationship with God. The communion which has delighted his soul, enlarged his mind, and expelled his fear, has been abruptly terminated. Acknowledging his responsibility for this severance of relations, he confesses his personal sin, which is too deep for definition.

We find an interesting example of this type of experience in the great penitential psalm, Ps. 51. In this classic poem of faith and penitence the psalmist admits his guilt and his sin, calling upon God to cleanse him thoroughly. He states that he cannot escape the unlovely specter of that sin—it is ever before him—and that he has sinned against God only. This assertion does not necessarily preclude the sin of ethical wrongdoing; it does, however, emphasize the exclusively theological character of the psalmist's sin. In searching for a reason for his feeling of guilt beyond the fact of his sin, he realizes that sin and guilt accompanied his very conception in the body of his mother (51:5). He asks God to create in him a clean heart and to renew a steadfast spirit within him, and thus gives a hint as to the nature and

---

[3] An exception may be seen in the case of Job (note especially chap. 10), who accuses God of displaying love toward him and then of arbitrarily withdrawing it.

origin of his sin. It has to do with his heart and his spirit, with his deepest self, upon which the spirit of God may operate.[4] This is confirmed further by the plea "and take not thy holy spirit from me." The culminating tragedy of his life would be the removal of God's holy spirit.

The prophet Isaiah, awed by the splendor of his vision of the Lord on a throne in the temple, "high and uplifted," confesses no overt sins which might have aroused and caused this display of the awful power of God—he does not come to the temple as a suppliant sinner seeking forgiveness. Yet, when the full impact of the vision strikes him, he bursts out with a startling expression, "I am lost." The symbolic removal of his guilt and sin by coals from the altar then follows. How should we interpret this surprising reaction of the prophet? It seems plausible to suggest that the vision of God excited in the mind of the prophet a new awareness of his true self, and of the fact of his previously hidden personal sin. He saw himself as a guilty person only because he saw God, the wholly other, whose holiness filled the whole earth. Through this cataclysmic experience the shocking meaning of past decisions, past procrastinations in obeying God, and past sins which may have seemed inconsequential sank deep into his soul; and he saw himself as he was—a sinful man.

What has been written on this aspect of sin as personal and spiritual may cause the conclusion that sin is inseparable from human nature, since all men, when confronted with evidence of the glory and holiness of God, are bound to acknowledge their own sinfulness. Is this not the logical conclusion from the fact of the fundamentally personal nature of sin as outlined and illustrated above? This raises the question respecting the locus of sin. Where does it reside; in the body of man, in his mind, in his spirit, or in his will?

THE LOCUS OF SIN

Does sin inhere in the physical nature of man? The universality of sin is explicitly stated in several writings of the Old Testament: "For there is no man that sins not." (I Kings 8:46; II Chr. 6:36.) "Every mortal on the earth had corrupted his life." (Gen. 6:12.)

> For there is no man on earth so righteous
> That he does good and never fails. (Eccl. 7:20.)

These are absolute statements whose intent is clear, but do they imply

[4] See pp. 41-42.

that by reason of his physiological nature man is prone to sin and will always do so? The weakness of the flesh is a characteristic biblical idea,[5] but this does not necessarily connote sinfulness. As seen elsewhere in our study, flesh is usually contrasted with spirit and particularly with the spiritual power of God. It is never clearly identified as the seat of sin or as the basis for sinful conduct. It is true that "all flesh is grass," but this does not mean that all flesh is therefore sinful. The same may be said about the biblical distinction between flesh and spirit. There is a contrast, but it does not take the form of sinfulness versus sinlessness.

The searching examination which the writer of Job makes when he faces his task of portraying a man with integrity and uprightness who is nonetheless afflicted by the Almighty gives him an opportunity to survey every facet of human character. He constructs his leading character—the type of a genuinely righteous man—and then creates the figures of antagonists who voice various accepted theories in explanation of Job's predicament. Eliphaz, for example, makes the point that man, being mortal, cannot be righteous when compared with God, who is immortal. He dwells in a house of clay—the human body—and is crushed as readily as is the frail moth (4:17-19). Eliphaz does not equate mortality with sin in this passage; he merely declares that man is frail and should not try to challenge the ways of God. Two other references in Job are sometimes taken to support a theory of original sin. Both observe that man appears in this world by the process of human birth, as though this in some way accounts for the brevity and trouble of his life.

Man, that is born of woman,
Is of few days and full of trouble. (14:1.)

What is man, that he should be pure,
And the child of a woman, that he should be innocent? (15:14.)

It matters little that the second verse quoted is probably a scribal gloss; it is a reflection upon the life of man in any case. The effect of these verses is not to produce a conclusion that sin is original in man because of corruption inherent in the sexual process of reproduction. The allusions to being born of a woman are simply intended to show that man is weak and mortal, not that he is sinful.

As to *sex* itself the Old Testament is far removed from later Platonic thinking by Christian theologians on this question. Matter is not

[5] See pp. 61-63.

intrinsically evil or corrupt, and carnality is not a sin in Hebrew thought. Israel's Scriptures contain hardly a hint that the life of sex per se is a life of immorality and sinfulness. A possible exception may be encountered in the Yahwist's narrative of the temptation in the garden, in which the eating of fruit from the tree of the knowledge of good and evil, according to one view, opened the eyes of the man and the woman to their sexual natures and possibilities. Thereupon life began for them. They experienced sexual knowledge, the hardship of toil in the fields, pregnancy for woman, and the rise of the arts and the crafts of civilization. All this led to disaster, climaxed by the great flood. But elsewhere the functions of sex, including intercourse, conception, pregnancy, the birth of children, are ingenuously displayed on the pages of the Bible. God makes barren women fertile; children are a blessing from the Creator; and the nation's founders are promised descendants as numerous as the sands of the sea. Nowhere is there any support for the Pauline language, "our sinful physical form" (Rom. 8:3); "to be physically minded means death, but to be spiritually minded means life and peace" (8:6). On the other hand, Paul's "honor God with your bodies" (I Cor. 6:20) is in agreement with Hebrew thought.

Opposition to sexual license is concentrated on its association with the *paganism* of the day. Baalism and related religious cultures were stigmatized by the spiritual guides of Israel as perverted and debauched. This attack was incurred by reason of baalism's attraction for the men of Israel, who saw in the agricultural gods a means of getting good crops, and who found in the prostitutes attached to their sanctuaries an outlet for their own sexuality. Sex, then, was fundamentally a religious question—its personal-ethical aspects lay in the background, if they were considered at all. An entirely frank exposure of the history of Israel from the standpoint of her sexual and idolatrous lust is given with uncensored fulness in Ezek. 23. Personified as Oholah (Samaria) and Oholibah (Jerusalem), the two kingdoms are revealed as submitting to their lovers from Egypt and Assyria and Babylonia. These lovers defiled Oholah and Oholibah with their lust till they were sated. They in turn doted on their paramours, "whose lust was as gross as that of asses or stallions." This allegory effectively combines the religious and the sexual significance of prostitution in ancient Israel. But the real sin is not sexuality; it is idolatry.

When we push our inquiry further in the matter of discovering the locus of sin, the relation of sin to the *will* and mind of man calls for consideration. In all of the discussion thus far the paramount value of man's loyalty and personal devotion to the object of his adoration and emulation has been stressed. This was particularly pronounced in the treatment of biblical idolatry, where it was noted that idols were really embodiments of human thought and desire. The chief sin was rebellion against God, the other-than-man, and the glorification of man-made images, who were gods in name only. These gods were made in the image of man—in the image of his mind, desire, and purpose. As a consequence of this type of idolatry man was outrageously guilty of giving himself the status of God and of exalting his own will as of supreme worth. This unseemly magnification of human desire arose from man's stubborn unwillingness to admit his human shortcomings and limitations. His mind was bent on evil continually, simply because he sought to do the will of man rather than the will of God. His will was sinful in its rejection of the divine will.

Thus sin has finally been traced to its source—the mind and will of man, which is corrupted by human pride and arrogance. This will is the spirit of apostasy and defiance abhorred by the prophets; it is the unresigned rebellion of men who have had a taste of power, and to whom the recognition of a higher power is utterly repugnant. An unusually forceful prophetic oracle on this subject appears in Isa. 2. On the day of the Lord's coming in all his glory, we are told, the pride and haughtiness of man will be humbled to the dust. Both men and the idols of their self-worship will rush into holes in the ground on that day. In his panic man will cast away

> His idols of silver and his idols of gold,
> Which he made for himself to worship. (2:20.)

Mankind will be ignominiously brought low. With telling cogency some scribe has added,

> Cease trusting man, in whose nostrils is breath;
> For of what account is he? (2:22.)

He sensed the all-important point—the pride of man causes him to trust in man rather than in God. His idols are pretexts for self-worship.

The sin of *pride* constitutes the principal religious message of the story of Babel (Gen. 11). In this ancient legend one finds an attempted explanation of the building of the city of Babylon and the construction of a *zikkurat* (artificial mountain-temple). We are informed that men once spoke only one language and lived together in one place. Gathering confidence from their numbers and their solidarity, perhaps induced by their ability to understand one another, men decided to erect a tower and to build a city. The tower, they hoped, would reach to the heavens. In this way they would demonstrate their ingenuity and strength and at the same time make a name for themselves. But the plans of men went awry when Yahweh entered the picture. Noting what man was doing he resolved to block the enterprise and to put a stop to this human attempt to exalt the creature and make him a creator on a par with God. So he "made a babble of the language of the whole earth, and . . . dispersed them all over the earth" (11:9).

The plans of God will stand firm while the imperialistic plans of mighty nations will be thwarted. Human pride on the national level cannot stand against the power of God who is Lord of history. Even Assyria, the great nation boasting arrogantly of its wisdom, military success and plunder, will bow before One who is mightier than that lion of the ancient world. God has used her against his own sinful people, but Assyria is blissfully unaware that she is being used:

> But not so does he think,
> And not so does he plan. (Isa. 10:7.)

On the contrary, he confidently asserts:

> By the strength of my hand have I done it,
> And by my wisdom, for I have understanding. (10:13.)

This smugness brings the retort:

> Shall an axe boast over the man that hews with it? (10:15.)

Pride is sin, whether it be the pride of an individual or of a nation; for it is the mark of presumptuous self-glorification whereby man tries to forget his lowly stature and to assert an impossible lordship which is not his to assert. A forthright and pungent summation of the meaning of pride as it affects man's relation to God deserves to be quoted here in full.

> Thus says the Lord:
> "Let not the wise man boast of his wisdom,
> Nor the strong man boast of his strength,
> Nor the rich man boast of his riches!
> But if one must boast, let him boast of this,
> That he understands and knows me—
> How I, the Lord, am he who practices kindness,

Justice, and righteousness on the earth;
For in these things I delight," is the oracle of the Lord.
(Jer. 9:23-24.)

Wisdom, power, and wealth are totally unreliable substitutes for the God of love and goodness, the splendor of whose righteousness convicts all self-made men of the sin of destructive pride. Only by the humble surrender of the human values he cherishes can man know the Lord.

THE OCCASION FOR SIN

This truth leads to the observation that the occasion for man's sin is his dilemma of godlikeness and creatureliness.[6] Man is a being torn between two worlds; the world of his physical, created nature which binds him inextricably to the earth and to things of earth, and the world of freedom and spiritual aspiration in which he may transcend the weakness of his flesh and put all things under his feet. In his refusal to accept the fate this apparent duality of his being imposes upon him he commits sin, either by extravagant self-assertion in the projection of his will, or by deliberate titillation of his sense organs in the hope of anesthetizing his spirit into forgetfulness of his origin and nature. This self-assertion appears in the biblical literature as human pride or as the pride of idolatry. Through the glamorous and sensuously delightful worship of the baals man in the Old Testament finds self-fulfillment without suffering the self-humiliation accompanying the adoration of a God transcendent to man and able to annihilate his self-deception by the blazing light of his holiness.

Man wills to heap up wealth—wealth in land or wealth in gold and silver—principally as a means of confirming his secret belief as to his masterly powers; and if he puts some of this gold and silver upon images carved from wood, this act further strengthens his deception with respect to his godlike nature. Or man creates an elaborate sacerdotal system with impressive ritual, richly robed priests, and solemn incantations. This too is so patently the work of his brain and hands that the thrilling spectacle it affords gives him an added sense of well-being and power. This feeling is intensified to the degree that the religious system he has produced pronounces no ethical indictment of his pattern for living. The gods of Canaan, of Egypt, of Assyria, of Babylonia were worshiped by means of such a ritual. They incarnated no ultimate righteousness for the regeneration of men; in them men saw themselves and were satisfied. Beneath this satisfaction, however,

[6] For a stimulating treatment of this subject, see R. Niebuhr, *The Nature and Destiny of Man;* Series I, *Human Nature* (1941), pp. 15 ff.

was painful restlessness which could not be quieted. Man never forgot the paradox of his being; his Scriptures made that impossible, at least for the Israelite. At the height of his attainments—as witness David or Solomon—he was most sensitive to criticisms of his illusions of grandeur or of his unfounded assumptions of authority. Both individual kings and the nation they ruled chafed under the rankling harangues of the prophets. The violence of their repudiation of prophetic criticism was in direct proportion to the uneasiness of their consciences, we may well believe. The anger which occasionally broke out against these caustic critics was not just the natural reaction to adverse criticism; it was even more the deeper disturbance of minds not sure of their ground and fighting to maintain the illusion of assurance.

With the increase in man's disquiet came a commensurate increase in the diligence and aggressiveness with which man prosecuted the various enterprises his will had brought into being. To the degree that other wills stood in the path of his success he ruthlessly overrode them, if and when he could. This was the occasion for the widespread practice of social injustice so wholeheartedly hated and vigorously attacked by the prophets and others of like mind. Men took the blessing of God seriously and literally as they recalled that he had given them power and had urged them to fill the earth, subdue it, and have dominion over fish, birds, animals, and reptiles; but they went beyond this permissive decree and tried to bring their fellow men under their dominion also. Using due process of law, or ignoring it, men in political positions, in commercial life, and in organized religion violated human rights and enslaved the weak and defenseless. These evidences of social injustice are symptomatic of the sin of pride, which refuses to believe that man is a creature whose only possible salvation is humble dependence upon the God who made him.

5. Salvation in the Old Testament

SALVATION signifies the help that men receive from their religion. It may be defined so as to concentrate attention upon deliverance from evil in the future life, or it may be made more inclusive to embrace also escape from the evils of this present world. It may be freely used for the secular or mundane activities by means of which man struggles to emancipate himself from ignorance, prejudice, fear, and insecurity with the help of forces in the natural order which are amenable to his control. On the other hand, salvation may relate exclusively to the process instigated and continued by a nonhuman Power believed to have a will independent of man's and a purpose which transcends his. If this Power is defined with the theistic vocabulary of the Old Testament, salvation must be regarded as strictly theocentric as to the nature of the process, its goals, and its driving force.

Salvation of one kind or another appears in religions universally, although religions which stress a personal God and the possibility of human intercourse with him are usually called religions of salvation in contrast with those that do not. Since *human need* appears in every culture and community without regard to race or degree of civilization, some form of salvation will also appear. If this need is reduced to its lowest terms, the fundamental drives of mankind for physical, sexual, and social satisfaction are encountered. For the realization of these drives and the satisfaction of the needs which they represent man turns to religion as an important resource.

Salvation is a general term, then, covering the nature of the several human needs and the activities which must be carried on to meet them. These activities, when the term salvation is used in the religious sense, involve both the deeds of God and the response of man. The local Chamber of Commerce, the Rotary Club, or the American Federation of Labor may engage in programs for community betterment; but their work cannot be spoken of as salvation, except in a broad and practically meaningless sense. Man's efforts to improve the social order or to perfect the mechanical tools with which he earns a living, although they bear upon the subject of religion, are not in themselves aspects of the experience of salvation. The biblical vocabulary of salvation is a strongly theological vocabulary with a decided emphasis upon the work of God in helping men. When men work for their own salvation—as far as the men of Israel are concerned—they are accused of idolatry by their prophetic contemporaries. The final doom which will reward their folly is vividly portrayed. Thus this chapter on salvation must inquire into the part that God plays, and then it needs to investigate the question of man's participation in the process. Before this inquiry is undertaken, however, a brief statement will be made outlining the goals of salvation as emphasized by the people of the Old Testament.

GOALS OF SALVATION

Salvation is often identified with *national victory* by the biblical writers. The saving activity of God culminates in conquering the foes of his people, the record often informs us. This victory is regarded as the direct result of the work of God on behalf of his people. It may be withheld if the nation is guilty of disobedience. Defeat and servitude to another nation are frequently described as the consequence of sin. The Israelites are urged to go into battle with the assurance that God is on their side. On the eve of a battle a priest is to say to them, "To-day you are on the eve of a battle against your enemies; do not be faint-hearted, nor afraid, nor alarmed, nor stand in dread of them; for the Lord your God is going with you, to fight for you against your enemies and give you victory [salvation]." (Deut. 20:3-4.) In the recurrent cycle of evildoing, punishment by subjection to the enemy, and repentance followed by deliverance through the coming of a savior—a cycle which characterizes the conception of early Hebrew history held by the Deuteronomic writers of the book of Judges (3:7-11; 3:15; 6:36; 7:7; 10:11-12)—we have another example of salvation as victory over the enemy.

Deliverance from the foe follows political subjection to that foe as a consequence of forsaking God and following after false gods. In the time of the monarchy this meaning of salvation as military victory or national deliverance continues in effect. In the eighth century, when Jeroboam was king of Israel, although he did "that which was evil in the sight of the Lord" (II Kings 14:24), he was permitted to restore "the territory of Israel from the entrance of Hamath to the sea of Arabah" (14:25) pursuant to the word which God had spoken by his servant Jonah, the son of Amittai. In this way God saved Israel by the hand of Jeroboam, not by the chance and fortunate combination of favorable political, military, and economic forces which appeared to guarantee victory, but by the divine decree designed to prevent Israel from being wiped off the face of the earth.

In like manner, at the time of Assyria's invasion of Judah under Sennacherib, God announced his intention to preserve his city Jerusalem. "By the way that he came, by the same shall he return; but he shall not come into this city, is the Lord's oracle. For I will defend this city to deliver it for my own sake, and for the sake of my servant David." (II Kings 19:33-34.) To carry out this purpose, we are told, the angel of the Lord killed in one night 185,000 Assyrian troops (19:35).[1] In the late apocalypse found in Isa. 24-27, the salvation of the Lord follows the defeat of Moab, which is trampled down "as straw is trampled down in the water of a dung-pit" (25:10). These mighty deeds worked against the enemy naturally permit Israel's God to be called a "victorious warrior" (Zeph. 3:17). The writer of the ancient psalm incorporated both in the collection of psalms (18:46-48) and in Second Samuel (22:47-49) without hesitation ascribes to his God the power to free him from his enemies and to give him vengeance over his adversaries. This God he calls "the God of my deliverance." It is the God of salvation who assembles the exiles and frees them from the nations by his power (I Chr. 16:35).

Long life and prosperity constitutes further evidence of the content of salvation conceived in terms of goals rather than as process. While this conception of material blessings runs through the literature rather extensively, it is especially emphasized in Deuteronomy, from which several citations will be made. The commandment enjoining honor toward parents is appropriate here. "Honor your father and mother, as the Lord your God has commanded you, that you may live long and prosper in the land that the Lord your God is giving you." (5:16; cf. 5:33.) God is giving Israel a land filled with wealth, great cities, houses full of riches, vineyards and olive groves, none of which was created by the Israelites, but all of which were placed at their disposal by the lovingkindness of their divine Savior (6:10-12; cf. 8:7-10). This God will abundantly bless them if his ordinances are heeded, as he promised their fathers. "He will bless the offspring of your body and the produce of your soil, your grain and wine and oil, the issue of your cattle, and the progeny of your flock, . . . not a male or a female

[1] Traditions are in conflict as to this. Note in II Kings 19:7: "Behold, I will put a spirit in him, so that he shall hear a rumor and return to his own land, and I will cause him to fall by the sword in his own land."

being barren among you or your cattle. The Lord will also free you from all sickness." (7:13-15.)

The ideal life, the gift of the great savior God, is poetically and extravagantly presented in the following psalm:

Our sons are like plants grown large in their youth;
Our daughters are like cornices carved after the fashion of a palace.
Our garners are filled to overflowing, garners of all sorts.
Our flocks increase by thousands and tens of thousands in our fields.
Our oxen are heavily laden.
There is no riot and no alarm,
And no outcry in our streets.
How happy the people that are in such a state!
How happy the people whose God is the Lord! (144:12-15.)

Numerous, lovely children, abundant crops, large herds and flocks, ample goods for the market, a land at peace—how happy indeed are the people who have a God who loves them so much!

THE DIVINE PURPOSE OF SALVATION

Along with political freedom, victory over the enemy, material prosperity and general well-being the idea of salvation has numerous other meanings which can best be brought out by a discussion of how salvation takes place. This entails a consideration of the divine purpose in God's giving his people the salvation of prosperity, victory, and the other consequences of his activity. In particular we should note that the objective of God's interaction with his people and of theirs with him is the glorification of his name and the development of an obedient and righteous nation. There is nothing inherently deserving in the national character which induces God to choose this particular group for his redemptive purposes. In fact, there were times when the conduct of the nation was so rampantly evil that no basis whatsoever for the divine favor could possibly be discerned. Yet the fact of the favor, amazing as it was, was a demonstrated and demonstrable fact of history. There being no empirical justification on the human level for God's amazing grace, Israel's thinkers found it in the very nature of their God. As a consequence two great obligations and passions assumed a central place in their conception of salvation. One was the duty and joy of obedience to the God of righteousness, and the other was the passion for personal communion with this God.

Although Israel time and again had proved herself unworthy to receive the benefits of God's love, she had received a revelation of the way of life God esteemed most highly—the way of justice and mercy. This she had learned from her prophets and seers and through her history. To experience the fullness of salvation, therefore, she could do nothing less than to strive to follow this way. Thus the life of righteousness was exalted in this people's literature. Only by living such a life could final victory be assured; only by *ethical obedience* could men and women find the personal peace and power which their hearts craved.

This view of salvation is outstanding in the extant records; it runs through the canonical books and is present even in those writings which contain a pronounced materialistic note. Physical blessings, in the book of Deuteronomy for example, are never promised without qualification. "You must keep his statutes and commands" (4:40); "You must walk wholly in the way that the Lord your God has appointed you" (5:33)—these are stipulations that blessings are conditioned upon ethical behavior. Such exhortations appear with almost monotonous frequency.

The second obligation laid upon a people to whom salvation is to come is that of direct and *personal communion with God*. Let us look at this point for a moment. In the land of Canaan Israel is to seek God faithfully and diligently and is promised success in her quest if she seeks him with her whole heart and mind (4:29). She must love her God with all her mind, and heart, and strength (6:5). Continuously conscious of the absolute holiness and goodness of her God, Israel must keep herself holy and upright, maintaining a relation of sincere loyalty to him. So even in the priestly book of Leviticus provision is made for personal religion and communion with God. After various injunctions have been given, their religious purpose is indicated in words declaring the supremacy of God—"since I am the Lord" (19:16; cf. 19:2, 12, 14). Many are the psalmists who proclaim triumphantly their delight in practicing the presence of God. One of these finds God in the sanctuary for which his heart longs. Once there, he can cry:

> My heart and my flesh give a shout of joy
> for the living God! (84:2.)

In the midst of terrifying calamities and awful fears another psalmist can calmly declare, "Into thy hand I commit my spirit" (31:5). The presence of God is his salvation.

The above sketch of the general content of the idea of salvation serves to identify the end result of a process rather than the process itself. Deliverance from evil—whether that evil be national defeat, famine, poverty, personal fear, or illness—is the negative side of experience. When the positive side is recorded, we find that salvation involves ethical and spiritual results also. The "saved" community is burdened by the obligation to incarnate the principles of social justice believed to represent the will of God, and the "saved" individual has the joy of knowing the very presence of God in his life. But in any case, whether negative or positive, salvation seems to be conceived as something given by God, either as the result of his goodness or as a reward for righteousness and piety.

Yet it is questionable that such an influential and useful word can be disposed of so readily. If religion is a continuing and living experience, and if salvation is the heart of that experience, its dismissal as simply signifying the particular consequences of a prescribed mode of behavior is highly unrealistic. The limited number of passages already discussed contain hints that salvation is far greater than a more or less tangible reward for good conduct. By tentatively defining salvation as the good which comes to men in their *life with God,* we are able to avoid the artificial separation between processes and their consequences, which underlies the general misunderstanding of the Old Testament as reflecting a religion primarily of concrete rewards for good conduct. Such a definition as the one proposed is admittedly highly over-simplified; but the subsequent development of the subject will supply its most serious deficiencies, it is hoped.

A cogent interpretation of salvation in the Old Testament must be closely associated with the ideas of God, man, and sin found in this literature. The theology of its writers is not composed of separate gems of religious truth strung upon a string of logic; it is the articulate statement of the meaning of a special historical experience which reflects what God is and does for man. From the nature of God, man and sin and salvation take their distinctive meaning, as do the other ideas to be discussed later in this work. More specifically, then, we may ask, How does the conception of salvation depend upon the nature of sin? Sin, we have seen, is man's refusal to recognize his creaturehood, and his proud assertion of his spiritual uniqueness and freedom. He pretends he is God and proceeds to create images of himself in the form of economic or political power, intellectual systems viewed as sacrosanct, and moral codes replacing the divine righteousness, thus seeking to prove to himself and his fellows that he is God rather than a creature of God. He uses his freedom idolatrously and unethically, encroaching upon the freedom of others whom he may exploit and enslave. This is sin. In view of this, what is salvation?

Salvation obviously must include the arrival of a sense of humility and dependence upon God as a consequence of the breakdown of pride and arrogance. It requires an honest admission of man's creatureliness and an acknowledgement of the weakness and limitations which this condition imposes upon man. It presupposes the surrender of the will to God and the full acceptance of the divine will as determinative for all of life. It demands complete submission to God as the arbiter of man's destiny and the reorganization of life in harmony with this surrender. All of this involves adjustments of a difficult and complicated personal nature, calling for psychological changes, radically revolutionary ethical commitments of a new self seeing values in a new light, and a transformation of man's volitional nature in a response to goals and influences originating in the being of God. Such a change is incredibly fantastic when man's moral and psychological resources and limitations are considered. Salvation from sin appears to be impossible in view of these enormous difficulties.

But salvation is not a kind of psychosomatic therapy by means of which health of mind and body may be restored. Such a restoration is conceivable, but it makes use of the work of God rather than of the psychiatrist. Only through the action of a higher Power outside of himself can man come to that final humility which is the basis and the starting point of salvation. Nothing less than the penetrating light of God's condemning and illuminating holiness can reveal man to himself and show him his sin. Only the revelation of the majesty and mercy of God can break man's pride and destroy his sin. With this in mind, as a true expression of Old Testament belief, we must now examine biblical assertions about God as savior and redeemer of men. What does God do in bringing men to the point of confessing their sin of self-will and receiving the good which may come to them in their life with God? We must remember, in this connection, that what the Bible says God *is* really amounts to saying what he *does*. Terms of description are really terms of function and behavior.

GOD AS SAVIOR

Here it is well to distinguish between the so-called attributes of God, described in Chapter 2, and the traits or appellatives applied to him in the present discussion of salvation. Properly this material and that already presented on the nature of God belong together. The division has been made for the purpose of impressing upon the reader that the God of Israel is most adequately understood in terms of his work as savior. In this phase of our treatment we are concerned with the everlasting God of justice, creative power, and holiness *as he seeks to save men* from their sins and to help them live a new life. As the Hebrews saw this God in action in their personal lives and in their national history, they recorded what they saw, in dynamic terms testifying to the faith that was in them and to the God of salvation who was the author and object of that faith. This testimony, therefore, is weighted with religious rather than theological or philosophical terminology. Nevertheless it is of unusual value for our purpose of discovering the part played by the divine Actor in the mighty drama of salvation.

Logically we may begin our survey by studying the use of the title "savior" or the verb "save" in connection with God. In the days to come God will reveal himself as savior, establishing Jerusalem as an immovable tent, and a quiet home; and as judge, commander, and king, he will bring salvation (Isa. 33:20-22). On that day the glory of the Lord will be revealed; feeble hands will be strengthened, tottering knees made firm, and fearful hearts given peace, when God comes to save Israel (35:2-4). In the chaotic days of Cyrus' startling military victories Israel was commissioned to testify to the uniqueness of God her savior:

> Before me was no God formed,
> And after me there shall be none:
> I, I am the Lord,
> And apart from me there is no savior. (Isa. 43:10-11.)

God will oppose the enemies of his people with all his might, so that "all flesh shall know that I the Lord am your savior" (49:26). Out of his great pity and love God became the savior of the household of Israel. Through no intermediary but directly by his own presence, he saved them; by his love he redeemed them (63:8-9).

The restoration of the exiles is the work of God the savior. Everyone is to "shout on the top of the mountain" and be glad because the Lord is bringing them from all parts of the earth—the blind, the lame, the pregnant women—a great company returning to Zion after years of heartbreaking absence: "the Lord has saved his people" (Jer. 31:7-8). By giving them a ruler from the line of David, God again demonstrates that he can save them from being scattered like sheep in foreign lands (Ezek. 34:22). He will deliver his people from the lands to the west and to the east; and they shall dwell in Jerusalem.

> And they shall be my people, and I will be their God,
> In faithfulness and righteousness. (Zech. 8:8.)

When God saves—that is, delivers—Zion, he will rebuild the cities of Judah (Ps. 69:35); and, in spite of rebellion against him, he delivered them at the Sea of Reeds for his own name's sake (106:7-8). A prayer is said to this savior God:

> O God, in thy plenteous grace,
> Answer me with thy saving faithfulness. (69:13.)

His salvation is close to those who reverence the Lord (85:9). In quiet confidence one saint of old declares,

> The Lord is my light and my salvation;
> whom shall I fear? (27:1.)

He is a God deserving of great praise, eliciting songs of gratitude to the rock of Israel's deliverance. To the successful warrior he is a rock and the God of his deliverance, before whom the alien enemy fades away (Ps. 18:46-47). As a consequence of forgetting the God of their salvation the apostate nation will suffer famine and ruin (Isa. 17:10). Defeated Israel, overthrown by her enemies, announces that she will confidently wait for the God of deliverance, assured that he will appear with his saving power in due time (Mic. 7:7). This God of salvation is petitioned by the exiles to save them, that they may give thanks to his holy name (I Chr. 16:35).

All the nations of the earth should be glad, for God judges justly and leads aright. His treatment of his own people will mean that his salvation will be made known among all nations (Ps. 67:2). Trust in God is the assurance of salvation from the wicked (37:39-40). By his grace and faithfulness the God of the psalmist gives victory and salvation (40:10). So eager is another devout man of Israel to praise God for his deeds of salvation that he declares that if he were a skilled writer and lived to a ripe old age, he would be kept fully occupied recording God's righteous acts toward him (71:14-16). Salvation as the activity of God, then, on the basis of these references, means deliverance of the nation throughout its history; and the glorious culmination of this experience in the restoration of the exiles, as well as release from personal afflictions such as human enemies, fear, and uncertainty.

GOD AS FATHER

The divine savior of Israel is the father of the nation, who gave being and life to its individual members, and who controls, guides, and watches over the entire community, punishing, rebuking, and blessing it. The concept of the fatherhood of God is clearly at home in the Old Testament, although it is not as pronounced as it might have been had the baalism of the day contained no similar designation for its male deity (Jer. 2:27). The meaning of fatherhood as applied to God may be observed from the following quotations:

> Is this the way to treat the Lord,
> You foolish and senseless people?
> Is he not your father who created you,
> Who made you and fashioned you? (Deut. 32:6.)

> He found them in a desert land,
>
> . . . .
>
> He encircled them, he cared for them;
> He guarded them like the pupil of his eye. (32:10.)

> And I thought, "Surely you will call me 'Father,'
> And will not turn back from me." (Jer. 3:19.)

> Have you not now been calling to me,
>   "My father! the comrade of my youth?" (3:4.)

In a more joyous mood the writer acts as the spokesman of God, who says,

> I will lead them to streams of water,
>
> . . . .
>
> For I have become a father to Israel,
> And Ephraim is my first-born. (31:9.)

And in Isaiah,

> Thou, O Lord, art our Father,
> Our Redeemer from of old is thy name. (63:16.)

> Yet now, O Lord, thou art our Father;
> We are the clay, and thou art the potter—
> We are all of us the work of thy hand. (64:8.)

Or again,

> "But if I be a father, where is my honor?
> And if I be a master, where is my reverence?"

Says the Lord of hosts to you,
O priests, who despise my name. (Mal. 1:6.)

Have we not all one father?
Did not one God create us? (2:10.)

In the psalms we find,

Sing unto God; praise his name!

. . . .

A father to the fatherless and the judge of widows
Is God in his holy dwelling. (68:4-5.)

In the above citations God as father is revealed to be the creator and fashioner of the nation. He cares for, and watches over, Israel and requires love and loyalty of his children; he is also redeemer and determiner of their fate. In at least one instance he is the father of all. mankind. To the weak and needy he shows fatherly kindness, and of the defenseless he is the champion against the oppressor. Thus he exhibits important functions with respect to the salvation of men.

The Hebrew verb *pakadh* (attend to, visit, muster, visit with the intention of punishing the guilty, appoint—in the favorable sense) gives additional information as to the saving function of God. In the references used here, God's loving care and interest in men and in Israel are aptly pictured. In the first of these passages God has aroused wonder in the heart of one man over the fact that human beings have been singled out for special attention and favor.

What is man that thou shouldst think of him,
And the son of man that thou shouldst care for [visit] him? (Ps. 8:4.)

Job wistfully reminds God of the tender relations which had existed between them in the past, when he says,

Life and love hast thou exercised with me,
And thy watch-care [visitation] has preserved my spirit. (Job 10:12.)

The word may indicate a gracious act performed by God on man's behalf, as in this instance where Sarah has prayed for a son, "The Lord dealt with [*pakadh*] Sarah, as he had said; the Lord did to Sarah as he had promised" (Gen. 21:1).

Joseph was at the end of the road of his life when he spoke to his brothers, "I am about to die; but God will be sure to take note of [*pakadh*] you, and take you out of this land" (Gen. 50:24). We may see here the providential care of God toward the people who were to be the object and the means of his salvation. In a personal vein the term is used by Jeremiah:

> Thou knowest, O Lord!
> Think of me, and visit me;
> Avenge me on my persecutors. (15:15.)

In this petition of a harassed man driven frantic by his enemies the effective presence of God is desired for the accomplishment of vengeance. Nevertheless the possibility of this presence and its potency to influence events is positively believed and accepted by the prophet.

To accomplish his purpose of freeing the exiled Jews, God plans to *visit* them: " 'As soon as Babylon has finished seventy years, I will visit you, and will fulfill my gracious promise to you, by restoring you to this place. For I know the thoughts I cherish toward you,' is the oracle of the Lord, 'thoughts of good and not of evil, directed toward giving you a future and a hope.' " (29:10-11.) In his letter to the exiles Jeremiah voices the good will of God, who intends to come to his nation with the gift of deliverance in his hand in order to re-establish them in Jerusalem.

A poet acquainted with drought and crop failure must have written a part of Ps. 65. His faith impels him to write:

> Thou makest the dawn and the sunset to shout with joy.
> Thou visitest the land and makest it overflow. (65:8-9.)

The blessed downpour of rain, which softens the earth and revives plant life, accompanies a visit from God—it is his gift to men. A more personal note is struck in another psalm, where the author contemplates the divine deliverance of Israel and prays for the opportunity to share in it:

> Remember me, O Lord, in thy favor toward thy people;
> Visit me when thou deliverest them. (106:4.)

Similarly a man of God confesses that the holy one has come to chasten and purge him of evil:

> Thou hast tried my heart, thou hast visited me by night;
> Thou hast purified me by fire;

Thou dost not find iniquity in me;
My mouth does not transgress. (17:3.)

Such a visitation brings salvation in a spiritual rather than a political or physical sense. In a considerable number of passages containing *pakadh* the meaning "visit in order to punish" is to be noted (Jer. 6:15; 49:8; 50:31; Ps. 59:5; Amos 3:14; Hos. 1:4; 2:13; Exod. 20:5; Deut. 5:9; Isa. 10:12, etc.). The significance of these will be dealt with later.

GOD'S LOVE AND GRACE

We have seen how God as father and savior does not remain aloof from men; it is his nature to participate aggressively and creatively in their lives, giving of himself for the sake of their redemption. He "comes" to them with a decisiveness and a certainty of action that cannot be ignored. The language describing the event of salvation leaves no doubt in the reader's mind as to what is meant—God does not vaguely inspire men to help themselves: he is actually present and gives help in time of need. This biblical belief prepares the way for examining certain terms in the Hebrew Bible which express the love of God. The motivating forces behind the choice of Israel as the covenant people were the hidden purpose of God and his manifest love for this people and, through them, for all men. This inquiry is necessary in connection with the idea of salvation, for the good that men experience from God, which may be called salvation, is simply the evidence of the divine love in action upon the stage of history. As the men of Israel pragmatically learned the truth of the meaning of salvation, they put it into words by talking about the love, the mercy, or the grace of God.

We will note first a term used less often of God, but frequently of human relationships, the word 'ahav (love). When applied to God it expresses a redemptive purpose in his mind and effective historical action through his power. The merciful God, the creator of man, the only God revealed himself to Israel because he loved them; and because of his love he brought them out of Egypt, it is disclosed in Deuteronomy (4:37-38). It was not because they were the greatest of all peoples—far from it—that the Lord chose Israel, but because he loved them, we are informed (7:8, 13; 23:5). God loves the Israelites though they are untrue to him (Hos. 3:1); when Israel was a child, he came to love him (11:1); he loves them freely, and this love will cause him to heal and to forgive them (14:4). God does not love the way men love; his love is not meted out in the hope of a return; it magnificently overlooks the opportunity for hatred and vindictiveness.

> How can I give you up, O Ephraim!
> How surrender you, O Israel!
> How can I treat you like Admah!
> How make you like Zeboim!
> My mind turns against me;
> My sympathies also grow hot.
> I will not carry out my hot anger:
> Nor will I again destroy Ephraim;
> For I am God and not man,
> The holy one in the midst of you.
> (Hos. 11:8-9.)

Israel is precious in the sight of God. His Creator has redeemed him, called him by his name; and God attends him in every misfortune and hardship. He is not to fear, for God is with him, rescuing from every land the people whom he loves, and whom he created and formed for his glory (Isa. 43:1-7). God has loved Israel with an everlasting love, so that he will restore him and permit him once more to rejoice in the land of his fathers (Jer. 31:1-3). In all of these passages the love of God for men—confined largely to Israel—was projected into the historical situation in the form of guidance and actual political or social deliverance. Here salvation is the convincing consequence of the expression of love, as it is of other functional characteristics in the divine nature.

A much more common and religiously valuable word for love in the Hebrew Bible is *hesedh,* often translated "lovingkindness." "Condescending love" or "gracious favor" might better express what the word means, however. It comes close to Paul's use of *charis* (grace) in the New Testament. As applied to man its meaning is to do a favor for another. For instance, Jonathan says to David, "If I should die, may you never cut off your kindness [*hesedh*] from my house" (I Sam. 20:15). Hosea shows us what he believes to be of great importance in the life of a nation when he announces that there is no fidelity, no "kindness" and no knowledge of God in the land (4:1). When the throne of David is re-established, it will take place by means of "kindness" and faithfulness (Isa. 16:5). In Proverbs "kindness" and "good faith" are consistently juxtaposed (3:3; 14:22; 16:6; 20:28). In other places the word is used in connection with terms for righteousness, mercy, and compassion. It is thus a word for human relations where decency, courtesy, and good will prevail. Notwithstanding its ethical use for human relations it is predominantly a word for the outreaching love of God, denoting his grace, mercy, and redemptive power. Its use to convey this thought, with particular reference to redemption or salvation, should now receive our attention.

God is man's strength, his fortress, his "gracious" God, a refuge in time of danger (Ps. 59:17). Saving grace is God's, not man's; the sons of men are not trustworthy, but the grace of God is sure (62:9-12).

> For with the Lord is grace,
> And with him is plenteous redemption. (130:7.)

The Lord was kind to Joseph in prison (Gen. 39:21); through the Sea of Reeds God led the people whom he wished to redeem in his grace (Exod. 15:13); in kindness God draws Israel to himself (Jer. 31:3). Ezra was enabled through the grace of God to obtain the favor of Artaxerxes, the Persian ruler, in rebuilding Jerusalem (Ezra 7:28); the king who trusts in the Lord will be confirmed by the "grace" (goodness) of God (Ps. 21:7); and the psalmist who trusts in him may pray, "deliver me through thy grace" (31:16). The love or grace of God is exceedingly precious, another psalmist tells us (36:7); by day and by night the consciousness of the divine love makes the believer rejoice (42:8); God's grace is a source of amazement over which men may ponder in the temple (48:9). This grace comes to men as an answer to prayer (66:20); a worshiper prays,

> Show us thy grace, O Lord;
> And grant us thy salvation. (85:7.)

Thus he connects this word with the manifestation of salvation. Fidelity, righteousness, and peace are thought to be in intimate association with grace (85:10); God's mercy and grace make men shout with joy (90:13-14): his grace is seen in the wonders of his liberating, life-giving work among the sons of men (107:8, 15, 21, 31); and grace as actively potent is invoked by one petitioner to destroy his adversaries (109:26).

God's gracious love is extended to those who seek redemption and forgiveness for their sins (25:7).

Have pity on me, O God, in accordance with thy grace;

. . . .

Wash me thoroughly from my guilt,
And cleanse me from my sin. (51:1-2.)

This love is evinced in the faithful covenant-keeping character of God:
by faithfully keeping the promises made in the covenant bond, God
shows his love and kindness.

> Though the mountains should remove,
> And the hills should waver,
> My love shall not remove from you,
> And my covenant of peace shall not waver. (Isa. 54:10.)

God keeps loving faith with those who love him; he keeps his covenant
and shows kindness (*ḥesedh*) to his servants (Mic. 7:18; Deut. 7:9,
12; I Kings 8:23). Although a great and terrible God, he keeps his
gracious covenant with those who love him (Neh. 1:5); and in confessing sin on behalf of the Jews, Daniel recalls that God is loving
and faithful in maintaining the covenant (9:4). God's love is said to
be as great as the heavens (Pss. 57:10; 103:11); the earth is full of it;
it will endure forever; and it is exceedingly good. Grace, therefore,
is the active love of God to man, unmerited by him, working for his
redemption, and stimulating in him words of wonder and joy. It is
what men discover in the heart of God when they personally experience
his gift of salvation.

Two other terms, *raḥamim* (compassion) and *ḥanan* (show favor,
be gracious), may be brought into this discussion. As to the first, its
root is the same as the root of the word for womb and may suggest
brotherly or maternal feeling, that is, the feeling proper to those
coming from the same womb, or to the one from whose womb man
comes. In any case, love or compassion is its meaning when used of
God. *Raḥamim* may denote the divine pity or fatherly mercy, likewise
mercy as opposed to anger, or the merciful forgiveness and redemption
of Israel. It also stands for the compassion resulting in the furtherance of life and is connected with God's forgiveness; because of it
God forgives men and delivers them from evil. God's anger linked
with his mercy is preferable to man's violence in war; compassion is
equivalent to God's everlasting love; Israel, called "the unpitied," will
receive a new name and be called "my people." The compassion or
mercy of God directs him to listen to the pleas of men; the mercies
and compassion of God never fail, and they have continued from of

old (Isa. 63:7; Pss. 77:9; 79:8; 86:5; 119:77; Dan. 9:9; Neh. 9:28; II Sam. 24:14; Isa. 54:8; Hos. 2:23; Ps. 69:16; Lam. 3:22; Ps. 25:6). The other word, *ḥanan,* has a usage practically identical with *raḥamim* in the Old Testament, although it finds a place more often in the ordinary intercourse of men or between men and God. We may cite the benediction from Num. 6:24-26 by way of illustration:

The Lord bless you and guard you;
The Lord make his face to shine upon you, and be *gracious* unto you;
The Lord lift up his countenance upon you, and make you prosper!

Aaron was instructed to use this blessing for the Israelites. When Hazael of Syria subdued Israel, God was gracious and permitted Jehoash to defeat Ben-hadad, the son of Hazael, and to recover certain cities of Israel (II Kings 13:23).

The God of justice can be expected to be gracious and compassionate to all who wait upon him (Isa. 30:18); the exiles may call upon God to be gracious to them and to be their strength and salvation daily (33:2). His grace is assurance that he will hear men's prayers (Ps. 4:1); it also gives confidence that God will deliver the oppressed, and that he will have pity on the sufferer whose bones are wasting away (6:2). The consciousness of his mercy sustains a man upon his sickbed (41:3-4); it is a consolation for the victim of devastating slander who knows that he may take refuge in the strength and protecting mercy of God (9:13; 25:16; 26:11; 30:10; 31:9; 56:1; 57:1, 4); the God who is "slow to anger and rich in grace and fidelity" is also merciful and full of pity (86:15-16). The eternal God will arise and have pity on Zion (102:13); and his graciousness is found in God's self-determining will rather than caprice or human entreaty: he is gracious to those to whom he is gracious—that is his prerogative and his glory (Exod. 33:19).

GOD'S FAITHFULNESS

As is well known, the word which formally concludes Judaeo-Christian prayers is *amen,* from a root meaning "confirm, support, be established." This verb and two related nouns, *'emeth* and *'emunah* (firmness, truth, faithfulness), are used by several Hebrew authors who desire to convey the idea of the faithfulness of God in carrying out his promises of salvation or his trustworthiness in a variety of situations. One author actually uses the root as a title for God—God of amen—"faithful" (Isa. 65:16). God is also called a trustworthy God (Deut. 7:9); the Holy One of Israel, who is faithful as a redeemer and savior, a faithful (dependable) witness against the people if they do not conform to the word of Jeremiah (42:5); one who is trustworthy and never deceives (Deut. 32:4); as dependable as a rock; a wonderful God who fulfills plans made long ago to cast down proud cities (Isa. 25:1); and a help for the living, whose grace and faithfulness cannot be made known in Hades (Ps. 88:11).

Still other passages show the use of this root in the religious vocabulary of the Old Testament: God's faithfulness is established in the heavens, and it is a faithfulness far more wonderful than that claimed by any other deity (Ps. 89:2, 5); the foundation of his throne is righteousness and justice (89:14); grace and faithfulness go before him as royal heralds; his commandments are sure (119:86); and his faithfulness is for all generations (100:5). The psalmist delights in proclaiming his grace in the morning and his faithfulness every night (92:2); God comes to judge the earth with righteousness and its peoples with faithfulness (96:13). He will give everlasting joy to his people, for the God who loves justice will faithfully keep his covenant with them (Isa. 61:8); and his Messiah will be clothed with a girdle of faithfulness around his waist (11:5).

Some twenty times the words for grace and fidelity are used together as signifying to men God's great power to save and protect his own. God is rich in grace and fidelity (Exod. 34:6); he showed his grace and truth to Abraham (Gen. 24:27); he is slow to anger and abounding in grace and fidelity (Ps. 86:15); Grace and Fidelity are personified and are charged to protect the righteous king (61:7). All honor is due the God of Israel because of his grace and faithfulness, in contrast with the idols, which have mouths, eyes, and hands, but can do nothing for those who foolishly trust them (115:1-8). Grace and faithfulness are God's messengers and agents of salvation (57:3); God, the creator who made heaven and earth, who renders justice to the oppressed, preserves fidelity forever (146:6). The term meaning faithfulness, therefore, has a rich variety of uses, especially in the Psalms. When used by itself, or in conjunction with the words for grace, righteousness, and salvation, it strikingly reveals the redeeming God, whose unfailing love brings hope and joy to men.

GOD AS REDEEMER

Another term of interest in this study of salvation is the word for redeemer (*gâ'al*). Frequently it is used to express deliverance from death. So it is found with a negative connotation in Hos. 13:14:

Shall I rescue them from the power of Sheol?
Shall I redeem them from death?

Redemption in the sense of deliverance from other kinds of evil is also found in the records. This may include the rescue of the Jewish people from foreign enemies (Jer. 50:34) or of the righteous from the wicked (Ps. 69:18). The difficult passage in Job 19:25—which should perhaps be translated, "But I myself know that my Vindicator lives: and as a later one he will arise upon the earth"—contains the Hebrew term for redeemer, whose etymology need not concern us here. The meaning seems to be that after Job's death God, acting as redeemer or next of kin, will vindicate Job by testifying to his righteousness upon his grave. It is not redemption in any real sense, but simply vindication which is advertised to the world. In Isaiah, God receives the title of redeemer—principally with the idea of restoring Israel—only in the exilic and postexilic sections (41:14; 43:14; 44:6, 24; 47:3; 48:17; 49:7, 26; 54:5, 8; 59:20; 60:16; 63:16). Their context in this book states how God rescues and gathers his scattered people, and that, in the time of Cyrus, as redeemer he declares himself to be the only God, who stretches out the heavens and so maneuvers the events of history that he drives diviners crazy. He teaches and leads the Israelites, takes vengeance upon their foes, seeks to remove transgression from Jacob, and is the mighty One of Jacob.

One of the most familiar biblical terms, found frequently in both the Old and the New Testaments, is the one translated usually "righteousness." The Hebrew word *ṣedek* and the related word *ṣedakah* carry the idea of rightness, justice, righteousness, deliverance, or victory, depending upon the circumstances in each case. This root is often used in close connection with other Hebrew expressions bearing upon the idea of salvation. We find, to be specific, that the God who has chosen Israel to be his servant promises freedom from fear and weakness through his direct support and strength: "I will uphold you with my victorious right hand" (Isa. 41:10), he tells his servant. Here *ṣedek* is rightly translated "victorious," to signify the power of God directed toward the conquest of evil and the triumph of the righteous. The righteous God is the victorious God, fully competent to save his people, as the events of history prove, if we may believe the words of the context.

In the same historical context as the passage quoted above, we find Second Isaiah facing the import of the coming of Cyrus in its possible effect upon the fortunes of the exiles and upon their faith. He concludes that Yahweh is the prime mover in this event, and that he has thus demonstrated his victorious power and his supremacy over other so-called gods.

> Let the skies rain deliverance;
> Let the earth open her womb,
> And bring forth salvation;
> Let her cause deliverance also to spring up—
> I the Lord have created it.[2] (45:8.)

Deliverance (victory) and salvation are here and elsewhere in the work of this unknown prophet brought together as inseparable parts of the same whole—the whole being the reality of the righteous God at work for the salvation of men.

In the Psalms righteousness finds a place in the prayers of needy and stricken men who cry out to God for help. Some examples follow:

O Lord, lead me in thy righteousness, because of my enemies. (5:8.)

Through thy justification, deliver me! (31:1.)

Thy right hand is full of righteousness. (48:10.)

In thy righteousness, rescue me and deliver me!
Incline thy ear unto me and save me! (71:2.)

And through thy righteousness are they [temple worshipers] exalted.
(89:16.)

Lo, I have longed for thy precepts;
Revive me through thy righteousness. (119:40.)

In thy fidelity answer me, and in thy righteousness! (143:1.)

The word evidently has the power to inspire in men an assurance that God will reply to their petitions for help under various circumstances. It is certainly not an abstract virtue or ethical attribute which is in question here; rather the very nature and work of God are at stake. When *the whole being of God is bent on salvation* to men, then his righteousness is operative. The vindication of the righteous, the triumph of good over evil, the restoration and reconstruction of human life according to a divinely conceived pattern working itself out in history—these are the happy results of God's victorious righteousness.

[2] That is, accomplished the advent of Cyrus. Note also 51:5-6.

133

GOD'S FORGIVENESS

Forgiveness also is the work of God rather than of men and is properly a part of this exploration of how God saves men. Words having such meanings as "pardon, cover over (make propitiation), take away guilt, ransom" appear in this connection. Shades of meaning are discernible, running all the way from the removal of ceremonial guilt to the restoration of the soul to a right relation to God. Since our concern here is only with forgiveness as an activity of God, the elaborate sacramental system of the priests will not be considered at present. As was seen to be true of other verbal symbols of divine activity, also here the words used are largely functional in announcing men's conception of the effects upon them of the work of God rather than descriptive of the process producing these effects. This need not be regretted, however, for it underscores the fact of a biblical God who is a living, personal, righteous power, creatively sharing in the life of men. Thus what God does for and with men is what he means to them and is what he actually is, provided we humbly acknowledge the limitations of language and of human knowledge in reaching for the highest truth in the universe.

Returning to the task in hand—that of noting the ways in which various words for forgiveness are used in our literature—we may first observe the use of the Hebrew word *salaḥ* (pardon). Thus we find that God agrees to pardon the people's sin of disloyalty and distrust in the desert, in accordance with the request of Moses (Num. 14:20). This God does out of the abundance of his grace. This pardon is not unconditional, however, as far as the removal of punishment is concerned. The older generation will not be allowed to see the promised land. As a consequence of pardoning Israel, God makes a new covenant with them and promises to go with them in their migration to a new home in Palestine (Exod. 34:9-10). Solomon's prayer in dedicating the temple includes the request that prayer in the temple should insure the divine forgiveness for any sin which may have been committed (I Kings 8:30). God, another writer exults, pardons abundantly when the wicked turn to him and forsake their wickedness (Isa. 55:7-9). This divine magnanimity is characteristic of God's nature in contrast to man's.

The Lord does not pardon when sins like those of Manasseh have been perpetrated against both human beings and God (II Kings 24:4). Pardon will never be extended to those who serve other gods; on the contrary, every conceivable curse will fall upon them (Deut. 29:20). If the prophet can find one man who does justice and aims at honesty in the streets of Jerusalem, God may pardon the city (Jer. 5:1). But pardon cannot be granted when rank adultery and idolatry are profanely flaunted in the very face of God; for these evils punishment is unavoidable (5:7-9). The guilt of a nation whose spirit has been renewed will be pardoned, and its sin will no longer be remembered (31:34). Pardon for guilt and sin, to be followed by reinstatement in the favor of God and the blessing of material prosperity, is stressed in the book of Jeremiah, as the references cited show (33:8; 36:3; 50:20). Related terms, in addition to *salah*, to convey the idea of the removal of guilt and the redemption of the individual could be collated.[3] However, the results would not be greatly different from those already obtained. Let us now proceed to a brief and general interpretation of the material accumulated on the subject of forgiveness.

In the Old Testament, generally speaking, forgiveness involves the removal of guilt and certain consequences of sin, although not all of these, by any means. This is clear from a reading of Exod. 34:7: "The Lord, the Lord, a God compassionate and gracious, . . . rich in grace and fidelity, showing grace to the thousandth generation, forgiving inquity, transgression and sin, *without leaving it unpunished, however*."[4] God forgives guilt and sin, but he upholds his ethical nature by meting out punishment severely to the third and even the fourth generation. Pardon and forgiveness are obviously conditioned in an ethical way by the conduct of men. If they persist in their wickedness, God will not pardon them. Only if they repent can pardon be granted. Thus pardon is not based arbitrarily upon chance or whimsical desire. Neither can it be experienced when men do not seek it ardently. Often it is seen as God's answer to prayer by the individual on his own behalf or on behalf of the nation, as in the case of Moses.

The effects of pardon, as we have seen, are only in part the remission of sins and the cancellation of penalties for wrongdoing; in part they must also be the inauguration of a right relationship with God which is ethical, and which requires the facing of the terrible reality of evil in human hearts and lives. If penalties are not removed entirely, pardon can have little meaning without the creation of this relationship. Some of the psalms explicitly state that this relationship is the greatest consequence of pardon, and others tacitly convey this idea. Likewise it may be inferred from many other parts of the Old Testament

[3] Note especially: *Padhah* (ransom) : Deut. 7:8; 13:5; Mic. 6:4; Ps. 78:42; II Sam. 7:23; Neh. 1:10; Zech. 10:8. *Nasa'* (take away—guilt) : Gen. 50:17; Exod. 32:32; 34:7; I Sam. 15:25; Hos. 14:2; Job 7:21; Ps. 32:5; Mic. 7:18. *Kipper* (cover over, atone) : Deut. 32:43; Ezek. 16:63; Ps. 65:3; Dan. 9:24; Jer. 18:23.
[4] Here and elsewhere italics in biblical quotations are mine.

that love and loyalty to God can thrive only where sin has been pardoned through the personal appeal of the sinner and the personal response of the merciful God. Pardon, then, is the forgiveness afforded by the love and grace of the savior God, communion with whom is impossible in the absence of commitment to his way in ethical obedience. God shows himself merciful to the merciful; only the righteous and the pure in heart can see God. Pardon makes possible the ethical precondition to such a vision of God.

THE COVENANT

Every feature of salvation comprehended in this essay as developed thus far derives its value for Old Testament theology from the prominence of the covenant between God and man as the basis for a continuing, redemptive relationship. No other aspect of Israel's faith is so conspicuous as this, and no more fruitful inquiry can be made than to search the Scriptures for light on the covenant idea. Within the scope of this idea may be found all that is relevant to the basic religious beliefs of Israel and to the faith by which she championed them. If salvation is the outstanding concept of this faith—as the mass of material in this chapter indicates—the making of the covenant at Sinai is the crucial historical event which made this faith possible. The covenant of Sinai may be compared with other covenants entered into by clans or tribes and their respective deities. It was not uncommon for a tribe or even a nation to "cut a covenant" of blood with its god to insure establishment and maintenance of mutually beneficial relations between the parties. The god of the tribe became a member of the tribe through ties of blood which could not be broken. This god was obligated to take vengeance on the tribe's enemies and to come to its assistance whenever needed.

Such blood covenants existed by the hundreds in the ancient world of the Hebrews. What marks the Hebrew covenant as unique is the appearance of a new conception, which may be negatively stated— that God was not automatically obligated, upon request, to help his people. His proffer of help depended upon the merits of each case, which were determined by a standard of measurement derived from the objectively righteous will of God rather than community mores and customs. To know that will was of supreme importance, for no other way of guaranteeing salvation existed. How this will became known to the Hebrews was a source of perpetual amazement to them throughout their history. Their wonder and gratitude are found in their folklore, their poetry, their prophecy, and their wisdom writings,

moral freedom, with its possibility of sin and tragedy and its omen of the need of salvation. Being a creature, man could not know through his own efforts the meaning of his creaturehood and the way to fulfillment. Only the Creator could impart such knowledge.

In the Old Testament there are specific media of revelation, some of which fall into the background, while others become increasingly important in the history of Israel's religion. In the literary documents, especially the Pentateuch and the prophetic books, the method of revelation by *direct communication* is widely indicated. God speaks to whom he will—to Abraham, to Moses, to Aaron, to his prophets—in a friendly, personal, and even intimate fashion. There are no stage settings as a rule; spectacular displays of power are relatively few in number. We simply read, "The Lord said to Moses," or "God said to Jacob," and are then informed of the content of the divine utterance. The human listener usually takes the whole matter in his stride, listening calmly or, on occasion, even talking back, as witness the bargaining of Abraham for the lives of the men of Sodom (Gen. 18:23-33) or the arguments presented to the Lord by a reluctant Moses (Exod. 3) or a timid Jeremiah (1:6). So commonplace is this pleasant conversational method whereby men are informed of the divine will that it may be regarded largely as a literary device of the authors and redactors using it. This is probably the case, at least in the Pentateuch. In other books the situation may be somewhat different.

Other methods of revelation make use of *dreams and angels*. As examples of the former the stories of Joseph and Daniel are relevant, to say nothing of the story of Jacob, the swain whose pillow was so uneasy that he dreamed and saw processions of angels upon a ladder. Angels are numerous in the records, although they have a highly undifferentiated function—to act as messengers of God—while in the postcanonical books they receive special functions and personalities (Book of Jubilees). Sacred places serve as a means of revelation also, usually in conjunction with other media. So at Bethel Abraham receives a theophany, and at the temple in Jerusalem Isaiah has a vision of the Lord. Sanctuaries are viewed as the abode of the gods, and it is reasonable to communicate with them there.

Wonder-working also impressed men as evidence of the activity and nature of God. The Egyptians were witnesses of devastating plagues whose purpose was to impress them with the power and purpose of Israel's God and to induce them to release his people. The pestilence, the hail, and death of the first-born were revelations of the will of God as well as inducements to the Egyptians to change their plans concerning the enslaved Israelites. Since the working of wonders usually meant special manipulation of the processes of nature, this type of revelation can be associated with revelation through nature itself. The splendid creation hymn extant in Ps. 104 witnesses to the creative power of God and reveals the greatness and orderliness of his work.[7] That Creation affirms the justice as well as the power of God may be seen in the book of Amos. This prophet relates how God sends or holds back the rain, controls insect pests in order to destroy gardens and fields, and releases a pestilence, all for the purpose of inciting in Israel a lively repentance for sin and an earnest desire to return to the path of righteousness (4:7-11). Thus natural forces are used to effect the salvation of men and to reveal their Savior in the power of his righteousness.

In the law codes and in the psalms which eulogize the Law one notes an additional medium of revelation. The Law itself is alleged to represent the very will and being of God, response to which by man makes his salvation sure. The psalmist cries,

> Oh, how I love thy law! (119:97.)

> How sweet are thy promises to my palate. (119:103.)

> My flesh creeps in awe of thee. (119:120.)

> And thy law is thy truth. (119:142.)

> Thou art near, O Lord. (119:151.)

> Thy faithfulness is for generation after generation. (119:90.)

To this deeply sensitive and religiously awake soul the Law was, in effect, God's means of communicating with him, of restoring his soul, and of inciting in him the mood of adoration and praise. By means of the Law he knew the kind of behavior which God viewed with approval; he saw behind it the great Lawgiver and Redeemer of men. Observance of the Law is highly rewarding, since it renews life, gives wisdom, rejoices the heart, and enlightens the eyes; yet to win assurance that one's whole life and thought are acceptable to God, who is revealed through the Law, is the greatest longing of man (19:7-14).

[7] That this psalm rests upon an Egyptian hymn to the sun god Aton does not argue against this conclusion, since the psalm has been adapted to the faith and genius of the Hebrews.

Man may love the Law because it mediates the divine will and presence to him. Functioning in this way, it is an instrument both of revelation and salvation.

A special kind of revelation has been preserved and exalted in the Old Testament—*the prophetic vision*. When God has need of a spokesman to announce his word to the nation, we are told that he raises up a prophet for this purpose. To this prophet he communicates his desire and the import of the message he wishes him to proclaim. It may be a message—and it often is—which is difficult to deliver because it cuts across strong public sentiment and popular practice, or because it is directed to a political-social situation which has serious and baffling ramifications into the economic structure and the dominant cultural patterns of the time, and therefore demands boldness in attack on the part of the prophet. For this very reason the prophet's vision and the call which sometimes accompanies it have defied psychological and historical analysis. After the full weight of criticism's data has been applied to the prophet's consciousness at the time of the vision-experience for the purpose of determining the prevalent cultural ideas, political events, biographical material, and other possible influences, the character of the vision as a revelation from and of God may go unnoticed by the modern scholar. As far as the prophets themselves are concerned, this last point is of major significance. In fact, this matter of a divine revelation is all they see in the vision. Of course, following it, they reflect upon its relation to their own personal plans and to the nation's fate and embark upon a course of action as a result of it; but it is God to whom they yield, not circumstances.

A few examples of revelation through prophetic vision may serve to clarify and reinforce this part of our study. The oracles of Balaam—of uncertain date, but valuable because they record important traditions of prophetic behavior under the influence of the spirit of God—contain several evidences of revelation from a superhuman source (Num. 24:3-5, 16). Balaam had been employed by the king of Moab—on the basis of the prose narrative incorporating the poem—to prophesy against the Hebrews; but he found himself unable to do so, regardless of the importunity of his employer or of the location of the sanctuary from which he pronounced his oracles. In every attempt the oracle was favorable to the Hebrews, since, as Balaam said to Balak, "Whatsoever the Lord declares, that I must do" (23:26). His own will had nothing to do with the purport of his words. On the contrary, the oracle of this man, "who had evil designs," arose from a vision of the Almighty which caused him to hear the words of God, "prostrate, but with eyes opened." Balaam's experience seems to contravene all that is known relative to the process whereby an intelligent person arrives at an opinion about a nation other than his own, which becomes the basis for an emphatic judgment on that nation's character and destiny. It sets aside rational methods of knowing and substitutes the irrational or the suprarational.

The case of Jeremiah is relevant at this point. Without the dramatic setting of physical prostration, ecstasy, and a dazzling theophany—as was the case in the Balaam oracles and in the experience of Isaiah and Ezekiel—there is the same absolute conviction that God has spoken in words which must be obeyed and proclaimed. Vacillation stemming from timidity and fear becomes certainty; life finds a new and terrifying direction leading to association with kings, involvement in national and international affairs, the hatred of friends, and vile imprisonment. The tender-minded youth becomes tough-minded; the sensitive, shrinking soul becomes a "fortified city, an iron pillar, and a bronze wall" (1:18). Through Jeremiah, thus transformed—and the process of transformation can be traced through its biographical, spiritual, and psychological phases—were communicated to the world to become a precious heritage mighty truths about God and man which penetrated into the very fabric of modern man's religious and political thought and life. The Word of the Lord which came to this prophet in the experience of his call, and in other crises of his life, was a revelation from God, a disclosure of his will, and an impartation of the very life of the divine savior.

Revelation in the Bible, as described and defined above, was received through many media—nature, law, abnormal and normal mental experiences such as prophetic visions, wonderful deeds, historical events, and the direct experience of God. But the principal purpose of revelation was not the disclosure of truths or of doctrines about religion. In spite of the delight of the saints of Israel in receiving the word of God, or the agony of fear or frustration which this word brought to the prophets, revelation did not take place to lift men's souls or to harrow their feelings. Its sole purpose was the *gift* of the life of God to the life of men. That this gift came to the whole life of men meant that it affected their intellectual powers also and stimulated some degree of reflection as to the divine nature. Thus revelation resulted in the discovery of truth, while it primarily confronted men with the reality and the demands of God. This gift of the life of God was radically serious for the human enterprise, since it divulged to them their true natures as dependent beings standing in desperate need of salvation. Revelation made known the way of salvation as it presented to men the holiness and righteousness of God, the meaning of their sin, and the call to judgment and repentance.

MAN'S PART IN SALVATION

In view of the foregoing description of the meaning of salvation, it seems to be an inclusive experience which is begun, continued, and ended through the initiative and authority of God alone. Salvation proceeds from *his* will, *his* purpose for history, and *his* revelation to men. Undeniably this is a correct evaluation of the Old Testament viewpoint, any minimization of which would be a distortion of the biblical truth. When the inquiry into the part taken by God in the salvation of men is completed, is not the entire discussion completed? But if salvation is the sum total of good which God brings to men by his self-revelation and self-originated activity, it cannot possibly preclude human participation and a human response whose nature is determined by the meaning of man. As the being of God predetermines the content of the concept of salvation, so the facts of human nature indicate what man must do to be saved. He is a sinner; hence he needs salvation. He is a free, ethical person; hence he may repent of his sins and turn to God for forgiveness. The fact is, salvation can have no meaning unless the participation of man with his capacity for willful pride, his longing for personal success and social pre-eminence, and his helplessness without God is taken into account. Both proud self-assertiveness and helpless dependence are involved in his experience of salvation. When these come into conflict—and this is bound to happen—the spiritual preparation has been made for redemption and a life of fellowship with God and man.

There is no established *order of events* in the soul when redemption occurs, as far as Old Testament thought is concerned; but there are events of a destiny-making nature without which salvation is impossible. These consist of an overwhelming, inescapable awareness of the coming of God in judgment to the individual and of the gulf that yawns wide and deep between the two, a shattering of the will of man in soul-shaking repentance and contrition as the full horror of human sin is exposed to the light of God's ineffable holiness and justice, an accompanying confession of rebellion against God by a soul stripped of all sham and self-deception, and an unreserved commitment to the service of God in personal loyalty and ethical obedience. This commitment causes the individual to plunge headlong into the endless struggle for human betterment, although the broad principles behind this struggle are of greater interest to the men of Israel than the detailed blueprint. Dedication and loyalty to God awaken the human spirit to its possibilities and needs, moving it to turn to God repeatedly in confession and thanksgiving, in prayer and worship, by means of private religious exercises and in public ceremonies.

This rather formal and extreme statement of the matter should not be misunderstood. Not every account of salvation in the Old Testament exhibits all of the stages named above; in fact, possibly only one or two of these steps may be named, although the others may be implied. Further, not every individual whose salvation is narrated in the biblical books experiences the divine activity with the same sharpness and poignancy as may be noted in a few remarkable cases. In spite of these undeniable facts Israel's literature makes it clear that repentance, confession, commitment, obedience, private and public worship represent acts which man will and must perform when he is faced by the God who is both his creator-judge and his merciful savior. The language used here refers to man as an individual; it must not be forgotten that our sources think of the individual and the community interchangeably and fail to make the modern distinction between the two as sharply opposed entities. Thus the Hebrew terminology of salvation may be applied with equal pertinency to both, unless any particular textual context determines otherwise. This view does not water down the biblical idea of personal responsibility by any means. Indeed the consciousness of community accentuates it and gives it meaningful and concrete direction for effective social expression.

The salvation of Israel depends, first of all, upon its *acceptance of the coming of God* in wrath and in judgment. The concept of judgment belongs both here and in the subsequent discussion of the kingdom of God in the Old Testament. Since it will be elaborated later, a briefer reference here will suffice. The righteousness and justice of God, when flaunted by sinful men, cannot fail to constitute the reason for his wrath and judgment upon them; else the world would be a moral chaos, a desolate waste as far as truth and goodness are concerned. This judgment of God is inescapable, as is vividly portrayed in the book of Amos:

No single one of them shall escape,
Nor shall a single one be delivered.
Though they dig into Sheol, thence shall my hand take them;
And though they mount up to the heavens, thence will I bring them down.
And though they hide themselves on the top of Carmel.
Thence will I search them out and take them.

Though they be concealed from my eyes on the floor of the sea
There will I command the serpent and it shall bite them.
Though they go into captivity before their foes,
There will I command the sword, and it shall slay them.
And I will set my eye upon them
For evil, and not for good. (9:1-4.)

This fact of certain doom is burned upon the consciousness of Israel by the prophet of the God of justice, who announces to his people—and to all men, if we take seriously the universal scope of justice—that judgment for sin is at hand. On the day of judgment

the pride of man will be brought low;
And the Lord alone will be exalted. (Isa. 2:17.)

"By the sword shall you fall, and over all the borders of Israel will I execute judgments upon you; and you shall know that I am the Lord." (Ezek. 11:10.) The supreme righteousness of God will be vindicated by his judgment upon a sinful people and upon sinful individuals. Ps. 38 is as personal a psalm as can be found, although some commentators see in it the personification of the nation's woes; and it depicts the gruesome details of some loathsome disease, in all likelihood, which is the sign of the wrath of God upon a sinner (38:1, 3, 4). Inferentially all men and each man must stand in the presence of this God of wrath before they can know salvation. When the texts of many psalms, for example, are examined, this may not appear to be too obvious, for the spirit of self-righteousness too often emerges in the writings of the very pious. Yet in Israel's distinctive faith that God is a righteous judge one finds the basis for the unavoidable conclusion that in a direct and personal facing of this judge lies the first step in the experience of salvation.

The moral majesty and power of the God who comes in judgment convicts men of sin. This is why God's spokesmen enunciated so vigorously and persistently the truth of God's holiness and righteousness. They wished to prod the people into wakefulness that they might become conscious of the God who was their judge, and who held before them the way of life rather than death. By means of this consciousness the certainty of judgment and the weight of human sin were pressed home to the minds of men. When they saw themselves as God saw them, the burden of their sin was too great to bear, and *repentance* became a way of release. Repentance is more than regret or even contrition for past sin; it involves admission of sin, self-condemnation, and turning toward a new way of life in which sin has no part. The Old Testament writers saw this clearly in speaking for God.

The word correctly translated "return" contains the essential meaning of repentance as used by them. "Afterward, the Israelites shall return and seek the Lord . . . ; they shall hasten eagerly toward the Lord, and his goodness in the days to come." (Hos. 3:5.)

> Return, apostate Israel,
> . . . .
> For I am full of kindness, . . .
> I will not keep up anger forever.
> Only acknowledge your guilt,
> How you have rebelled against the Lord your God.
> > (Jer. 3:12-13.)

> If you return, O Israel, . . .
> If you put your detestable things out of my sight,
> > and waver not;
> If you swear, "As the Lord lives," in truth,
> > in honesty, and in uprightness;
> Then shall the nations bless themselves in him,
> > and in him shall they glory. (4:1-2.)

The single act of returning to the Lord is really extremely complex, for it marks a deep recognition of the demands of God, an admission of sin, an act of repentance, and a reorganization of life. Israel, if it returns, must understand what it is doing. This is put negatively in Isa. 6:10:

> Make the mind of this people gross,
> Dull their ears, and besmear their eyes,
> Lest they see with their eyes, and hear with their ears,
> And have a mind to understand, and turn, and be healed.

Without understanding, salvation is impossible.

Repentance signifies turning to the Lord and the complete abandonment of idolatrous beliefs and practices, which have led the people astray and corrupted the entire nation. Solomon's dedicatory prayer in the temple contains typical elements relative to repentance and salvation (I Kings 8:33-34, 46-50). After suffering defeat by an enemy, Israel may confess its sin, turn again to God, and pray for forgiveness, presumably with the assurance that its prayer will be heard. "If they return to thee with all their mind and with all their heart," forgiveness may be granted, the petitioner confidently believes. Nonetheless at least one prophet knows how the iron shackles of habitual sin can imprison the spirit of man:

> Their deeds will not permit them
> To return to their God.
> For an apostate spirit is within them,
> And they do not know the Lord. (Hos. 5:4.)

When sinful acts are repeated and fixed habits are formed, repentance becomes increasingly difficult and finally impossible, because men who repent must turn to God "with all their mind and with all their heart," an impossible psychological demand—at least from the human stand-point—when the heart has been stubbornly set on sin through the years.

As sin is the deliberate substitution of the will of man for the will of God in a variety of forms, such as idolatry and the will to power, so repentance is profound regret for that sin and a revolutionary re-placement of God at the center of life. This calls for emotional and rational adjustments as well as social and institutional changes which are radically disturbing, and which may not appear on the surface in the biblical books or teachings. If we probe the full meaning of these teachings, however, repentance is seen to possess these wider ramifi-cations into the life of the self and the life of the community. Not only are individuals exhorted to repent and to turn to God in faith and hope; the structure of the community is to be leavened with the spirit of jus-tice and lovingkindness also. This makes it clear that repentance has a deep rootage in the spirit of man and in the institutionalized sin which gives expression to that spirit.

After repentance, as already noted, a life of *loyalty* and obedience to God ensues. By an act of faith and of the will man manifests his re-pentance and his desire to live a new life. He has received in the form of a revelation the knowledge of what is good:

> You have been told, O man, what is good:
> Yet what does the Lord require of you,
> But to do justice, and to love kindness,
> And to walk humbly with your God? (Mic. 6:8.)

He is to walk in trust and obedience in the way of the righteous God. The prophets announce the great ethical demands of this God and urge the people to observe them (Amos 5:24); the legalists codify these demands in direct relation to the practical exigencies of community life and proclaim the validity of their codes (Deut. 5:1); the priests define the ritualistic requirements for life in the holy community and prescribe the conduct becoming to a people whose God is holy (Lev. 19:2); the wise men outline in the form of aphorisms and axioms sensible principles for daily living that is pleasing to God (Prov. 3:1-4); and the psalmists declare that he who worships in the temple must have clean hands and a pure heart (Ps. 24:3-4). The reality of salvation is contingent upon a complete dedication of life to God in unhesitating and thoroughgoing ethical obedience to his righteous will. Repentance is a fraud without this regeneration of heart and conscience. If men return to God in honesty and uprightness, they must put away their detestable things and serve him alone. They are to be circumcised in their hearts and then yield themselves in the performance of just and compassionate deeds to the God who is "the God of gods, and the Lord of lords, the great, mighty, and awful God, who is never partial, and never takes a bribe, who secures justice for the orphan and the widow, and loves the resident alien in giving him food and clothing." (Deut. 10:16-18.)

Genuine loyalty to God, therefore, reaches to the heart and involves personal and inner acquaintance with his greatness and goodness. The technical biblical term "knowledge of God" carries this personal connotation in the Old Testament. *Knowledge* of God is not only rational; it is close to the intuitive and mystical, implying a rapport with the mind of God which permeates the entire being and gladdens the heart. We may observe the use of this word in the book of Hosea, where it occurs several times. Speaking of a future time when Israel would be betrothed to God forever in faithfulness, the prophet announces that she "shall know the Lord" (2:20). Again, the prophet asserts that there is no fidelity, kindness, or "knowledge of God" in the land (4:1), and that his people are destroyed for want of knowledge (4:6). They do not know the Lord, for a spirit of faithlessness resides in them (5:4). In seeking reinstatement in the divine favor the nation cries,

> Come, let us return unto the Lord. (6:1.)
> Let us know, let us press on to know the Lord. (6:3.)

God tells the people that he delights

> in piety, not sacrifice;
> And in the knowledge of God, rather than burnt-offerings. (6:6.)

The note of obedience is struck in Jeremiah when that prophet—addressing Jehoiakim—eulogizes Josiah, king of Judah, after his death:

SALVATION IN THE OLD TESTAMENT

> "Did not your father, as he ate and drank,
>   do justice and righteousness?
> Then all went well with him.
> He defended the cause of the poor and needy—
> Then all went well.
> Is not that how to know me?"
>   is the oracle of the Lord. (22:15-16.)

Knowledge means an intimate, spiritual relationship and personal loyalty that produces conduct in harmony with the will of God. It is not found when halfhearted allegiance is mixed with the worship of other gods. Rather it suggests an absolute devotion, unequivocal in its demands. When men seek the Lord with all their hearts, such knowledge is the result.

Trust is also a factor in man's salvation. It does not mean faith in any technical or mysteriously abstruse sense, but is simply confidence in the justice, goodness, and providential mercy of God. It is an attitude of soul and mind indicating a willingness to believe and to accept as true the claims and deeds of God among men. It accompanies loyalty and active obedience to the personal object of loyalty—the God of eternal justice. So Hezekiah "trusted in the Lord, . . . for he was loyal to the Lord, he . . . kept his commandments" (II Kings 18:5-6). On the occasion of the Syro-Ephraimitish war the prophet Isaiah counseled Ahaz to hold fast to faith in God and not to give way to fear of his two political enemies. He put it negatively:

> If you do not believe,
> Surely you shall not be established. (7:9.)

At the time of another national crisis—perhaps the coming of the Assyrians in 701—Isaiah took the opportunity to declare,

> By returning and resting shall you be saved,
> In quietness and confidence shall be your strength. (30:15.)

Not in the noise of political strife, nor in the sound of marching troops with their armored chariots and siege weapons, will victory and peace be found. Rather it will come with quiet trust in the overwhelming power of the faithful and righteous God, confidence in whom is far better than trust in horses and chariots.

Trust in God is more certain to bring desired results than reliance upon men's own understanding; those who know the name and the glory of God are those who trust in him. The fathers of the Israelites trusted in God, and they were set free; the two great requirements of religion are to trust in the Lord and do good. Man is undependable, God alone being trustworthy; happy is the man who puts his trust in him (Pss. 9:10; 22:5; 37:3; 40:4; 56:4; 84:12). Thus the attitude of trust pervades the psalms. God's promises are sure to be fulfilled for those who believe in him. He is a God who keeps his covenant with his people, bringing to them the blessing of salvation in every area of their lives. If they believe this and commit themselves to him and to his way, life will be free from fear and anxiety. Each man may then say,

> I will lay me down and sleep;
> I awake, for the Lord sustains me. (3:5.)
>
> In peace will I both lay me down and sleep;
> For thou alone, O Lord, makest me dwell in safety
> (4:8.)
> Thou hast put joy in my heart. (4:7.)
>
> I have been young, and now I am old;
> But I have not seen the righteous forsaken. (37:24.)
> If my father and my mother forsake me,
>   then the Lord will take me up. (27:10.)
> The Lord is the refuge of my life;
>   of whom shall I be afraid? (27:1.)

In life, in death, in sickness and in health, in poverty and in wealth, he guides, restores, and comforts those who trust in him. Truly the righteous man shall live, both by his faithfulness and humble obedience to God and by his trustful confidence in the God of his salvation. He believes all that has been revealed concerning this God: he believes that God has confronted him in judgment, charging him with the sin of rebellion; he believes that God will receive his repentance and create in him a clean heart and a steadfast spirit; he believes that God will renew his spirit daily and give him courage to overcome all obstacles. To these things he does not simply give intellectual assent: his whole being shouts a ringing "Yes" to the claims and overtures of God, and he is dedicated heart and mind and soul to his holy cause.

In walking upon the way of salvation man is continuously impelled to *worship* and adore the Author of his faith, out of gratitude for God's unceasing love for him and from the sheer impulse to commune with the One who has become a light to his feet and the redeemer of his soul. This impulsion to worship breaks out particularly in the psalms where national aspiration and personal petition are inseparably associated. In private prayer and supplication, in public thanksgiving and confession, the mood of worship is revealed. Men confess their sin, pray for help in the presence of their enemies, ask to be preserved from sickness unto death, seek the welfare of the community, joyously sing the triumphs of the God of Israel, cry out in agony and doubt because of the evildoer's prosperity, praise their Maker and the Creator of the universe, wistfully long for the delight of worship in the temple, pray for their king, plead with God when maligned by their sharp-tongued neighbors, and utter piteous pleas for mercy and forgiveness. All this and much more pours out of the hearts of the men of Israel as they worship the God of their salvation.

With the adoption of the Deuteronomic Code, requiring the centralization of worship in the temple at Jerusalem, this institution received greatly enhanced prestige and at the same time found itself confronted by a new rival—personal piety in the home and the local community. The requirement that all of Israel must worship at Jerusalem could not be rigidly enforced. Persons living too far away either had to cease the worship of God or find a way of doing so in their own neighborhood and homes. There is no doubt that personal piety, aided by the emphasis upon inner, spiritual religion made by Jeremiah, flourished in competition with the ecclesiasticism of the organized temple religion. The book of Psalms may well contain devotional materials derived from both sources, although positive proof is lacking. The combination of individual piety and elaborate temple ceremonialism exists in a number of psalms. One devout worshiper calls upon men to "offer righteous sacrifices" and then testifies that God has put joy in his heart (4:5, 7). Another, influenced by the ethical passion of the prophets, meditates over the wonderful worship he has enjoyed in the temple in the past and asks, "Who may sojourn in thy pavilion, O Lord?" The answer affirms that only the good man, who is truthful, patient, neighborly, and just, can enter the temple (Ps. 15:24).

Other writers state that they will praise God in the great assembly (22:25), that they will bless the Lord in the congregations (26:12), that they desire to dwell in the house of God all their days (27:4), that they are sheltered in the temple from "the strife of tongues" (31:20), and that in the assembly they have confessed their faith in God, against whom they have committed sin innumerable times (40: 9, 12). Beyond question, here we find intense delight in a personal worship of God and a comparable delight in the formality and rich imagery of temple worship. The two are not seen to be incompatible, although here and there a note of conflict may be discovered (51:16; see Mic. 6:6-8). That the temple may mark the high point of intense personal piety is evident from a final quotation, in which firm faith in God is beautifully expressed:

> Send forth thy light and thy faithfulness; may they guide me,
> May they bring me to thy holy hill, and to thy dwelling-place.
> May I go to the altar of God, to God my highest joy. (43:3-4.)

Prayer in the Old Testament is a human activity which accompanies and guides the experience of salvation. We may first observe several examples of prayer outside of the book of Psalms before interpreting what may be selected from that book. Hannah's prayer for a son at Shiloh is a deeply moving one. She prayed with bitter tears to express the longing of her woman's heart and offered to dedicate the son God might give her to his service (I Sam. 1:11). When attacked by the Syrians, Elisha prayed for horses and chariots to overcome the enemy. He also prayed that temporary blindness seize his attackers (II Kings 6:18), and that life be restored to the body of the Shunammite woman's son (4:33). In the prayer of Ezra (9:5-15) we watch him fall upon his knees, after tearing his garment, and spread out his hands, as he confesses the sin and guilt of the nation. When the sick king Hezekiah prays, he reminds God that his heart has been perfect and obedient, presumably a condition deserving a favorable response to his prayer (II Kings 20:2-3).

In Daniel's long prayer (9:4-19) may be identified praise to God, confession of sin, acknowledgement of the justice of the nation's punishment in exile, a petition that the anger of God be turned away from Jerusalem, and that he make his face shine upon his sanctuary, forgive his people, and act promptly to save them. Solomon's prayer (I Kings 8:23-54) when he dedicates the temple includes praise to God; a request that the line of David be preserved; and a plea that the guilty be punished, that the nation be restored from the land of the enemy—an interesting reflection of an exilic or postexilic date of composition much later than the time of David—after it confesses its sin, for rain when withheld because of sin, for an equitable balancing of the divine mercy with the inner goodness of man, for a favorable reply when a resident alien prays toward the temple, for victory in battle, and for mercy toward a penitent people.

Except for Elisha's prayers, which strongly betray the effect of folk-lore, these prayers reflect the universal need of men for physical strength and health, for national security, and for the favor of God through confession of sin and forgiveness. They are uttered on formal occasions and also spontaneously, when the need arises. In the book of Psalms their frequency is much greater, but their quality is not markedly different. The psalms cover a very wide range of needs and interests, some of which have been noticed in the discussion of other aspects of salvation. Especial attention may be called to the spirit of sheer delight in communion with God in the psalms. The nearness of God is man's highest good (73:28); he has fullness of joy in the divine presence (16:11); and God's grace is better than life itself (63:3). In these prayers is also the element of self-criticism and soul-searching in the light of the demands of God. Overt sins and secret sins are held up to the divine scrutiny. Any trace of guilt or of evil is an abomination to God and must be washed away by confession and the merciful forgiveness of the Most High. No man can come to the altar of God unless he has a pure heart and clean hands. Only the upright can see God.

But most of the prayers in the Old Testament demonstrate that salvation is a process, including the activity of God and man's sincere response to this activity. To the degree that prayer measures this response in a personal and ethical manner prayer is essential to salvation. It lifts man's soul, in all of its nakedness, to God. In humility and faith it appropriates what God has to give, both of himself and of his righteous will, whether that will is exhibited in the form of moral precepts, retributive judgment, or material blessings. This concept of prayer rests firmly upon the nature of God as righteous, living will and upon man as rebellious sinner, although made in the divine image. Through Creation and revelation God relates himself to the world and by his own acts makes possible and even necessary the practice of effective prayer. When this revelation is received and validated in faith and empirical experience, it opens the channels of prayer for all men. Through the revelation the nature and conditions of prayer are laid down. Having received the revelation, Israel gives full assent to the possibility and necessity of prayer. No problems such as those arising in a scientific age interfere with this assent. Only the complete denial of the revelation could cause a rejection of prayer.

The concept of the *worshiping community* as understood in the Old Testament may properly enter into this account of salvation. We are not principally interested in the behavior of this community, rather in the meaning of its behavior in so far as it reflects the community idea. Much has already been said in the matter of Israel as a chosen people having special covenant relations with its God. The concept of choice or election set this people apart from other nations, both in its own thought regarding its manifest destiny and in the thinking of its neighbors. At first this nation was politically independent with a king of its own. Later when the nation fell, the idea of nationalism was gradually replaced by the concept of a holy community. This community was bound together by ties of tradition centering in a history marked by special acts of divine deliverance. It was also integrated by social and religious practices setting it apart from other communities and giving it a keen sense of uniqueness and mission.

The multiplication of hardships and calamities acted to intensify and deepen the feeling of solidarity and distinctiveness, so that the exilic period saw the appearance of a remarkable idea—that of vicarious suffering by the group as a means of redeeming the world. Israel's tragic defeat was transformed by God into a triumphant message and an effective instrument of salvation. "Through his [Israel's] stripes we [the nations] were healed." (Isa. 53:5.) The purified, spiritual community of Israel, chastened and cleansed by the experiences of the Exile, was the new holy community. For self-correction, self-analysis, and in order to win the favor of God, this community needed to utilize its energies in worship and religious instruction. For this purpose the rebuilt temple was at hand, both as an institutional reality and as a dynamic idea. Actual worship within its confines and according to its regulations, or the hope of future worship which sustained the exiles as they dreamed of the glories of the temple of Solomon, brought the nation nearer to God.

The sacrificial system and the complex ritual of the temple need not concern us here, except as these reveal the concrete, sensuous practices by which an entire community of diverse capacities and attainments on the part of its individual members could have the experience of worship. Whether the sacrifices offered on prescribed occasions were gifts, acts of communion with God—who shared a common meal with his worshipers, or whose symbolic animal body was shared by members of the community—or had some other function, is not too important for our purpose.[8] Here we may simply observe that these sacrifices were the tangible acts conceived as providing the sacrificer access to God and an assurance of his help to men. So they served an invaluable function in promoting the cause of the holy community, whose service to its members, to the world, and to God was dependent upon the preservation of its consciousness of uniqueness and special election.

This consciousness could hardly be fostered in a hostile culture,

[8] For a full discussion of the subject of sacrifice see Oesterley, *Sacrifices in Ancient Israel* (1937).

such as surrounded the exiles and the Jews of the dispersion, in the absence of the ceremonial rites of the Jewish temple. Full salvation could not come to Israel save as it consciously related itself and its purposes to God by practicing worship on a community-wide basis. Without insisting on this relationship Israel would disintegrate into a multitude of scattered, purposeless individuals whose original faith would be assimilated to other dominant cultures, so that it could make no real contribution to history. However, as a worshiping community the contrary is true: Israel's faith in the God of salvation has survived and is today the distinctive, driving spiritual force which alone holds out hope for the world.

6. The Kingdom of God

SINCE the exact phrase "kingdom of God" nowhere appears in the Old Testament, a serious question may be raised relative to the wisdom of including it in an outline of Old Testament theology. In justification it may be said that the ground work for the formulation of this concept has been laid in the Old Testament writings, even though the results were not labeled with the title by the biblical writers. The idea of the kingdom of God brings together illuminatingly within the scope of a single thought pattern the essential features of world redemption—in history and beyond history—as these were taught by Israel's religious thinkers. Here may be associated the major postulates of this people's faith relative to God, man, history, sin, and salvation. Such an association permits a view of the whole process of salvation in terms of its origin, its successive advances and recessions, and its ultimate goal in the triumph of God in history.

The fact that the modern interpreter is unavoidably called upon to attempt his own synthesis in the absence of a pre-existing biblical synthesis, and that he may fail to do justice to his sources, is a risk he must take, unless he abandons entirely the effort to find religious meanings and viewpoints in his materials. However, if his theological construction rests upon critically defensible data found in the records or upon valid and pertinent extrabiblical evidence, the result may be considered sound and useful to the wider purpose of identifying the elements of Old Testament theology. The raw materials out of which the concept of the kingdom of God is constructed themselves assume a life and meaning which they could not possibly have had in textual and logical isolation.

Further justification for this study lies in the curious fact that the principal teaching attributed to Jesus in the Gospels is that pertaining to the kingdom of God, according to competent New Testament scholars, although they find in the Old Testament only a very limited amount of material upon which Jesus could have drawn in developing his teaching. E. F. Scott's excellent work *The Kingdom of God in the New Testament* makes a brief statement as to the Old Testament background of his subject in a preliminary chapter. This is far from adequate, even in a small volume. Scholars have eagerly searched the Old Testament and other Jewish writings for the sources of Jesus' ideas, but for his greatest teaching they find little or no direct Old Testament support. When the historical, cultural, and religious continuity of the New Testament with the Old Testament is held in mind, such an omission is astonishing. The entire basis for the literary-historical study of the New Testament consists in the recognition of this continuity, as well as the continuity of New Testament life and thought with that of contemporary non-Jewish cultures. It may well be that the failure of Old Testament scholars at this point accounts for the shortcomings of their New Testament colleagues in slighting the Hebrew sources.

ISRAEL'S NEED FOR THE KINGDOM OF GOD

If we think of the kingdom of God as a social concept and as a fact of faith which includes in its range the experience of divine judgment, the conquest of evil through the direct activity of God or of his agent the Messiah, and the establishment of a new order involving radical transformation in national and international life, we may understand how the history of Israel prepared her for the reception of this idea. The historical experience of the nation was not conducive to dreams of grandeur or of world supremacy: in fact, this experience tended to cultivate a sense of defeat and failure in practically every enterprise in which nations hope to excel—the military, the political, the economic, and the social. The instinct of the native Israelites—not of the Canaanites, who were farmers—was toward peace. The Bedouin tradition which they brought into Palestine tended to persist in spite of cultural assimilation and social adjustment. Inferiority of fighting equipment and limitations in manpower also contributed to military weakness, as did Israel's vulnerable position on the land bridge between Asia and Africa. Defeat was a common experience consequently. The glorious periods when David and Solomon reigned, or the times of Jeroboam of Israel and Uzziah of Judah, were remembered the more keenly because of the dark days intervening and following. When it came to political shrewdness, both in domestic and in foreign affairs, the Hebrew kings often failed sadly. They rode roughshod over the sensitive feelings of freedom-loving tribesmen (I Kings 12:14); they flaunted the principles of justice and tried to set themselves up as despots, perhaps in an effort to make up losses in prestige and wealth on the battlefields of diplomacy (II Sam. 11:1–12:12; I Kings 5:13-18; I Kings 21).

In their relations with other nations the Hebrew kings were inept;

in fact, they were often outwitted or outnumbered when diplomacy was backed by military force. The last days of Israel witnessed the blundering of kings as well as the demoralization of the people, who lacked firm leadership. The same sorry spectacle was to be seen in Judah when at last she succumbed to the Babylonians. Rulers were unruly; they were more interested in pampering their own lust than in saving the nation. So they ground the face of the poor and played the tyrant over their subjects, who should have been treated as neighbors (Isa. 3:4-5, 15). In the meantime they vacillated stupidly in foreign relations, swinging toward Egypt and then toward Assyria or Babylonia in fear, uncertainty, and a complete lack of statesmanlike conviction. So Israel fell in 721 B.C., and Judah followed suit over a century later.

There was little opportunity to excel in the realm of trade, since Israel's location and geographical situation were not conducive to any great accumulation of surpluses which could be exported. The same was true of the southern kingdom to an even greater degree. These military, political, and economic factors lent themselves to the creation of social instability and ruinous class struggle, with the result that Israel and Judah were unable to produce a society well adjusted to the world and at peace with itself. Caught in the crushing power of opposing empires, inadequately endowed with the natural resources necessary to economic affluence, ineptly led by rulers incompetent to compete with other powers and baffled by circumstances beyond their control, and weakened by internal dissension, these Hebrew nations were trapped in history without the possibility of escape.

How, then, could the Hebrews find meaning and distinctiveness as a nation or as a people? [1] For a nation, as for an individual, a sense of worth is essential to survival. When every avenue of achievement is apparently blocked, destruction and defeat are inevitable. The interpreters of Israel's history—using the term "Israel" now to mean the entire people, regardless of northern and southern divisions—and the authors of the legends, folk tales, and poems used by these interpreters instinctively or deliberately reacted to *national frustration* by developing a myth of a golden age and by using this myth as the springboard for the projection of this golden age into a glorious future. The non-Hebraic sources which these writers used for the dramatic structure of this myth need not concern us; we are interested in the technique of transforming despair into hope which their work illustrates.

Did Israel face complete political futility? There was a time when this was not the case, and that time would recur in the future when the

---

[1] See Graham, *op. cit.*, for a full development of this point.

nation's aspirations would be vindicated and the world would hail her as victor. Were her armies repeatedly unsuccessful in the field? The day would come when the armies of the Lord of hosts would fight for her and completely vanquish her enemies. Did Israel know poverty and deprivation in comparison with the impressive wealth of her neighbors? In the future she would enjoy undreamed-of abundance, with each man sitting under his own vine and fig tree and even the harsh desert blooming like the crocus. Was she surrounded by idolatrous nations who corrupted her from without and contaminated her by causing apostate Israelites to infect her from within? The days were coming when all Israel would seek the Lord and enshrine his worship in their hearts, while all the nations would come to Mount Zion to learn his ways. This release from frustration, this golden age projected into the future, this hope of divine vindication in history and even beyond it belongs to the idea of the kingdom of God, for whose realization in thought and in time Israel's history of doom and defeat was an important preparation.

THE OFFICE OF KING

Our investigation requires a knowledge of the meaning of the term "kingdom" as used in the Old Testament, and also of the nature of the concept of king. The two are obviously closely related. Since the office of king is more concretely identifiable and is the historical antecedent of the idea of the kingdom, it will be examined rather fully in the hope that its development in Israel will throw light upon our general problem. Our search is handicapped at the outset by the deficiencies of the sources upon which we are almost entirely dependent. There is a decided paucity of detailed information dealing with administrative, political, and governmental phases of the nation's life. The numerous practical questions as to how the total life of the community was regulated, so important to the historian, are practically ignored by the biblical writers and editors. Their interest is strongly theological and religious; and they have but one question to ask of history, How did Israel's leading personalities, especially its rulers, fulfill the purposes of God with respect to his covenant with the nation?

We may ask, When did the office of king first appear in the life of the Israelites? Traditions now extant in the Old Testament show that early Israel, before its penetration into Canaan, was familiar with the office of tribal chieftain rather than that of king. If we suppose that a limited number of tribes entered Palestine with a Yahwistic tradition, and constituted a loose tribal confederacy, the idea of a king as a political fact could not have been conceived until this confederacy had become some kind of a monarchy. Only as extensive migrations into Palestine, together with the resulting merging and accommodations of opposing cultures, continued for several centuries did the social necessity for the office of king become sufficiently apparent to overcome the great obstacle of desert-bred tradition, which, even when the monarchy appeared, effectually prevented the permanent establishment on Palestinian soil of an absolute despotism.

In premonarchical Israel two tendencies were at work—one looking toward centralization of power, and the other moving in the direction of decentralization under the influence of the democratic impulse of desert tribalism. Neither tendency became completely dominant in Israel. Even though centralization seemed to win out at times, the concept of freedom and of local political autonomy limited the power of the king to a marked degree. The coming of the monarchy was accelerated by the force of political events in Palestine. The biblical account of the inauguration of the kingdom is not without inner contradictions, yet it strongly suggests that the threat of Philistine control over Israelite tribes was the occasion for its adoption (I Sam. 5–7; 10:1, 5). Saul's personal traits, his stature and strength, are also significant. He proved his fighting qualities in his raid against the Ammonites across the Jordan. He continued to demonstrate his abilities as a leader until mental disintegration set in. Significantly, he died upon a battlefield. His royal duties were largely military ones; other functions were performed, but they must have been limited in number.

The attitudes of the two early sources—the Yahwistic (J) and the Elohistic (E)—are of interest at this point. The J writer evinces no hostility toward the idea of a king for Israel; he simply recorded available tradition. On the other hand, the E writer is positive that to have a king would bring disaster, because it meant disloyalty to God. He presents a melancholy picture of life under a king. The king foolishly requested by the people would conscript young men for the royal army; he would impose heavy taxes upon the farmers; and he would virtually enslave his subjects in his passion for power. One suspects that this decidedly unenthusiastic view of the monarchy was not altogether the work of imagination or even of revelation: it contains evidence of painful reflection upon Israel's actual history prior to the time of the writer. The two sources agree that the establishment of the office of king and the creation of the monarchy was not a matter of indifference to God, and that he chose the first king, whether this was done willingly or not. It is noteworthy that the two leading personalities in the early monarchy

—Samuel and Saul—were either prophets or capable of having prophetic experiences (I Sam. 10:10).

We may now comment on the extent of the king's *authority* over the life of the nation, since this matter relates to the development of the prestige of the king's office, an office which reaches a high level when kingship is finally ascribed to God himself. At first the monarchy was greatly limited by reason of its infancy, the effect of the principle of freedom, and the limitations in the personality of the holders of the office. Saul's administration was unpretentious and unimpressive. Apparently he remained on his own estate and administered affairs of state —such as they were, in a simple economy—from there. His court was practically nonexistent, or at best was composed of a small group of officials. The limited power of the early monarchy may be emphasized by calling attention to the use of the term "king" to designate the rulers of countries adjacent to the land of Israel. The inscription of the Assyrian ruler Esarhaddon—681-668 B.C.—names the rulers of Tyre, Judah, Edom, Moab, Gaza, Askelon, Ekron, Gebal, Arvad, and Cyprus as kings.[2] These places include nations and small city-states. The word "king" is thus used loosely and identifies any ruler, no matter how insignificant he may be. With the growth of a ruler's wealth, gained by military conquest or by trade, his prestige and power also increase. Assyrian inscriptions and the biblical accounts themselves tell of the wealth of certain Hebrew kings. From Menahem of Israel, Tiglath-Pileser—745-727 B.C.—took tribute which included such items as gold and silver, lead, iron, elephant-hide, ivory, linen, colored wool, birds with wings dyed purple, horses, mules, oxen, sheep, and camels.[3] As for Solomon, his wealth and wisdom were proverbial (I Kings 10; 4:29-31.)

This accumulation of wealth and the power that it brought, as well as the personal *prestige* of the individual monarch, tended to inspire in the king's subjects the feeling of awe and fear which widened the distance between ruler and people. So there gradually emerged an idea of kingship surrounded with the emotions of reverence, fear, and self-abasement. And as the office of king became more and more glamorous and awe-inspiring, its power waxed stronger. It is not surprising that such power would be conceived as divine and become the object of religious emotions. In addition to exercising the religious functions of presiding at sacrifices and supervising the construction and dedication of religious buildings, the king, it is entirely probable, actually repre-

[2] G. A. Barton, *Archaeology and the Bible* (1916), p. 378.
[3] *Ibid.*, p. 367. Israel was but one of several contributors to this list.

sented God on certain occasions, especially at the celebration of the New Year Festival. This was the most dramatic and solemn festival of the entire year. If the king truly represented the needs and interests of the whole national community, the day when the people witnessed in the sanctuary a dramatic demonstration of God's promise that fields, herds, and wives would be fruitful during the new year, would surely be the day when the king's function as religious leader would rise to its climactic point. In the opinion of Oesterley, in the great drama re-enacted annually the creative power of Yahweh is recited by the actors; his defeat of the powers of evil and darkness is announced; and his victory over the nations is triumphantly declared.[4] In this ritual the figure of the king may have occupied a prominent place. We may think of the king as mounting the throne, after his coronation, to the accompaniment of choric shouts: "Yahweh is become king!" This would mean that in the human king was to be seen the actual presence of the Deity. This theory cannot be supported by absolute proof, but it is extremely probable, especially in view of the facts regarding the increasingly idealized concept of the office of king in Israel.

GOD AS KING

It was not a difficult step to apply to God himself these traits and functions of a glorified monarch who held in his hands the destiny of his people. For an indication of the tendency to characterize God in terms taken from experience with the monarchy, the psalms furnish the most material. In them we encounter such statements as:

God is king over the whole earth. (47:7.)

The Lord is king: he is clothed with majesty. (93:1.)

For the Lord is a great God,
And a great king over all gods. (95:3.)

We may note also comparable allusions:

My king and my God. (5:2.)

The Lord is king forever and ever. (10:16.)

The Lord sits as king forever. (29:10.)

[4] *The Psalms* (1939), I, 44-55.

It is thou, my king, O God,
Who orderest victory for Jacob. (44:4.)

The joy of the whole earth
Is the hill of Zion in the far north,
The city of the great king.
God, in her palaces,
Has shown himself a tower of strength. (48:2-3.)

The processions of my God, my King, in the sanctuary.
(68:24.)

God is my king from of old,
Who wrought victory in the midst of the earth. (74:12.)

I will exalt thee, my God, O King;
And bless thy name forever and ever. (145:1.)

Let the sons of Zion triumph in their king. (149:2.)

In the work of Second Isaiah, God is called the "King of Israel," or by a similar title (Isa. 44:6; see 41:21; 43:15). The E source in Samuel makes the same claim when Israel's stubbornness in demanding a human king is under discussion: "And you said to me, 'No, but a king shall reign over us,' although the Lord your God was your king" (I Sam. 12:12).

A group of passages with the general meaning that God will become, or has become, king is worth noting. Some of these may be quoted: "with a strong hand, . . . and with outpoured fury, will I be king over you." (Ezek. 20:33.)

And the Lord shall rule [become king] over them in Mount Zion.
(Mic. 4:7.)

For the Lord of hosts will be king on Mount Zion. (Isa. 24:23.)

The Lord shall reign [be king] for ever and ever. (Exod. 15:18.)

How beautiful upon the mountains
are the feet of the heralds,

. . . .

Who say to Zion,
"Your God has become king" (Isa. 52:7.)

The Lord is king; he is clothed with majesty. (Ps. 93:1.)

Tell among the nations that the Lord is [has become] king.
(96:10.)

The Lord reigns; let the earth rejoice! (97:1.)

The Lord is king; let the peoples tremble! (99:1.)

The Lord reigns forever. (146:10.)

In these references it has been seen that God is viewed as king of Israel and as king of the whole earth, who will reign forever in glory and majesty, and cause rejoicing because of the victory he will bring. He will far outshine an earthly king in the extent of his rule and in the wondrous salvation he will visit upon all who hail him as ruler and Lord. The political background of most of these citations is exilic or postexilic dependence upon a foreign power. The nation is no more, although its memory is held as a consuming hope and goal in the minds of the faithful patriots who cannot forget the days of freedom, which seem more glamorous than they actually were. There is no longer a king in Israel, no earthly throne from which a political ruler can issue his decrees. Then let the exiled and defeated people with one accord proclaim their new Ruler, who has always been their true Ruler: "Yahweh is become king!"

In this interpretation of the relation of God to Israel as a relation of king to his people, we have a firm basis for approaching the concept of the kingdom of God. In this relationship, in the idea of king in its developed and lofty spiritual sense, and in Israel's awakened consciousness that throughout her history God had, in fact, been her king, we have the preparation for a fuller understanding of the meaning of the divine kingdom. Postexilic writers came to believe that God's rule—to be so gloriously consummated in the future—had been in effect in the entire course of the nation's history. There had been no real interruption, in spite of external appearances. As they read the history of their people, they discovered that there was a history within a history, that within the changing forms of political and social life effected by environmental influences through the centuries—and constituting a history of a sort —there was a true history of God's eternal purpose for Israel. This was a spiritual history—a history of the kingdom of God—within the more obvious political history, consisting of migrations, wars, changing dynasties, and foreign entanglements. This is the history of the kingdom of God within the external political history. To trace its emergence and to delineate its features will be the task now.

THE POLITICAL KINGDOM AS GOD'S KINGDOM

There is a sense in which the idea of the kingdom of God never emerged in Hebrew thought, for it was always present. All of the literature is witness to the fact of a special, unified national experience which had a definite beginning, and which points toward a meaningful future. This experience lay deeper than the entertaining episodes in the narratives of the heroic exploits of Hebrew ancestors, although the narratives contribute to a knowledge of the spiritual events in which these ancestors participated. The stories of Abraham, Isaac, and Jacob, or of Joseph, Moses, or Samuel, are replete with colorful detail, delighting the heart of the *reconteur*. Yet they are essentially the record of the pilgrimage of a people torn by doubt, buffeted by misfortune, corrupted by paganism, and—often against its will—walking in the way of life and faith. Wistfully the J writer recounts the old tale of the garden of Eden, where man's first ancestor came to a knowledge of good and evil and was driven out of his first home. With a racial nostalgia and memory he recalls that age of innocence and peace when men and animals lived together, and together found sustenance from the plants rather than in the shedding of blood. In the garden of man's life was ample provision for every need: food, water, companionship with man and with God. This was the kingdom already full grown.

The evil choice that appeared to destroy it brought into being the kingdom of hate, murder, and overweening pride, to say nothing of pain and sweating toil upon weed-infested soil. But it was not destroyed, for out of the evil which man did, God created the good which he would do through the election of a people and preparation for his kingdom. Joseph tells the deeper truth about God's use of history when he says to his brothers, who have treated him with unforgiveable cruelty, "Do not be afraid: for can I take God's place? You meant to do me harm, but God accounted it good, in order to do as he has done today: save the lives of many people." (Gen. 50:20—1935 ed.) Cain's murder of Abel, the unendurable corruption of the human race which produced the flood, the pride preceding the futile attempt of men to build a high tower, the cunning of Jacob, the stupidity of Esau, the incest of Reuben, the murderous anger of Moses, the resistance of the pharaoh, the fleshpot sensuality of the Israelites, the Baal-loving arrogance of the tycoons of Samaria and Jerusalem, the pampered rich and the exploited poor—

these could not turn the God of history from his course and his purpose of establishing his kingdom.

Evidence accumulates to show that the political kingdom of Israel was always thought to be God's kingdom. The powerful opposition to the founding of the monarchy at the time of Saul, which was registered by the E writer and possibly others, is proof of this. When Samuel complains to God of the Hebrews' unfortunate insistence upon having a king, God tells him not to take it as a personal insult, for, he says, "They have not rejected you, but they have rejected me from being king over them" (I Sam. 8:7). Here is the assumption that the demand for a king was a revolt against, and a rejection of, a king already in power—God himself. The E source conveys the idea of a strong theocratic government over Israel, which has existed continuously, and which is being disturbed by the disloyal conduct of the people. Ever since the Exodus, at least, this relationship had obtained between God and his people. It is true that God had appointed human agents to interpret his statutes to his subjects, but these agents had never usurped his royal position as absolute ruler over Israel.

Moses, the greatest of these agents, had never instigated important programs on his own initiative; he had always referred problems of government to the Lord, from whom came the authoritative and final word for action. Consequently when Israel's political and economic needs—which were occasioned by the problems of settlement in a new country and by the weakness of the loosely organized confederation of seminomadic tribes who called themselves Israelites—became sufficiently intense, the necessity for a centralized form of government was created. The tradition that the coming of the monarchy was hastened by a popular desire to be "like all the nations" must be discounted, for this people was simply conforming to the principles of social organization in effect wherever circumstances similar to those confronting the Hebrews chance to arise.

These circumstances, decisive as they were, could not obscure the survival among certain Hebrew tribes of a belief that the God of the desert, from which they had migrated, had voluntarily chosen them, had presided over their fortunes, and had guided them into a new land. To these fierce, freedom-loving tribesmen God alone was ruler, and to him belonged the honor and the glory of being king. To accept an Oriental ruler like those governing Palestinian city-states or adjacent petty kingdoms was tantamount to opening the door both to the loss of their jealously guarded freedom and to the corruption attendant upon the concentration of power in the hands of a small clique or of an individual ruler. In as much as God was held to be the conserver of freedom and of social justice, the proposal to transfer his power to a human king outraged their religious feelings and violated their intense social conservatism. The only kingdom they could sincerely acknowledge was that of God. This is what tradition meant to the prophetic-minded Hebrews, even when the political monarchy had become firmly established.

From the surviving accounts of the origin of the monarchy the presence of the idea of the inner, spiritual kingdom ruled over by God alone can be detected. Undeniably authentic sources agree that the political kingdom derived its being from the intervention of God in the historical process. In other words, a divine-kingdom history was superimposed upon the history of the rise and fall of Israel's social institutions. In the language of the Bible the prophet Samuel, after pouring the contents of a vial of oil upon the head of Saul, said, "Has not the Lord anointed you to be a leader over his people Israel?" (I Sam. 10:1.) At this juncture in history the prophetic movement, whose purpose had been the conservation and propagation of Yahweh worship, created a political order whose head was a king, and whose authority and very existence derived from the permissive sanction of God—the actual head of the state. The monarchy endured on sufferance, never for one moment surviving or functioning in its own right. It was conceived in the mind of men as an instrument of control and defense, like similar instruments in the world of men; it was conceived in the mind of God as the embodiment in historical form of his holy purpose to save men and to inaugurate his kingdom.

The prophets represented, and put into concrete political form, this divine conception. Thus Samuel the prophet anointed Saul, and perhaps even selected him; he went to Bethlehem and anointed David after God had "rejected Saul from being king over Israel"; Nathan the prophet shared in the harem intrigues which put Solomon on the throne; Ahijah the prophet conspired against Solomon and helped place Jeroboam on the throne as king of the rebelling northern tribes; Elisha the prophet sent a messenger to Jehu to inform him that the time was ripe for a revolt against the house of Ahab, and thus started a royal bloodletting which practically wiped out Ahab's line (I Sam. 10:1; 16:13; 13:14; I Kings 1:22-28; 11:29-39; II Kings 9–10).

So the prophets had a hand in setting up and upsetting kings, in carrying out their purpose of pointedly and ruthlessly driving home their conviction that God was the real ruler of Israel. Admittedly this oversimplifies the matter. Many facts and factors are pertinent to a history of a monarchy aside from the factor of religious influence. However, this is not a history in the generally accepted sense: it is a search for the history within a history, the record of the spiritual kingdom of faith and divine judgment and redemption—a record lying hidden beneath the sensate history unfolding in time and space in the form of revolutions, regicides, and social change. The prophets' participation in the outer history of the monarchy underlines the monarchy's subordinate character and its subjection to the will of God as an instrument for accomplishing his purpose in history and beyond.

As understood by practically all Old Testament thinkers—assuming they thought about the matter at all—the monarchy endured the vicissitudes of changing fortune, not because of the ineffectiveness of kings or the ill fortune of unfavorable circumstances, but because of the often mysterious purposes of God. Externally the biblical writers saw in the rise and fall of the kings of Israel and Judah the exemplification of the rule of divine retribution. When a king sinned, if his sin was heinous enough, he lost his throne prematurely; or in the event that God saw fit to let him retain it, it did not pass to his sons. Revolutions were fomented for this apparent reason. If we study the evidence more carefully and more comprehensively, however, we find that it is not merely a law of retribution that is at work in history. There is a more fundamental law which tests the conformity of an event or a royal program with the pattern of the spiritual kingdom whose outlines, even before the Exile, were beginning to emerge in Hebrew thought.

Prophetic condemnation of Saul for taking a census or for sparing Agag, the king of the Amalekites, has no visible ethical basis, yet it does mark the presence of an active insistence upon the requirement of unhesitating and even irrational obedience to God on the part of every king. The earthly ruler may not forget the source of his authority or the insecurity of his exalted position. His throne is fragile, his seat insecure. Disobedience to God may quickly destroy it beyond hope of repair. When kings take their task and position too seriously and allow from their subjects the adulation due to God alone, punishment is swift and sure. An Ahijah may suggest to a superintendent of public works that he might become king, setting off a *coup d'etat* of revolutionary proportions; or an Elisha may hint to a general that Ahab can be toppled from his throne, along with various heirs apparent, thus making room for a successful rebel. Apart from human plans and ambitions these prophetic maneuvers serve God's purpose of providing a constant reminder that his kingdom is over all human kingdoms and is working as a leaven within them for purposes beyond the power of human reason fully to comprehend.

We have noted that the kingdom of God lay within the political kingdom made by man. This is evident from the religious meaning of the patriarchal stories in Genesis; from God's use of evil for doing ultimate good, from the emphatic objection of God—according to one source —to the establishment of the kingdom; from the existence of the biblical tradition that the kingdom was in opposition to the will of God, thus witnessing to the presence in Israel of men and groups sympathetic to this idea; from the influence of Yahwistic prophets in originating the monarchy; and from evidence of the divine control of its course through rebuke, qualified approval, punitive judgment, or catastrophic revolution. By these means we are able to determine that within a visible, observable history the spiritual history of the kingdom of God was making itself felt. It did not fully exist among men, for its complete design was conceived only in the mind of God; but its distinctive elements were slowly coming to light. As an illustration of this, the growth of a spiritual conception of the *duties of the king* may be considered. The king was not only to perform public religious duties, such as presiding over sacrifices. He was also expected, as this ideal grew, to live religiously as a person, holding before his subjects an example of piety and devotion to God.

The standard of approval used by the Deuteronomists in judging the reigns of individual kings bears on this theme. Many kings are condemned because they "did that which was evil in the sight of the Lord" (II Kings 8:18). The specific nature of what is "evil" or what is "right" is not always made clear, although some concrete illustrations are given. For example, the judgment on Jehoash's reign states that this king had been instructed by Jehoiada the priest, presumably in matters pertaining to correct forms of worship. It is said, however, "the high places were not taken away" (II Kings 12:2-3). A number of the kings of Israel did evil in not turning away from the sins of Jeroboam— obviously a reference to the deeds of Jeroboam I—who set up golden calves in Dan and Bethel, and made priests from the people without regard to the sons of Levi (I Kings 12:29-33). Evidently right conduct consisted in devotion to the one God and the rejection of the worship of Baals and Asheroth, the fertility deities of Canaan. Evil conduct was, of course, the worship of these gods and toleration of their temples, priests, and ceremonies. Involved in evil, as understood by these Deuteronomic theologians, was the matter of the right kind of religious loyalty. The kings were judged, not by their political astuteness, military leadership, or statesmanship, but by their obedience to, and worship of, the one God, Yahweh. Only as they showed themselves to be examples of this kind of piety could they receive a favorable verdict from their Deuteronomic judges. More than this, their commitment in personal devotion to God was the only way of winning his favor, as their proud recalcitrance earned his wrath. In this way the ideal of royal piety served to make prominent the king's humble submission to God and to emphasize the subordinate relation of the earthly monarch's kingdom to that of the divine King.

In the book of Psalms the king is presented as a pious, devout worshiper of God, standing in the need of prayer and offering prayer on his own behalf. If Ps. 18 is partly Davidic, it exhibits a king's utter dependence upon God for help and strength. God is described, in a series of metaphors, as the king's rock, a fortress, a high tower, and a refuge. God bows the heavens and comes down; he arrives with the accompaniment of storm, hail, lightning, and earthquake; to the degree that the king is righteous and pure he helps him by his mercy and justice; he girds the king for battle and gives him victory over his enemies. In the next psalm—20—under consideration the king's gifts and burnt offerings are named, and he is promised victory on the basis of trust in God rather than of reliance upon horses and chariots. The third—Ps. 21— of the royal psalms in our list tells how the king rejoices in the strength of God and in the gift of long life. This king is gladdened by the presence of God, in whose power and goodness he trusts both for personal strength and for victory in battle.

In Ps. 45, celebrating a royal wedding, the groom's virtues are extolled. He is a mighty warrior and a champion of truth and right. He loves righteousness and hates wickedness, and has been abundantly blessed by God accordingly. Finally, we discover in a prayer for a king—Ps. 72—the expression of extravagant hopes, doubtless a result of poetic Oriental hyperbole as well as the poet's natural desire to impress his royal patron. The king is to manifest justice and righteousness and peace, delivering the poor and the afflicted from the oppressor, and extending his rule to the ends of the earth. His ethical ideals and standards are to come from the very nature of the just God, we are informed. In the Deuteronomic tradition regarding David, and in the pronounced idealization of the psalms, we detect the development of this *spiritual* ideal of royal conduct and personality. David becomes the symbol of the kind of piety highly esteemed in the postexilic period of legalism, priestly ritualism, and mystical faith. He becomes a composite ideal for religious conduct and character for that period and, to a lesser degree, for the preceding period of the Exile and late monarchy. This is particularly noticeable in a study of the messianic literature.

The *ethical* as well as the religious ideal of royal conduct fits into our effort to show how the idea of the kingdom of God is latent within the external, political kingdom of written history. Piety, with its opposites disloyalty and apostasy, was not the only criterion for evaluating the reign of any given monarch, although it was, beyond question, the most important one. Closely allied with this idea is the ethical standard, so deeply rooted in the traditions and history of the Hebrew people. In Nathan's forthright attack upon the base deed of David against one of his subjects whose name was Uriah, we have an expression of what right conduct should mean to a king (II Sam. 11:1–12:25). David had lusted for Bathsheba, the wife of Uriah, an officer in the king's army at the front. He took the woman and ordered the officer into action in a military move that was almost certain to cause his death in battle. This despicable violation of the rights of a subject stirred up the wrath of the prophet, who minced no words in his bitter and unreserved denunciation. The king, who was supposed to defend the rights of his subjects, had set an example of cruel injustice by trampling upon them. He had flaunted justice and ordinary decency in his passionate desire for Bathsheba.

The case of Ahab's cruel whim and his queen's connivance in its realization also comes to mind (I Kings 21). Naboth's vineyard adjoined the palace grounds and had tantalized Ahab for some time because it wasn't his. A gnawing desire to possess it consumed his soul and finally put him to bed, ill from frustration. Through the ingenuity of his wife, Jezebel, he was given his heart's desire at the expense of the life of Naboth, against whom false charges of blasphemy and sedition were trumped up. Found guilty of these charges, he was promptly stoned to death, after the ancient Oriental equivalent of a trial had been held. Burning with anger and sent by God, the narrative states, the prophet Elijah faced the king and announced the utter annihilation of his whole house. We are not surprised that this event caused the historian to write, "There was absolutely no one who sold himself to do evil in the sight of the Lord, as did Ahab." While the rest of this section of the text names idolatry as the apparent reason for this drastic indictment, there is hardly any doubt that the injustice and cruelty of this act against a free subject is also a powerful factor. The king had offended the God of justice to satisfy his personal desire, and had set aside the ideal of royal righteousness cherished and defended in the prophetic tradition.

One more concrete illustration of the strength of this ideal may be included. We refer to the revolt against Solomon's authority which was instigated by the prophet Ahijah (I Kings 11:29-40). While the details of this affair are not fully known, it is probable that Solomon's heavy building projects, his use of forced labor, his ventures in foreign trade, his sumptuous court, and unsound system of taxation (4:7) did not endear him to his people. At any rate, Ahijah started a revolt among the northern tribes, and a new kingdom was born. This political upheaval—whatever the other contributing forces—has a direct relation to Solomon's indifference to the principles of justice which were an integral part of the Hebrew conception of a constitutional monarchy, and which limited the power of the king in the public interest. In all of these illustrations the imposition of the requirement of righteousness upon the king came from above as the command of God, the supreme king. This is the Old Testament view of the matter and supports the concept of a spiritual kingdom of God taking shape in history but not identical with it. The righteous king was the prototype of the later Messiah of God, who was to represent the full-fledged kingdom of God. In so far as he was motivated by concern for obeying the God of justice in his guidance of his subjects, such a king could promote and make visible the purposes of that kingdom.

THE CHOSEN PEOPLE

The kingdom of God within the kingdom of the monarchy is tied up with the conception of a chosen people, a holy community, whose destiny is closely related to the establishment of the divine rule upon the earth. Within the stream of history this chosen group was to become the nucleus of the kingdom. While this idea has other meanings and functions in the religion of the Old Testament, this is its most significant contribution to the understanding of Israel's fundamental beliefs. From the standpoint of God—the Bible would have us believe —his people Israel had been singled out for special attention, in order that the divine government might become a social and empirical fact in the world, as it was already an accomplished fact in the mind and will of God. This people was the medium for revealing to all the world the spiritual truths and the moral implications of this government, and also was the recipient of a direct revelation constituting its unique opportunity to show the world what that government could be in a definite historical culture. When they shrank from this mission in fear and reluctance, the God who had chosen them drove them to their task with the castigating lash of adversity and scornful condemnation, insisting that their election had nothing to do with special privilege and much to do with the painful obligation of obedience.

> You only have I known,
> Of all the families of the earth;
> Therefore, will I punish you
> For all your wrongdoing. (Amos 3:2.)

Thus punishment is promised because the nation which God had chosen refused stubbornly to exemplify the nature of the kingdom as the sovereign rule of the God of justice over the lives of men.

To this people, willing enough to reap the benefits of its favored position, promises of reward for obedience were held out. *If* they discarded their idolatrous beliefs and practices, God would lead them across the desert and into the promised land; *if* they showed kindness to the widow and orphan and the alien in their midst, they would be enabled to overthrow the nations in their path and establish themselves as a great people more numerous than the sands of the sea; *if* they washed their hands and cleansed their hearts of evil deeds and purposes, their nation would survive hostile attacks and gain world acclaim. But these were conditions, not unqualified promises. Their purpose was not to make it difficult for Israel to achieve her desires in the matter of earthly goods, political power, or cultural distinctiveness; instead they envisioned the chastening and spiritual disciplining produced by the failure of practice to measure up to the demands of God, as well as the actual and highly useful consequences which follow obedience in a moral order. In the incipient kingdom represented by the community of the chosen people—ideally depicted as obedient and righteous, but actually hardhearted and spiritually insensitive—the practical effectiveness and truth of social justice must be convincingly demonstrated. Failure here would undermine the historical purpose of the kingdom idea and invalidate its ethical foundations. It should be added that the demonstration of social justice can be both negative and positive, so that defeat in battle, invasion by an enemy, or internal social conflict, are arguments for the power of justice which are just as efficacious as victory, social stability, and prosperity. Punishment and reward are both appropriate in shaping the kingdom of God, of which the chosen people are the original nucleus.

THE KINGDOM OF GOD AS AN APPROACH TO HISTORY

We have been tracing the evidence for the kingdom of God in Israel's history and have found that it is by no means an imperceptible concept. While it has an inchoate form in the literature of the pre-exilic period, the essential elements are present and need simply to be subjected to the strain and pressures of the Exile to come to maturity and bear fruit. The flowering of the concept in the exilic period will be noted in a later part of this chapter. At present a different phase of the subject concerns us—the kingdom of God as history. We are not interested here in history as an unfolding and continuous record of man's life upon the planet or in Palestine, but rather with the assumptions with which this record may be interpreted. The philosophy of history expressly proposed and explicated by any individual, or implicitly contained in a piece of literature, seeks to find the principles of coherence and meaning, the application of which will associate in a single pattern or frame of reference the sum total of human experience or an important segment thereof. It uses chronicles, chronological tables, memoirs, letters, state papers, and all the source material usually associated with the scientific writing of history. This use of sources, however, follows a plan which is predetermined by the presuppositions about history which are held by the historian.

The customary methodology, now seriously criticized as inadequate and misleading, requires the creation of a chronological narrative in which one event after another becomes the basis for a running account of what happened at particular times and in particular places on the map. This is a kind of diary of the human race, written in the third person, although it may lack the intimate touch of a personal diary. Such an approach to history exalts the chronological-developmental principle, whereby a unilinear movement of events through the centuries—from the simple to the complex—receives a meaning derived from the evolutionary hypothesis. A view of history writing such as this betrays weaknesses at more than one point. We may merely identify one—that such a complex entity as social history can be explained simply by the assumption, implied or expressed, that time automatically guarantees better and better results in the human enterprise as the centuries pass.

To prepare ourselves for a more intelligent attitude toward the theory of history contained in the Old Testament, we might look for a moment at another modern approach to history which may be closer to what the Bible presents. This may be called by various names—an *organismic,* a spiritual, or a teleological conception of history.[5] With no thought of engaging in a technical and speculative analysis of the problem, it is suggested that this general view conceives of the movement of events—in an infinite variety of patterns and complicated interactions—toward the goal wherein the pattern is completed, in a manner similar to that which occurs when a single biological organism, with its intricate internal functions and its numerous responses to stimuli from without, fulfills its destiny in life. Under this conception of history the movement is not automatic and the end is not necessarily predictable, although certain adaptations of the theory may make it so, as is the case with the Old Testament conception. The biological analogy is unsatisfactory, although helpful; for the organism which is history is composed of psychological, sociological, economic, cultural, aesthetic, rational, and emotional factors in addition to that of biological vitality. In this view, the basic drive or the teleology of history's organismic responses is a differentiating feature distinguishing the variations of this general philosophy of history from one another. As we shall see, the Old Testament makes a unique contribution at this point.

The Old Testament is the first literature in the history of mankind to express a distinct and consistent idea of history, although prior mythologies in Egypt, Sumeria, Babylonia, and Syria suggest that history has some sort of meaning lying beyond any particular event. The J writer produces a sweeping, circular movement of history, which begins with innocence, moves through tragedy and evil, and returns to the primitive goodness of the garden in Eden, at least by implication. Man is good in the garden; he chooses evil, and civilization gets under way. Onward man moves, through one evil epoch after another, wistfully remembering his past, but unable to do much about returning to it because of his will to sin against God. He builds cities, founds the arts and sciences, and devotes all of his thinking to the matter of circumventing his Creator, so that the deluge comes. He survives this catastrophe through the grace of God and proceeds to build himself a tower, which he is not permitted to complete. Through it all there are periods of repentance and forgiveness in which the circle turns back toward the beginning of history, when God and man were at peace and

[5] See W. F. Albright, *From the Stone Age to Christianity* (1940); Shailer Mathews, *The Spiritual Interpretation of History* (1916); Paul Tillich, *The Interpretation of History* (1936); H. G. Wood (and others), *The Kingdom of God and History* (1938); N. A. Berdiaev, *The Meaning of History* (1936); S. J. Case, *The Christian Philosophy of History* (1943); C. H. Dodd, *History and the Gospel* (1938); G. W. F. Hegel, *Philosophy of History* (tr. J. Sibree, 1902).

there was no rebellion or sin. This philosophy is not less profound because it is naïvely presented in the form of legends and poetic oracles. It takes in the entire compass of history from the creation of the earth, and embraces all mankind from its common ancestor to the origin and development of the early monarchy of the Hebrews, touching on the rise of non-Hebrew nations as well. J's outline of world history is magnificently conceived and thrillingly executed, with subtle character delineation, rapidly moving narrative, and a deep awareness of the human and spiritual values in the drama of history. History for him is an entity, centering in Hebrew history, but viewed always in the setting of a special divine purpose which is ethical and redemptive.

The J writer is *prophetic* in spirit as he defends the worship of Yahweh and enunciates an idea of history which springs from his faith in this God. The great prophets and their anonymous successors made more articulate what this early thinker had implied or affirmed when he authored or compiled his materials, but they did not depart from his major point of view. They saw the grim fact of unavoidable judgment in the historical process and accepted it as proof of the divine sovereignty and righteousness at work in history. This process was cyclic and not unilinear, as they brought out when they contemplated the regularity with which judgment overtook the sinning nation. No amount of statecraft or other form of worldly wisdom could suffice to avert these periodic interruptions of routine buying and selling, living and dying. These judgments came as assertions of the transcendence of Israel's just God and as summons to repentance.

As an accompaniment of the judgment of God, which is primarily a decision of his righteous will, there came the act of punishment itself, which took the form of a calamity originating in nature, such as an earthquake, or a disaster of human origin such as military defeat, or a direct act of God such as the fire which devoured the great deep (Amos 7:4). After the calamity came restoration to the favor of God. This reconciliation is greatly minimized in the direct statements of such prophets as Amos and Micah (chaps. 1–3), who are more concerned with attacking national sin than with a promise of forgiveness; but it is not entirely omitted from their admonitions. Hosea and Jeremiah, as also the anonymous prophets and the apocalyptists, stress their belief in the possibility of restoration to God's favor, although the scholar cannot always be sure of the line of demarcation between their bona fide work and the additions of later editors and writers. No matter what the varying emphases of the individual books, in the teachings of most of the prophets—if not all—the cyclic conception of history may be detected. This includes the experiences of sin, judgment, disaster, and restoration in the life of the nation. For these champions of the religion of Yahweh history is an organic, unitary experience, integrated by its necessary dependence upon the will of a righteous, redeeming God, who is the principal causal force in the world of events where the history of the kingdom is unfolding.

The most studied and formal expression of this idea of history is presented in the *Deuteronomic* writings, especially in Judges and Second Kings. Under the influence of a clearly articulated theological position, these men of the Great Reform compiled and edited their sources with a single-minded purposefulness which left an imprint upon their work that cannot be missed by the reader. Their style and their theology are unmistakable. The first is marked by lengthy prosaic speeches, extremely verbose and loosely connected; the last by a belief in the unity of God, the unity of the sanctuary, and the social-ecclesiastical effects of these two ideas in promoting the unity of the people. The last point is implemented by the formulation of provisions for underprivileged groups—such as widows, orphans, resident aliens, unemployed Levites —and by practical adjustments in the rule requiring sacrifice of animals at the temple only. The literary work of these reformers exhibits the influence of the prophets and may be called prophetic in spirit, even though its legalistic material betrays also the interest of the priests.

The everlasting God of judgment, who is the Lord of history and the living God, is the clue to the history of mankind. This was the unique theological contribution of the great prophets of Israel. In putting this belief into the context of the biblical idea of the kingdom, however, the full meaning of the God concept must be duly weighed. In any case, the God of judgment, acting in a sensitive response to sin in history, is the God who is directly responsible for history's cyclic periods of sin, judgment, repentance, and reconciliation. The Deuteronomists would not be at home in the theological atmosphere which produced the optimistic line, "Through the ages one increasing purpose runs," for they witnessed the repeated defeat of this purpose and a series of retrogressions in man's spiritual history. They saw a revealed faith in the greatness and goodness of God at the beginning of history, instead of an achieved faith resulting from the belief in inevitable progress as man's reward for his effort and intelligence. To them the explanatory principles by which history could be interpreted were already at hand. The fact that man stupidly refused to use them in correcting his own participation in history does not argue against this conclusion. The prophets—and before them even Moses—had called men's attention to the headlong collision which history would experience when it crashed into the immovable rock of God's righteousness. That they blindly ignored this warning and acted as though the course of history was straight and smooth, bound to arrive at Utopia at last, shows the myopia of men too close to history rather than the unsoundness of the Deuteronomic-prophetic view.

An excellent summary of the meaning of human history as these quasi-historians saw it comes to our attention in Judges 2. This deserves to be reproduced in part:

The Israelites did what was evil in the sight of the Lord, by serving the Baals and forsaking the Lord, the God of their fathers, who had brought them out of the land of Egypt. . . . Then the anger of the Lord blazed against Israel, so that he delivered them into the power of plunderers who plundered them, and he sold them into the power of their enemies around them. . . . Then the Lord raised up champions to deliver them out of the power of their plunderers; but even their champions they did not heed; for they ran wantonly after alien gods. . . .

The Lord . . . would deliver them . . . during all the lifetime of the champion; for the Lord would be moved to pity by their groans under their tyrants and oppressors. But whenever the champion died, they would relapse. (2:11-12, 14, 16-19.)

In an Israelitish setting this compact and shocking revelation of man's conduct in history effectually epitomizes the significance of world history as the Deuteronomists saw it. Proof that this idea of history did have world-wide implications will be adduced in a later part of this chapter. Our quotation shows that the cycle of history is as follows: an original revelation and a covenant requiring obedience to the God who had initiated it, defiant rejection of God and the pursuit of false gods, the judgment upon men for their idolatry, suffering and repentance followed by deliverance through an act of God, and then rebellion once more. Thus history repeats itself, apparently with no variation except that consisting of the special modifications in the pattern of sin which might be effected by the peculiar circumstances of any given period or culture. Did the Deuteronomist foresee a breaking of this vicious circle and the final vindication of the God of history? Was the circle actually an ascending spiral, rising higher and higher to an ultimate goal of eternal peace and justice? Except for possible Deuteronomic glosses and editorial additions coming from later writers and displaying the spirit of the reformers of Josiah's time, the reply to this question cannot be categorical. Chapter 30 of the book of Deuteronomy—not a part of the original book—looks to a life of blessing and prosperity for an Israel who truly loves her God. We may only assume, on the basis of their faith in the living God, that these men believed in the final triumph of God in history. Those who edited their book, at any rate, thought that they so believed, whatever this may be worth.

When we turn to the *priestly* speculations about the meaning of history, we might expect to find a sharp difference from the beliefs of the prophets and the Deuteronomists. However, this is not the case, although detailed differences in matters of secondary importance are obviously present. Broadly, the priestly view of history comprehends a theocracy in which God would rule—and does rule—through consecrated men equipped with priestly lore, priestly skill, and holiness of person for their task of mediating to men the will of the holy God of Israel. These men, dedicated to the task of preserving the character of a theocratic community, would achieve this end principally by enforcing the minutiae of ritualistic rules set up to guarantee the universal practice of holiness in the community. The kingdom of God amounted to the extension and perpetuation of holiness in the whole world by means of the exaltation of the temple in Zion and of the priestly class within it. Every event was judged by its possible effect upon this grand conception. Every circumstance of Hebrew history was scrutinized to discover its bearing upon the glorification of priestly religion. Israel's leaders were judged from this standpoint. The records of their activities were even drastically revised if these were thought to be incongruous with the priestly ideal. David was thoroughly beatified, unofficially, by the process of expunging from his biography and history traces of unseemly episodes, such as his affair with Bathsheba, a story omitted by the Chronicler.

Of special interest for our purpose, perhaps because of its vividness of portrayal, is the *apocalyptic* literature of the Old Testament. This means in particular Isa. 24–27; Dan. 7–12; Zech. 9–14; Ezek. 37–39; and shorter units elsewhere in the canon (cf. Joel 2:28–3:21). Until rather recently the modern temper has dictated the selection from Scripture of "liberal" ethical passages as guides to faith and conduct, dismissing as meaninglessly fantastic the apocalyptic portions of the canonical books in both Testaments. Now the pendulum is swinging in the other direction, through more objective historical criticism, and through a new realization of the remarkable religious values contained in these writings. A literature which records the courageous faith of Jewish martyrs facing the stake and rack, as in the book of Daniel, or a fragment which depicts the monumental courage of the seer who overcame fear and death through his trust in the Lord of history, which comprises the apocalypse in Isaiah, cannot be neglected.

These books challenge us with their bold and inclusive theory of history. In them is presented the kingdom that is, and the kingdom that is to be. The whole world is the scene for the enactment of a cosmic drama involving all the nations and spotlighting one nation—Israel. All creation groans and travails to bring the kingdom to birth. Personal and national misfortune, victory and defeat in battle, terrors of earthquake, storm, and pestilence, famine, sickness, and death—all bear the meaning of the historical process which is the drama of the kingdom. History, while cyclic, comes to the end of the road and meets disaster and annihilation, only to emerge victorious over sin and death in the life of men with God beyond history and time, where it takes the full form of the kingdom of God. So the apocalypses offer the final answer to the question of history's outcome. Sin, judgment, calamity, redemption, and more sin! This is the deadly circle which God alone can break by bringing in a kingdom which supersedes the kingdoms of this world and endures beyond time and space.

THE FUTURE KINGDOM: ETHICAL, SPIRITUAL, UNIVERSAL

When these conclusions on the kingdom of God as history are summarized, it is found that a broadly consistent and unified idea of history pervades much of the Old Testament. This idea provides for the multiplicity and complexity of social, economic, and psychological factors involved in an organismic conception, and does not unrealistically oversimplify or idealize the total process. The contradictory and elusive forces in history which arise from the human will and nature are given full prominence, but it is not conceded that these forces are ultimately decisive. The reality of moral freedom and of environmental determinism is not forgotten, but neither are these the final word on the enigma of history. The key for solving this riddle is in the concept of God's kingdom, where the supremely decisive factor is the power and righteousness of the living God. His nature and his existence, as the essence of all being, give to history its organismic coherence, its teleological purpose, its ethical meaning, and its ultimate hope. This becomes clear when the full contour of the kingdom idea comes in view. The rule of God, who in judgment upon men seeks their repentance and obedience, and whose mercy and lovingkindness invites their complete commitment to his cause, is envisaged by the concept of the kingdom. The full accomplishment of this rule, when all is said and done, is the meaning and end of history.

Thus the kingdom, as it is—in the faith and hope of men and in the mind of God—and as it is to be, is held to possess an ethical and spiritual character. Since the nature and meaning of the kingdom in realized history have received our attention in a rather full treatment, the future kingdom may now be outlined as it is described in the Old Testament. Practically all of the prophetic books have addenda or original material on this theme. The book of Psalms is also useful, as are the apocalyptic writings and certain poems extant in the Pentateuch, such as that found in Deut. 32. In the psalms the idea of *equitable judgment* in the kingdom is conveyed (Pss. 9:8; 96:10). One poet cries,

> Let the nations be glad and sing for joy,
> Because thou judgest the peoples justly. (67:4.)

"Righteousness and justice are the foundation of his throne" (97:2), as the Lord reigns over the whole earth. He loves justice and he has established equity in his kingdom (99:4). The Davidic ruler over the future kingdom will inaugurate a reign of peace, justice, and righteousness, which will endure forever. The shoot from the stem of Jesse will rule with a strict regard for justice:

> He will not judge by that which his eyes shall see,
> Nor decide by that which his ears shall hear;
> But with justice will he judge the needy,
> And with fairness decide for the poor of the land. (Isa. 11:3-4.)

He will be reverent toward God and be governed by the spirit of wisdom and understanding which comes from God. The whole land will grow spiritually strong and will "become full of the knowledge of the Lord" (11:9; cf. Isa. 9:7; 54:14; 61:1-3; Jer. 23:5-6; 33:15-16).

An exquisite poem surviving in the book of Isaiah portrays the rule of righteousness in the future kingdom:

> Until the spirit be poured upon us from on high;
> Then will the steppe become garden land,
> And the garden land be counted an orchard.
> And justice will dwell in the steppe,
> And righteousness abide in the garden land;
> And the effect of righteousness will be peace,
> And the product of justice quietness and confidence forever.
> My people will dwell in peaceful homes,
> In secure abodes, and in quiet resting-places. (Isa. 32:15-18.)

In this poem, and in the others cited, the kingdom is described as the reign of God over a righteous people who turn to him constantly in love and obedience, and whose chief delight is to serve him faithfully. Justice will promote *peace,* and peace will promote *prosperity* in the kingdom of God.

This prosperity will be a source of unending wonder and joy in the kingdom because of its sheer abundance. The ancestral traditions with regard to the physical delights of life in Canaan, a land flowing with milk and honey, were repeated in the literature of hope, glorifying the coming kingdom. The kingdom is both spiritually and materialistically conceived by the writers of Israel. There will be a permanent government able to provide plenty for all. Rain will fall and the wheat crop will be heavy; the cattle will have ample pasturage; the streams will be brimming with water (Isa. 30:23-26). The desert shall blossom like the crocus; for water will break out in the waste places, and flocks will be able to feed and to drink in desolate places formerly occupied by ostriches and jackals (35:7). The afflicted nation, in the day of God's glorious coming, will receive wonderful compensation for its sufferings (60:17; 65:20-23):

> Behold! I am setting your stones in emeralds,
> And will lay your foundations in sapphires;
> I will make your pinnacles of rubies,
> Your gates of carbuncle stones,
> And all your encircling wall of jewels. (54:11-12.)

Lavish plenty will result from the miraculous fertility of the soil, as the plowman works on the heels of the reaper, and the worker on the wine press overtakes the man planting the vineyard. New wine will literally drip from vine-covered mountains, and gardens will give fruit to their owners (Amos 9:13-15). Indeed the kingdom will mean a time of unparalleled plenty, prosperity, and happiness, the gift of which, however, is dependent upon the practice of the divine justice in human relations. We cannot divorce the ethical-spiritual aspect of the kingdom concept from the materialistic and physical features which the idea undoubtedly possesses.

The very concept of the chosen people as the nucleus of the kingdom of God precludes an exclusively *nationalistic* order. A redeemed Israel is the beginning, not the end, of the kingdom process God is furthering in history. This kingdom is finally to embrace the world and all its inhabitants, as is explicitly stated and frequently implied in various parts of the Old Testament. Nevertheless, the student may readily come to an opposite conclusion when he faces what is admittedly a statistical preponderance of evidence for nationalism or particularism. Harshly God himself demands that the people exterminate their foes on every hand; Saul is punished for sparing the life of Agag the Amalekite; severe maledictions are called down upon Assyria, Babylonia, Tyre, and Egypt in the oracles against foreign nations found in the major prophetic books; and association with foreigners may be a capital offense (Deut. 13:10). In the last instance cited we should heed the context, which pronounces the sentence of death upon any Israelite enticing another to serve alien gods. It is not the intercourse with foreigners itself which is condemned, but the religious consequences in the form of idolatry which could ensue.

There is no denying that Israel thought of herself in exclusive terms and believed herself to sustain a special relation to her God. The fundamental idea of the covenant presupposes this. It is also beyond argument that many of this nation's spiritual leaders easily succumbed to the temptation to interpret the covenant in a narrowly national sense. Other leaders were aware of the danger and warned their contemporaries against it, threatening dire disaster for the abuse of special privilege. Their word of warning was remembered—especially after events confirmed it—and recalled on later occasions (Jer. 26:18-20). The bitter misfortunes the Hebrews suffered at the hands of their enemies, and their inability to conquer adversity in a political or cultural sense lent intensity to their fury and hatred of things foreign. This is psychologically explicable, but it should not obscure an equally understandable fact of Israel's history—her faith in a God of justice and lovingkindness. In this faith *universalism* is implicit.

A kingdom of God founded upon the justice of God embraces all mankind, when its meaning is fully understood. God's relationship to a particular people is not one of necessity but of choice, conditioned by ethical qualifications. This surely implies that all men of good will and devoted to justice can belong to the kingdom. Distinctions of race, nationality, color, or class are irrelevant in the sight of the sovereign Ruler of this kingdom. Justice knows no geographical limits: it is universal in its potentialities for good. The chosen nation's experience of this God therefore beat against the wall of national pride and exclusivism, breaching it in more than one place. We may note, for example, the poem testifying to the poet's fervent hope for world peace under the aegis of Israel's God (cf. Mic. 4:1-3—note the reversal of this spirit in Joel 3:9-11):

> Then will he [the Lord] judge between the nations,
> And will arbitrate for many peoples;
> And they will beat their swords into plowshares,
> And their spears into pruning-hooks:
> Nation will not lift up sword against nation,
> And they will learn no more the art of war. (Isa. 2:4.)

Searching further for evidence on universalism, we note that the messianic leader is to be the herald of peace for the nations, that God will be exalted in the earth, and he will make wars to cease, destroying the instruments of war as he opposes the makers of war between nations (Zech. 9:10; cf. Isa. 9:6). The writer of the book of Jonah shows us a Jewish particularist or nationalist who believes that his faith is too pure to be taken to the hated foreigner—the Assyrian. In a short but inimitable narrative we are shown the ugliness of a soul warped by self-regard and embittered by mistreatment at the hands of the enemy. In a vivid contrasting picture we see also the compassion of the God, whom this bigot has worshiped without recognizing the international import of his worship—this God's compassion which includes even the age-old enemies of his people. God protests to Jonah:

You have had pity on the gourd, for which you did not toil; nor did you raise it; which grew in a night, and perished in a night! And should not I, indeed, have pity on Nineveh, that great city, wherein are more than a hundred and twenty thousand infants, that cannot distinguish between their right hand and their left, and much cattle? (4:10-11.)

We must not forget another missionary document in the form of a short story whose theme is the sacrificial devotion of a daughter-in-law, who was a Moabite, to a Hebrew mother-in-law (Ruth 1:16-17). In ancient Israel it was indeed a remarkable situation which permitted one to say of the infant son of a young woman, a foreigner and a widow at that: "May the boy's name become famous in Israel! He shall renew your [Naomi's] youth, and be the stay of your old age; for your daughter-in-law, who loves you, has borne him, who herself is more to you than seven sons." (4:15). And the story ends, with the exception of the added genealogy, with these significant words: "He [the infant] was the father of Jesse, the father of David." This story was possibly written as a polemic against the decree of Ezra (10:1-17) against mixed marriages, which resulted in wholesale annulments.

Among the other Old Testament allusions to universalism, that in Ps. 22 should receive special attention. In this psalm it is stated that the ends of the earth will turn to God; its families and nations will worship him because he is their ruler, and the kingdom belongs to him. This tells of a universal acknowledgement by the nations that God through his kingdom has sovereign sway over them, and that he alone must be worshiped. We also find, in surveying the psalms, that God will be exalted among the nations of the earth (Ps. 46:10); he rules over the nations as their king (47:7-8); his way of salvation is to be made known among the nations (67:2); the kingdoms of the earth are to sing to God (68:32); all the nations he has made will bow down before him and honor his name (86:9); all the families of peoples are to ascribe to him glory and strength (96:7); all the peoples are to see his glory and righteousness (97:6); and that his kingdom rules over all (103:19).

It is evident that the worshiping Israelites could not refrain from bursting into rapturous utterances acclaiming their God king of the whole earth. The unrestrained outbursts of the soul contemplating its God are not to be compared with the precise, controlled pronouncements of reason and logic, which are interested more in analysis than in adoration. But even praise and earnest prayer have their ideological foundation and thought forms. The psalmists' extension of the domain of God into the uttermost parts of the earth is not merely rhetorical extravagance; it is also a sober judgment of reason as to the meaning of the nature of God, who is creator, ruler, and savior. This wider meaning of the power of God was brought home forcibly to the exiles when new cultural contacts were made and the barriers of a former parochialism were broken. The exiled Jews found a world big enough to act as the new theater for divine action and populous enough to offer him the praise due his glorious name. In this wider world the kingdom could be consummated when all the nations learned to exalt the God of Israel and to proclaim him as their Lord and king.

So Israel discovered its mission within the framework of this idea of universal kingship for its God. In an epochal statement of national destiny and world mission this people announces to the world its full acceptance of the principle of universalism (Isa. 53:4-12). The witnessing nations in wonder indicate their final understanding of Israel's mission, as they behold its suffering and affliction:

> Yet it was our sickness that he bore,
> Our pains that he carried;
>
> . . . .
>
> He was pierced for our transgressions,
> And through his stripes we were healed.

And the God, who at this moment in the history of his kingdom has revealed this international insight, makes it still clearer:

> Through his affliction shall my servant, the Righteous One,
> bring righteousness to many.

Thus Israel, redeemed and chastened, is conceived as the servant with a mission of salvation to the world.

We must pause to remark upon the essential relationship existing between particularism and universalism, with special reference to the problem as it takes shape in the Old Testament. The two ideas are treated as though they represent two different orders of experience or two social philosophies diametrically opposed to each other, if one may judge by modern attempts to disparage the so-called particularism in the Old Testament. Nothing can be farther from the truth. Actually the two are aspects of the same type of experience—an unquenchable devotion to the God of justice and mercy. Even when this devotion stops at national boundaries, it may be real and highly effective. Unless the spirit and the practice of religion are rooted deeply in domestic soil and produce the fruits of righteousness in local and familiar institutions and places, they can hardly take root and bear fruit in a foreign land. Only as the men of Israel learned the lessons of piety and ethical behavior in the market place at Bethel or in the temple in Jerusalem could they conceive of the practice of their religion and its extension in lands far away. In the cultivation of these localized loyalties connected with their national faith, they received the conviction and the desire to bring all men into the fold and to see the nations streaming to Zion.

This is the only kind of universalism that is worth thinking about—a universalism which takes the universal elements of a particular and highly cherished religion and works for their propagation and general adoption in all parts of the world. The Old Testament knows nothing of an attenuated or diluted faith, toned down to make it fit humanity's various cultures and interests; it knows only the faith of Israel—a faith in a merciful and redemptive God who seeks the salvation of all men on his terms of judgment and repentance. This literature is not interested in world brotherhood or in glittering generalities about democracy and justice and peace; but it is vitally concerned that sinful men turn to the God of justice and peace and thus make possible the coming of his kingdom, in which nations shall learn the art of war no more, and social inequities shall be removed. This is the true universalism of the Old Testament, and it is truly embodied in its conception of the coming kingdom of God.

MYTHOLOGY

It has been suggested that this kingdom points beyond history for its denouement; that is to say, that it presupposes an eschatology or set of assumptions concerning the end events of history. Since only some of these assumptions rest upon historical experience, and others are derived from mythology, the mythological aspects of the kingdom idea will first be considered. Much of ancient Near Eastern mythology harks back to a general motif of a duel between two gods, one regarded as the giver and preserver of life and the other as the author of chaos and darkness. The well-known creation epic of the mortal duel between Marduk and Tiamat of the Babylonian pantheon illustrates this theme. It occurs in various versions and in different countries within the cultural orb of the Near East. Of particular interest is the discovery of the mythological tablets at Ras Shamra, the site of ancient Ugarit, on the coast of north Syria.[6]

In these texts—so far as their translation is possible—one encounters characters and names familiar to the student of the Old Testament. There is Anath, who fought the dragon; El, the wise one and father of years; as well as Tannin and Lotan (Leviathan), the two dragons of the north; and also Baal, the creator of thunder. These deities have varied and fluctuating functions, for the concept of personality was highly fluid when the tablets were composed. The goddess of life and order could also be a bloody goddess of violence and death. It is a singular fact that the biblical parallels to the Ras Shamra texts are largely confined to the Israelite literature of the exilic and postexilic periods, and that references in the earlier prophetic books and in the Pentateuch are scarce or completely absent. This remarkable circumstance may be explained by the extension of Phoenician (Canaanite) trade and wealth into nearby countries in the period 800-500 B.C. Cultural achievements of the Phoenicians naturally spread also. Later in this chapter a few specific parallels to Old Testament mythology found in the Ras Shamra texts will be noted.

There is no doubt that the Hebrew Bible was affected by the ancient *myth of creation* cited above. Hugo Gressmann believes there was an original myth of a great world catastrophe, but no single primitive eschatology. This explains why prophetic accounts of the final fate

[6] Available texts for the scholar include: J. A. Montgomery, Z. S. Harris, *The Ras Shamra Mythological Texts* (1935); H. L. Ginsberg, *The Ugarit Texts* (1936, in Hebrew); Charles Virolleaud, *La légende phenicienne de Danel* and *La légende de Keret* (1936); H. Bauer, *Die Alphabetischen Keilschrifttexts von Ras Schamra* (1936).

of the world vary considerably, he believes.[7] The biblical references to a myth of catastrophic and cosmic proportions should now be examined. Only typical passages will be noted. Without regard to the chronological order of the sources, let us first note Gen. 1:2, which states that the darkness was covering the abyss. Literally translated, the passage reads: "Chaos hovered over [brooded over] Tehom [Tiamat]." Tiamat and Tehom—translated "the deep" or "abyss" in most versions—are etymologically identical, a fact which suggests that the priestly writer used the language of the Babylonian creation myth in composing his own version. He so ably transformed this myth, however, that its presence is not easily recognized. The translation of Deut. 33:13 also has interest in this connection:

> And of Joseph he said,
> "Blessed of the Lord be his land,
> With the wealth of the heavens above,
> And that of the *abyss couching* below."

This strongly suggests a monster of the deep.

The word *tannin,* usually rendered "dragon," occurs in the priestly creation story (Gen. 1:21), perhaps for the purpose of showing that the God of Israel was the creator of all things, even of the "sea-monsters," creatures possibly drawn from some primitive mythology by the Hebrew writer. This cannot be demonstrated, although another possible subtle allusion to non-Hebrew polytheism is hinted at in the language of this story. We are told that the sun and the moon were assigned to rule the day and the night. In view of the Babylonian gods represented by the heavenly bodies, this is an interesting way of putting it. To return to *tannin,* in Job a complaint is directed to God:

> Am I the sea, or a dragon,
> That thou appointest a watch over me. (7:12.)

In this instance the juxtaposition of the words may show that Tannin is the primitive god of the deep, which must be watched lest it destroy human beings. Paralleling this verse is a reference to Leviathan in Job 3:8, where men "skilled in arousing Leviathan" are mentioned. These two monsters or deities—Tannin and Leviathan—may be identical, both referring to a god of the primeval deep, perhaps later demoted to the status of a demon.

The mythological origin of parts of Ps. 74 is evident also. We read,

[7] *Der Messias* (1929), p. 145.

"Thou didst crush the heads of the dragons upon the waters." (74:13; cf. 74:14.) This is particularly significant in view of the eschatological meaning of the preceding verse. Leviathan appears here, also, and is described as having more than one head. This reminds the student of the Ras Shamra inscriptions, from which the following is taken:

> Thereupon Anath caught sight of the God
> Upon him with her feet she trampled,
> Violently she broke [his] back. . . .
> The pinnacle of his back quaked,
>   the tendon of his loins.
> She raised her voice and cried, . . .
> "I have destroyed the Sea-Dragon [Tannin], beloved of El,
> I muzzled Tannin, I muzzled him!
> I have destroyed the winding serpent,
> Shalyat of the seven heads." [8]

We encounter the dragon and the serpent—Tannin and Leviathan—in the apocalypse of Isa. 24–27 also.

> On that day will the Lord punish,
> With his sword which is hard and great and strong,
> Leviathan the fleeing serpent, Leviathan the coiled serpent;
> And he will slay the dragon that is in the sea. (27:1.)

Evidently these must be destroyed before the rule of God can be consummated. Rahab is another monster deity connected with Tannin (51:9). God is urged to awake and to act as he had acted in the "generations long gone" when he hewed Rahab in pieces and pierced Tannin. This mighty deed of old is associated in the mind of the writer with the deliverance God will effect for his people. Bildad's speech in Job describes the wonderful power of God, in whose presence man can hardly hope to receive justification, and adds:

> Through his power the sea was stilled,
> And by his skill he smote through Rahab.
> . . . .
> His hand slew the fleeing serpent. (26:12-13.)

Rahab is connected with the sea—perhaps the name originally applied to Tiamat—and makes the sea rage. To still the waves God crushed

[8] W. F. Albright, in *Bulletin of American Schools of Oriental Research*, No. 84, pp. 15-16; used by permission of the author.

Rahab; he also scattered his other foes (Ps. 89:10). The overthrow of the god of the great deep is essential—according to substantial textual evidence—to the coming of the kingdom of God among men. Is it possible that the text of Rev. 21:1—"and there was no longer any sea [god of the deep]"—is also a mythological allusion to Rahab or Leviathan?

The Old Testament is the product of a general Near Eastern culture, and it would be surprising indeed if it should show no trace of its background. The limited number of passages cited above proves conclusively that parallels do exist. The myth played an important part in the development of Israel's religion and literature, although direct evidence of borrowing is sharply reduced by the strong monotheistic and nationalistic bias of the writers. Within the Hebrew tradition itself, however, the myth is an approved vehicle for representing in dramatic terms the cosmic struggle between good and evil. The myth of creation, of the events in the garden of Eden, of the flood, and of the Tower of Babel vividly depict to men—as no abstract philosophy could possibly do—God's redemptive purpose and man's spiritual history in relation to this purpose. The term "myth" as used here, it should be explained, does not mean a fable or an unproved event. It identifies with convincing clarity the most momentous truth in history—the truth about God and his way of salvation. The myth may further man's understanding of the kingdom and direct him in the course which it takes through his history and that of the world. By means of the myth he learns of the universal power and reality of sin; he faces the fact of its rootage in the very stuff of the cosmic order; he comprehends the wonder of God's grace in overthrowing evil and in showing him the way of his salvation; and he comes face to face with himself as one who flaunts this grace and rebels against him who offers it.

By taking the meaning of the myth in the Old Testament at its face value, and not as it is recorded in the dictionary, we find that it points back into history to the first cosmic event in the history of the kingdom of God and identifies God's own successful assertion of his powerful goodness against the forces of evil at the dawn of Creation. The throes of his struggle with the powers of darkness as told in the myths of Creation—the overthrow of Rahab, Tiamat, Tannin, or Leviathan— are the measure of his triumph and the assurance that the kingdom of his planning will materialize in history. So the kingdom begins in the very nature and will of God. As it proceeds toward fulfillment, it encounters the barriers of man's will; it often suffers severe setbacks from the resistance of sin and the perversity of men; but it always moves toward its goal. The myth teaches that the God who has overthrown the demonic powers of darkness holds in the strength of his hand and in the firmness of his purpose the certainty of the kingdom's coming.

We have discovered how this kingdom appeared in history at the time of the early patriarchs, and the Exodus from Egypt, and in the monarchy. And we have seen its more vigorous vitality in the faith and life of the Exile and in the period after the Exile. During all of this time the idea of the kingdom came to assume increasingly the character of a projected hope rather than an actual and contemporary social experience. Men looked beyond the failures and disappointments of their own history and fixed their eyes upon what was to come. They dreamed dreams and saw visions of the future world upheaval which would presage a world of peace and justice. They deliberated over the "last things" and more sharply defined earlier ideas in the light of their growing eschatological expectations and beliefs. What had already appeared incidentally or casually in the earlier literature was reinterpreted and given a new emphasis in speculation about the future.

THE DAY OF JUDGMENT

The kingdom of God contemplates a final vindication of righteousness and of the righteous after great tribulation and sorrow. Before the complete rule of God can be effected, the earth will be laid waste, and many of its inhabitants will be wiped out. So in one apocalypse we read,

> The mirth of the world has gone;
> Desolation is left in the city. (Isa. 24:11-12.)

The sword of the Lord will be glutted with blood; terrible beasts [9] will devour much flesh, trampling what remains under their feet (Dan. 7:3, 8); fire will devour before the foe; and the nations will gather in the day of battle when God judges the peoples (Joel 3:9-12). In the appalling world war which will herald the coming of the kingdom, the Lord of hosts will protect his people and cause them to drink blood like wine (Zech. 9:15). This description is taken from apocalyptic sections of the Old Testament, which use vivid, picturesque language, often cryptic in meaning, and which depict a powerful God who moves suddenly in history, through calamities and dreadful wars, conquering evil and vindicating the faithful. The end of history does not come quietly like a sunset; its vast and terrible meaning requires it to come

---

[9] These beasts are symbols of dominant political powers known to the second-century author of Daniel.

with bloody wars, terrifying earthquakes, and consuming pestilences. The death of the world demands appropriate stage setting, such as widespread confusion in nature as well as in human life. We read that the world languishes;

And the foundations of the earth tremble. (Isa. 24:19.)

The earth reels like a drunkard. (24:20.)

The mountains melt like wax before the Lord. (Ps. 97:5.)

The mountains saw thee; they writhed with pain. (Hab. 3:10.)

The moon stood still in its dwelling. (3:11.)

There will be portents in the heavens and on the earth—blood, fire, and smoke; the sun will be darkened, and the moon will become the color of blood (Joel 2:30-31). All nature thus shares the terror and panic of the world's end and the kingdom's eschatological beginning.

The turmoil and convulsion of the world is a fitting reaction to the evil which has been regnant in it during its entire history. Nothing less than a world catastrophe could reveal the dreadful effects of human sin. The powers of this world had, with every indication of success, gone their way in the adventures of empire, conquest, and lucrative trade, caring no whit for the human wreckage their headlong course left in its wake. Bankrupt in morals and in spirit, they recklessly persisted in following the dictates of their own pride and in rejecting the God of their salvation.

Would their sinful efforts finally be crowned with success? Could evil organized on a world-wide basis vanquish good and forever prevent the kingdom's coming? Israel's men of faith and vision answered with an emphatic No! The successful outcome of the kingdom's history was assured by the power of a God both holy and righteous. He had, in the beginning, conquered at the time of Creation the invisible powers and principalities of darkness. Were the political powers, created by mere men, as potent as these? Thus the mythological basis for eschatology in the Old Testament guaranteed the full consummation of the purposes of God at the end of history.

Upheavals in the natural order and world-wide social chaos demonstrated the awful judgment of God upon sinful men. These disturbances meant that the *day of the Lord* was at hand, and that this day was darkness rather than light. The popular hope that the day would bring the fulfillment of man's dreams of wealth and power was doomed to disappointment. The prophet Amos took this commonly held expectation and reversed its meaning by injecting into it a distinctive ethical content. To him it was a day of utter destruction, accompanied or introduced by such ominous calamities as a locust plague, a fire devouring the deep, and the vision of the Lord with a plumb line in his hand, announcing the certainty of the nation's ruin (7:1-9). It was to be a day of unspeakable horror for stubborn and unrepentantly wicked Israel, whose leaders and their sycophantic followers had persistently displayed a shocking disregard for human values and the demands of God. By their licentious living and the idolatry which sanctioned it they fully merited the terrible end which was about to overtake them. In refusing to heed the spiritual warnings of disaster, they were bringing upon themselves the day of doom. Therefore, "Prepare to meet your God, O Israel," the prophet is compelled to cry out (4:12).

Amos gives us little information of his conception of the nature of the kingdom to follow this national debacle. Does the rule of God end with this blow to the nation's life? There is no textual support for a belief that he expected the kingdom of God to arise from the ruins of Israel—indications to the contrary are glosses. The prophet was engrossed in the certainty of the coming judgment—perhaps depicting the day with the imagery of mythology—and in the majesty of the divine righteousness which no human will could profane with impunity. Somehow the living God of justice would continue to rule over history despite the power of collective organized sin.

Zephaniah takes up the idea of the day of the Lord, so radically reinterpreted by Amos, and describes it in lurid and forceful language. It is to be completely devastating—"I will utterly sweep away everything"—and is speeding fast (Zeph. 1:2). It will be a day of terror, trouble, distress, desolation, and gloom; the blood of sinners will be poured out like dust; and even the earth shall be consumed. Possibly the righteous and the piously humble—or even a larger remnant—will escape to become the center of the new kingdom and the instrument of a world religion. After the earth is consumed, the peoples will receive the gift of a new speech, a vocabulary of the religion of a redeemed Israel, with which all of the faithful will be able to call upon the name of the Lord (Zeph. 3:9). The ideas in this book are unfortunately scrambled, a condition perhaps partly attributable to the work of copyists and partly to the prophet's own state of mind. But the fact remains that—in his thinking—an Israel purified and humble will arise after the dreadful day and overcome its foes, either by attracting them to its religion or by their destruction at the hands of God. Then God will make his people

> a praise and renown
> Among all the peoples of the earth;

when he turns their captivity (3:20). Finally his kingdom will prevail over the whole earth. The writer of the book of Joel stresses the conquest of foreign nations as a preparation for the coming of the kingdom: after a decisive holocaust, in which the nations shall be cut down as the sickle cuts the grain, Israel will have permanent peace in a prosperous land, dripping wine and flowing with milk.

The conditions of *life in the new order* to follow the day of the Lord are barely mentioned or even hinted at by the earlier prophets. Other writers, however, are less restrained in their descriptions. By bringing together the main teachings and descriptions of these writers a fairly clear picture of the postjudgment kingdom can be secured. It will follow a return from the Exile and the dispersion (Isa. 66:20-23); it will entail the overthrow or the conversion of foreign nations; it will emphasize the virtues of piety and simple justice toward the needy; it will have its seat in Jerusalem, which will be a transformed city. Zion, the mount of God, will be the hub of this city's life. From it will radiate the influence of the divine government, taking the form of a miraculous transformation of nature, and social control by means of an elaborate hierarchy of priests living at the temple. To this temple the nations will stream and learn the lessons of justice, peace, and genuine piety. This kingdom will be an earthly rule, therefore; although in some of the writings this earth is to be transformed after the old order has passed away (Isa. 65:17).

Possibly influenced by mythological ideas, many biblical writers say that the new earth will be inhabited by peace-loving creatures (Isa. 2:4): both men and animals will be pacified in the kingdom (11:6-9; Ezek. 34:28). A remarkable river will flow from the temple, refreshing and fructifying the trees and plants in the whole land (47:1-12). So the kingdom will bring to pass revolutionary changes in nature and in the hearts of men (Ezek. 11:19; 36:26). The law and knowledge of God will be written upon human hearts (Jer. 31:33); justice and mercy will dictate social conduct and determine men's relation to God (Mal. 3:3-4). Sorrow and sighing will flee away:

> There shall no more be heard in her the sound of weeping,
> nor the sound of crying;

for young people and children will not die until completing a full life span (Isa. 65:19-20). In short, it will be a world in which the full lovingkindness and righteousness of the redeeming God will be felt by men in their every activity and relationship.

MEANS OF ESTABLISHING THE KINGDOM

Before this chapter is brought to a conclusion, the question as to the method of establishing the kingdom should be answered. While the answers vary, two major solutions can be noted. First, the kingdom's coming in the future may be due to the *direct action* of God. This is the view of most of the sources in the Old Testament. God may use the method of war or of natural calamity to effect his purposes; he may call Assyria the rod of his wrath (Isa. 10:5); he may summon to his dreadful service the hosts of God (Ezek 38:3-4), or cause an eclipse of the sun to be the forerunner of his terrible day (Joel 2:31; Amos 8:9). He is the Lord of history and of nations, directing their fate according to his holy and righteous purposes. Direct action is entirely reasonable, from the viewpoint of the biblical writers who believe in such a God.

Secondly, the kingdom may come by means of the use of a *personal agent* of God, such as a Messiah or Servant. The word Messiah means "anointed," and it is used rather often to denote one of the kings of Israel (I Sam. 24:6, 10; 26: 9, 11, 16, 23; II Sam. 1:14, 16). When the consummation of God's rule was believed to extend beyond the trials of the present into a happier future, however, the *messiah* concept was carried over into the eschatological terminology of biblical thought. The characteristics of the ideal king, as understood by the faithful worshipers of Yahweh, came to be symbolized by this term. What was deemed to be good in the character of a living king was incorporated into an ideal for judging all kings and for describing the coming messianic leader of the kingdom of God. This ideal was derived, not only from social and political experience during the monarchies, but from the theocratic assumptions underlying the kingdom-concept. The good king was judged in the light of the nature of the good God. The divine justice, mercy, and compassion were held to be essential for God's messianic vicegerent on earth. This may be confirmed from specific textual citations.

The era of peace is to come through the leadership of a "wonderful counsellor, Godlike hero," a "Prince of peace," who will reign upon the throne of David forever, in justice and righteousness (Isa. 9:6-7). It is added, we should not forget, that "the zeal of the Lord of hosts will do this." Again, we read that a ruler from the house of Jesse will possess wisdom, knowledge, reverence, and justice, for he will rule with equity and absolute fairness over a peaceful kingdom (11:1-9). The same emphasis upon the character of the Messiah is made in the book of Jeremiah, where it is said that a Davidic king, reigning justly, will cause Israel to dwell in security in the days that are coming (23: 5-6; 33:15-16). The messianic king will come from the house of David to re-establish the ancient Davidic rule in the name of the Lord, his God (Mic. 5:1-3). There is also a strong suggestion in Haggai and Zechariah that a messianic rule will be set up over the restored Jewish community after the Exile. God promises to shake the heavens and the earth, to overthrow the kingdoms of the nations, and to take Zerubbabel, his servant, and make him like a seal ring. (Hag. 2:21-23; Zech. 4:6-10). After rebuilding the temple, this servant shall reign upon his throne (6:9-13). The messianic king is to come humbly upon an ass, yet vindicated and victorious (9:9). He will bring peace to the nations "from the river to the ends of the earth" (9:10; cf. Pss. 2, 110, viewed by some as messianic).

In these passages the messianic figure usually comes from the line of David and rules over his restored people in justice and peace, always receiving and holding his authority from God. This figure lacks the distinctiveness and the personal power which are requisite for the inauguration of a real government. He is largely a symbol of a ruler who humbly relies upon the God who sent him. He doesn't actually found the kingdom: that is the work of God himself. He appears to be entirely human rather than supernatural, if we except the figure presented in the book of Daniel, where "one like a man" (Son of man?) approaches the Venerable One (God) and receives from him "dominion, and glory, and kingly power," and the submission of all peoples as the basis for an everlasting kingdom that cannot be destroyed (Dan. 7:13-14). This being, coming with the clouds of heavens, is clearly of supernatural origin. But even in this case, his authority is a delegated authority: he has no power apart from God. It is God who actually sets up the kingdom, in the last analysis.

The other type of personal agent selected by God for establishing his kingdom is identified by the word *Servant*. "Servant of Yahweh" may be a phrase designating priestly singers in the temple (Ps. 113:1), the prophets (II Kings 9:7), or particular individuals, such as Jonah or Isaiah (II Kings 14:25; Isa. 20:3); the nation may be so identified also. Most of the latter instances occur in Second Isaiah (41:8,9;44:21; 49:3; 44:1, 2; 45:4). The word is used in a specialized sense to refer to an ideal Servant going on a mission to the nations and bringing to them the light of salvation through his sacrificial suffering and martyrdom (Isa. 42:1, 49:5-7; 52:13–53:12). No matter how this Servant is understood, his function is to aid in the realization of the kingdom, especially in its more universalistic and spiritual aspects. Viewed as the redeemed, chastened, and spiritualized Jewish community within the larger community of exiles, the Servant exemplifies to the world his *raison d'être*—the furtherance of the rule of God over the lives of men. His character and holy purpose as conceived in the Old Testament records were so significant that they stimulated later theological thinking and produced a great variety of opinion, since Jewish exegetes tried to identify his figure as an historical person. It is not surprising that the early Christians were also influenced by this fascinating character as they sought to state the meaning of the personality of Jesus in the language of their Jewish faith.

It may be admitted that this rapid sketch of the idea of the kingdom of God in the Old Testament has required a rather superficial treatment of important questions. The reason for this treatment—the amount and variety of the material—in itself leads to confusion on the part of the student. He may well ask, Is there one conception of the kingdom, or are there several? In summing up, it may be helpful to point out indications of broad and fundamental agreement in the sources, and deliberately to omit evidence of contradictions which may be seen to be less important than when they were first noticed. The records agree that the rule or kingdom of God is in effect among his people and will continue to be, after the breakdown of the nation. This kingdom evinces the spiritual and ethical values inherent in the divine nature as society conforms to the divine will. It is a durable kingdom, so that it continues through the ages to manifest these values. It is a nationalistic kingdom, founded upon the covenant relation between God and Israel; but potentially it includes all men, regardless of nationality or race. All men, by repentance and loyalty to the God of Israel, may become members of a spiritual Israel, and thus citizens of the kingdom. In this kingdom peace, justice, and wholesome piety will prevail; and the social consequences of peace and justice will be apparent—economic prosperity, social stability, human happiness. This is the kingdom which, with rigorous justice, tests the political and cultural kingdoms of man; this is the kingdom which is within men of good will and fidelity; and this is the kingdom of men's dreams and their noblest reflection, which will one day be a social reality upon the earth. Does it endure beyond the grave? Chapter 7 will deal with this question.

7. *Death and the Hereafter*

THE Book of life is a Book of death, every page and chapter testifying to the presence of that dread enemy of mankind. Death stalks on practically every page; for death is a part of life—life with its greed, passion, hate, lust, war, rapine, slaughter, and death. Men die under all kinds of circumstances: at a full old age, in youth at the hands of an enemy, upon the battlefield, under an assassin's dagger, or by a fatal disease. They are struck by weapons, storms, earthquakes, epidemics, and famine. They die naturally or supernaturally through the wrath of God. Death never takes a holiday, but is continuously on the march, cutting down its victims with inexorable certainty. Since the Bible is not romantic fiction of the happy-ending school, nothing less than this can be expected. Complete realism in the Old Testament view of life requires that every grim and every glorious detail of the human adventure be adequately recorded. As with the other elements in this drama, so with death: no formal philosophy setting forth final meanings and relationships of meanings can be found in this literature. Death is a fact of experience which unequivocally carries its own meaning when it comes. Yet it must be placed within the framework of general Old Testament thought if its complete significance is to be comprehended.

ATTITUDES TOWARD DEATH

We may first inquire as to the various attitudes toward death which may be found. A common attitude is that of *indifference*. This conclusion may be unfair to the records whose preoccupation with other themes may have permitted only casual allusions to the fact of death, in the same manner in which a novelist or historian might develop his subject and note the coming of death to his characters without going into an interpretation of the philosophy of death. The purpose of the writer in question as he selects and develops his material is a primary principle governing its interpretation. With this word of caution, let us proceed, provided the necessarily tentative nature of these conclusions is recognized.

We may take the illuminating narrative of the struggle between Jacob and his brother Esau for their dying father's blessing (Gen. 27) as an illustration of the attitude of indifference. Although Isaac was about to die, his sons and their mother were absorbed in their own ambitions and in plotting for preferential treatment. The sale of the birthright for a mess of pottage, the disguise of Jacob by the use of a hairy goatskin, and the bribe given to the old father in the form of a tasty stew are in the foreground of the story. The father's death is important to the narrator only because it provides the occasion for some choice chicanery. When a plague hit every household of Egypt and killed all the first-born, instead of giving any hint of joy or grief at the horror that had come, the Israelites proceeded promptly to loot the stricken Egyptians, the story frankly tells us (Exod. 12:29-36). And when the Israelites saw the Egyptians who had pursued them to the Sea of Reeds lying dead on the seashore, they sang a song to the Lord (Exod. 14:30–15:21). Death was unimportant, save as it intervened to deliver the men of Israel from their enemies.

In the book of Numbers a revolt of 250 laymen against the exclusive authority of the priestly hierarchy was effectually suppressed, it is said, when Moses invoked the terrible power of God to destroy the offenders (16:30). Moses asked those loyal to the regime in power to withdraw from the area where the rebels lived, and then called upon the earth to open and swallow them! Thus Korah, Dathan, Abiram, and "their wives and sons and little ones" were hurled into Sheol alive. It is of interest that, in thus punishing these sinners or rebels, Moses called upon "the God of the spirits of all mankind." There is no pity here for individuals—women, young children, and infants; there is rather a harsh defense of the established priestly order in this priestly book.

The revolt of Jehu against the house of Ahab was a bloody one and apparently had the complete approval of the religious conscience of the day; in fact, it was instigated by the prophetic leaders and spiritual guides of Israel. Jehu's purge wiped out the entire house of Ahab and liquidated hundreds of the priests and followers of the Baal (II Kings 9:1–10:36). The mood of the story is one of exultation over the glorious victory of Jehu. Clearly the vindication of Yahwism by the defeat of baalism was of much more interest to the chronicler of this event than the death of many important people. The death of his brother Abel created no remorse in the heart of the murderer Cain; he was wrapped up in thoughts of his own fate at the hands of God. After giving a surly reply when God asked where his brother was—"Am I my brother's keeper?"—Cain burst into open protest upon hearing the divine verdict, "My punishment is too great to bear" (Gen. 4:9, 14). We may also recall the stoicism rather than indifference of Abraham when he was required to sacrifice his son Isaac (Gen. 22). The apparent indifference here is probably the result of the storyteller's skill in omitting details and leaving something for the reader's imagination.

It is evident from reading the Bible that there are many things more important to its authors than death. Let us now note some of the *offenses* against the Law which were punishable by death. These include forgetting God, disloyalty, false prophesy (Deut. 13:5), apostasy in one's family (13:9), making an entire city apostate (13:16), the worship of the host of the heavens (17:3-5), rebellion against a priestly judge (17:12), presuming to deliver an oracle in the name of God when God has not authorized it (18:20), false testimony, disobedience of children (Deut. 21:18-21), and kidnaping fellow Hebrews (24:7). To maintain loyalty, faithfulness, the true worship of God in family and nation, and the authority of true prophecy, the penalty of death may be imposed. These matters affect the security of the entire community, and the fate of the individual must always be subordinated to this goal. Beyond these pre-eminently social values is also the supreme value of communion with God, an experience which delights the heart of the believer and gives him confidence in the face of death. There is also the matter of human love. As strong as death is, love matches it in strength and exceeds it in its power to interest mankind, as the following poetic fragment affirms:

> For love is as mighty as death,
>   as strong as Sheol.
> As for passion, its bolts are bolts of fire,
>   furious flames,
> Many waters cannot quench love,
>   nor rivers overcome it. (Song of S. 8:6-7.)

Death is a matter of comparative indifference and seldom a subject for profound reflection in the Old Testament. Life goes on, and death cannot seriously retard its progress through the centuries of history. When death is actually faced, however, it may be either accepted or rejected; for when it confronts the individual, it can hardly be ignored. An old man, full of years, may accept death. So we read: "This was the total length of Abraham's life—one hundred and seventy-five years. So Abraham came to his death, dying at a ripe old age, an old man, *satisfied with life;* and he was gathered to his fathers." (Gen. 25:7-8.)

Such a state of mind is also implied in the accounts of the deaths of other Israelite leaders. Joseph completed a full and satisfying life before being gathered to his fathers (Gen. 50:26); although greatly mourned, Jacob died at an advanced age, after having given life and faith to stalwart sons (49:33); and Moses, although deprived of the happiness of leading his people to journey's end, died in peace at the age of 120 years, "his eyes undimmed, and his virility unabated" (Deut. 34:7).

Death may be accepted with quiet confidence or with outspoken pessimism. We have observed the reaction of an old man contemplating his own death. Let us now note the reaction of another type of old man, who includes in the consideration of his own death reflection over the death of all creatures. The writer of the book of Ecclesiastes gives the impression of having reached a position of social prestige and great wealth after a life devoted to these ends in Jerusalem. His was an inquiring mind, possessing a cold curiosity which deprived him of the happiness he so self-consciously sought. He investigated all things—an ambitious undertaking—and set his mind to the acquisition of wisdom. He also reflected upon the best way to enjoy wine, women, and song, and finally concluded that nothing in the whole world had meaning or real value (2:1-11). There is one fate for man and beast, for wise and simple, righteous and wicked; so what is the value of life? Death ends it all, and after death there is no remembrance of anything that man has done during his life. Life is a vicious circle: the sun rises, and the sun sets; rivers flow, yet the sea is never full; man is born, and he dies. Death is an undeniable and final fact which nullifies and invalidates all existence, and painfully and wearisomely shows the futility of everything.

Here and there the records reveal a refusal to accept death without challenging its power over men or without demurring. The *grief* of individuals at the loss of friends or members of the family can hardly be construed as proof of the existence of a general protest against death; at the most it certifies to a feeling of personal loss which is irremediable. Nonetheless, such grief betrays the perennial surprise and the painful unexpectedness of death. Upon hearing of the supposed death of his son Joseph, "Jacob tore his clothes, and girded himself with sackcloth, and mourned for his son for a long time. His sons and daughters all tried to console him, but he would not be consoled." (Gen. 37:34-35.) The grief of Joseph over the death of his father is also emphasized in the narratives of Genesis. We are told that there was a period of national mourning in Egypt over this event (50:2-3). Weeping followed the death of Moses (Deut. 34:8).

No more tenderly poignant expression of grief may be found in literature than the poem in Second Samuel, one of the few poems that can be positively assigned to David as author:

> O, Jonathan! by your death am I mortally wounded,
> I am distressed for you, my brother Jonathan!
> You were exceedingly dear to me.
> Your love was more marvelous to me than the love of women! (1:25-26.)

We may also refer to David's lamentation over the death of Absalom. This is a moving sorrow on the part of a weak father whose inept handling of a spoiled son became notorious throughout his kingdom. "And thus he said, as he wept, 'My son Absalom, my son, my son Absalom! O that I, even I, had died instead of you, Absalom, my son, my son!'" (II Sam. 19:1.) Obviously we have in these instances simply the expression of a deep sense of personal loss and not a generalized attack upon, or protest against, death itself.

The *opposition* to death found in the Old Testament usually takes the form of action to ward off the death of particular individuals, or of legal prohibitions against murder. So Reuben counsels throwing his brother Joseph into a pit instead of killing him (Gen. 37:22), and the Decalogue prohibits murder (Exod. 20:13). Agag, about to be killed —sacrificed—before Yahweh, comes to his executioner trembling and says, "Surely death is bitter" (I Sam. 15:32). The prophet Elisha weeps at the thought of a Syrian invasion of Israel and the prospective death of young men, women, and children that will follow. Hazael of Syria says to Elisha, "Why does my lord weep?" And the reply comes, "Because . . . I know the evil that you will do to the Israelites: their fortresses you will set on fire, their choice young men you will slay with the sword, their little children you will dash in pieces, and their women with child you will disembowel." (II Kings 8:12.) Yet this is really opposition to a cruel and untimely death rather than to death itself. A desperate plan to circumvent almost certain death is devised by four lepers of Samaria in a time of famine aggravated by a siege of the city. They stand at the entrance to the gate and debate the alternatives. If they go in, they will perish in the famine that has fallen upon the city; if they remain without, they will also starve or be killed; if they desert to the Arameans, the latter may not kill them, or they may. In despair they choose the last alternative, saying: "If they kill us, we shall but die" (II Kings 7:4).

In only one book does one find a *longing* for death. In Job the leading character is in such a desperate plight that he earnestly desires
death. God has attacked him through the loss of possessions and social
standing, through a dreadful disease and a vicious assault upon his
last defense—his integrity as a man. In his agony he considers his unendurable fate and cries out:

> O that God would consent to crush me,
> That he would let loose his hand and cut me off! (6:9.)

He adds,

> Why did I not die at birth,
> Come forth from the womb and expire? (3:11.)

> I myself loathe my life. (10:1.)

> Lo! he will slay me; I have no hope. (13:15.)

Having searched futilely for a ray of hope in every conceivable direction—faith in a good God, help from his friends, the possibility of recovery from his sickness, and reinstatement in his former home and
community through the justice of God—Job can see but one way out:
the way of death. Such a choice, made as the result of the consideration
and rejection of other alternatives, in itself shows Job's evaluation of
life. Death is the final alternative, to be chosen after all other avenues
of deliverance have been tried and found wanting. Life is normally desirable, and would have been cherished by Job had only one boon been
granted—the personal consciousness of the justice of God in his treatment of his creatures. It is the certainty that this consciousness can
never again be his that drives Job to utter his piteous words.

For purposes of comparison it may be helpful to discuss briefly attitudes toward death which are not at home in the Old Testament, but
which have appeared in various periods of subsequent history and in
the modern day. Except in the case of Job life in the Old Testament
documents is viewed as good, a gift of the Creator, which is not to be
despised or rejected. When God made his Creation, including man and
woman, he saw that it was good. He blessed the man and the woman
and urged them to multiply upon the earth. This positive optimism is
shown in the disfavor with which *suicide* was viewed. Few cases of
suicide are recorded in the Bible. On the field of battle, when he had
been seriously wounded, Saul asked his armor-bearer to run him through

with his sword, lest the Philistines torture and make sport of him. This the terrified armor-bearer refused to do, so Saul took his sword and "fell upon it" (I Sam. 31:4). The purpose of this suicide was to save a soldier's honor.

There are many crises in human life in Israel's history, the solution of which—under any other view of death than that prevailing in the Old Testament—would have involved self-destruction. This book is a bitter, deadly record of the worst evils that can befall mankind: hunger, plague, disease, slavery, concubinage, prostitution, sin, spiritual conflict, personal disintegration. In all of these circumstances life is held to be better than death, and suicide is unthinkable. The single person in the Old Testament—and perhaps in all literature—who most fully typifies mankind's complete misery and pain is Job. But even he never for a moment considers the way of suicide. His only escape is by an act of God: if only God would take away his hand and let him die! And the writer of Ecclesiastes, whose philosophy is most modern because most pessimistic, decides—in spite of his unqualified futilitarianism—that life is preferable to death, so he continues to live.

Preoccupation with the affairs and duties of life, along with the typical pragmatic-positivistic nonmystical world view of the Semitic mind, prevented that glorification and romanticization of death which became evident in certain periods of Christianity under the influence of Hellenistic dualism and its Christian aftermath—asceticism. For biblical man life consisted in personal surrender to the demands and obligations of group living, and in performing the functions of social-ethical persons whose welfare and destiny were wrapped up in the fate of the community. This was the world of the men of Israel; in it they fulfilled their true being; from it escape was impossible. So they met the challenge of life squarely and eagerly, never losing the thrill of its conflict and high adventure. Biblical man's culture and temperament denied him the opportunity to take flight into unworldliness, there to contemplate in peace the beauty of holiness. He was unable to find release from the prison house of his body for his struggling soul through a blessed death.

It is evident that Israel's saints did not defer the day of the blessed consummation when they would be with God to a post-mortem period following the struggles and sorrows of life: they looked for this consummation in the only time they had—the present of their earthly existence. Their enjoyment of God was too severely ethical to be relegated to an unknown future. They were sinners, who had sinned against God in determinable, measurable ways. They were penitent sinners, whose penitence must be expressed in the ethical and social situation in which sin had been committed. They were pardoned sinners, whose pardon affected their performance of good in the community of God. Their joy in God thus was the joy of living persons, behaving as spiritual as well as physical organisms in a concrete historical community. Hence they adored and glorified God in this life, which was the only life they had, as the life of the present must always be the only life man has.

We may, then, say that the typical Old Testament attitude toward death was that of *common sense,* relatively unaffected by reflective or philosophical thinking. Death was accepted as a fact of life, unavoidable, unsought, but not to be denied when it came. It was recognized that the gods lived forever, and that men were mortal, but no complaint was lodged against the gods on that score. Could men be like gods? Obviously not, but man's mortal lot was not protested, as a rule; it provided ample room for the unfolding of his talents and the expression of his legitimate desires. The world was good, and God was good; it would be impious and ungrateful to declare otherwise. Recognizing the prevalence of this attitude of mind, we may now give particular attention to special concepts and customs relative to death and the dead, for the sake of a better understanding of the Old Testament's teaching on this question.

THE CULT OF THE DEAD

In Israel and throughout the Near East the cult of the dead flourished among the people. In non-Israelite countries it amounted to a state religion and was fully supported by the heads of government. Burials in royal tombs indicate the prevalence and prominence of this cult. The best known of these are, of course, the Egyptian; but elaborate burials in ancient Babylonia and Assyria as well as Hittite land should not be overlooked. If we judge from the placement, garb, adornment, and equipment of the bodies found in excavated sites, proper ceremonial burial was considered essential to life hereafter. Equipment and utensils buried with their owner would accompany him to the abode of the dead and there serve as they had in life. Offerings were brought to the place of burial, apparently as food for the departed, but also, according to some authorities, as a propitiatory sacrifice. The cult called for ceremonial acts to ward off possible dangerous attacks by the spirits of the dead. Loud shouting, shaving of the head, cutting or mutilation of the mourner's body, and tearing the garments come within this category. The spirits of the dead were thought to live, at least for a period of three days, near the grave, and must be approached circumspectly lest they become angry and harm the survivors. This cult of the dead is possibly the historical beginning of religion, with its gods, its rituals, its priestly classes, and its creeds. Leaving this question to the historians of religion, we may simply note that this cult became fully entrenched in the indigenous culture of the Near East—which Israel shared in Palestine—and developed its own institutions, such as the order of necromancers or communers with the dead.

Among the leaders of Israel's religion there arose a powerful *opposition* to the cult of the dead. This opposition, according to the Bible, was the result of necromancy's intimate association with alien faiths and cults. It symbolized the lower gods of their enemies and for this reason must be extirpated. This accounts for the comparatively small number of allusions to this cult of the dead in the Old Testament. Those which can be found, however, reveal its influence and merit study. For example, after being told by Yahweh that he should not take a wife, the prophet receives the following instruction:

> Do not enter the house of mourning, nor go to lament,
>   nor bemoan them:
> For I have withdrawn from this people my good will,
>   my kindness and pity.
>
> . . . .
>
> Both high and low shall die in this place,
>   and shall not be buried;
> None shall lament for them, nor gash himself,
>   nor make himself bald for them;
> None shall break bread for the mourner,
>   to comfort him for the dead;
> And none shall give him the cup of consolation to drink,
>   for his father or mother. (Jer. 16:5-7.)

The importance of *proper burial* is stressed in the next passage cited:

> Of morbid deaths shall they die,
> And shall be neither lamented or buried,
> But shall lie like dung on the face of the ground.
>   (Jer. 16:4.)

Or,

> With the burial of an ass shall he [Jehoiakim] be buried,
> Dragged and flung out beyond the gates of Jerusalem.
>   (22:19.)

One of the crimes Amos denounces violently is the defilement of the body of a king. Moab is to be punished

> Because he burned the bones
> Of the king of Edom to lime. (2:1.)

The ghastly death of Jezebel, whose blood-spattered body was partly devoured by dogs, is not less ghastly and horrible because of the impossibility of finding enough fragments to bury (II Kings 9:30-37). The kindly act of David in burying the bones of Saul and Jonathan, which had hung at Beth-shan, is commemorated in Second Samuel (21:13-14.) Inferences from these references are precarious, but interesting and irresistible. This care in providing proper burial and the evident horror at mistreatment of a corpse may have been based upon the belief that burial permitted the spirit of the dead to be at peace, while improper treatment made it restless and probably angry. That this theory presupposes a belief in survival cannot be denied.

The practice of necromancy certainly is derived from such a presupposition. The visit of Saul to the necromancer at Endor is a case in point. The purpose of the visit was Saul's desire to confer with the departed Samuel. When his spirit materialized so that the witch could recognize it—Saul evidently failed to do so—a voice gave the requested counsel to the king (I Sam. 28:3-25). The fear evinced by this witch when asked to raise up Samuel and to commune with the dead is based upon the action of the king, who had banned necromancy from the land by royal decree. If this is historical, it indicates the prominence of necromancy and its hold upon the people, as does also the law contained in the Code of Deuteronomy: "There must not be found among you anyone who makes his son or his daughter pass through fire, a diviner, a soothsayer, an augur, a sorcerer, a charmer, a medium, a magician, or a necromancer" (18:10-11). These practices are said to be an abomination to the Lord.

SHEOL

Perhaps because it was too far removed from the affairs and interests of men, the abode of the dead, called "Sheol" in the Old Testament, does not receive the condemnation which is extended toward necromancy and the cult of the dead in general. At any rate, the word Sheol appears frequently in the Old Testament. An account of these appearances is appropriate at this point. First, we find that the term Sheol has an etymology which may come from a root *sha'al* (inquire, place of inquiry) or from *sho'al* (hollow hand, hell). These are very dubious, however. The meaning of the word can best be understood by examining the various situations and contexts in which it is used in the biblical text.

We find that several passages use the word in a purely *figurative* manner. This is the case in the following:

> A fire shall blaze within me,
> And burn to the very depths of Sheol;
> So that it shall consume the earth and its produce,
> And set the bases of the mountains on fire. (Deut. 32:22.)

Here the depth and the destructiveness of God's anger are described. Ahaz, king of Judah, is urged by Isaiah to ask a sign from God as deep as Sheol or as high as the heavens (Isa. 7:11). The psalm found in the book of Jonah reveals a similar use of the word Sheol:

> From the heart of Sheol I called for help; . . .
> For thou hadst cast me into the depths, into the heart of the sea,
> And a flood encompassed me. (2:2-3.)

Amos mentions the inescapable judgment of God and declares that even by digging into Sheol men cannot escape his anger (9:2-4). And the psalmist is impressed by the completeness of God's care for him when he cries:

> Whither shall I go from thy spirit?
> And whither shall I flee from thy presence?
> If I ascend to the heavens, thou art there!
> If I make Sheol my bed, thou art there also. (139:7-8.)

Sheol connotes the deepest recesses of the world, as the heavens refer to the highest reaches of the known universe. This is a genuine clue to the location of the abode of the dead.

Many verses could be presented to support this idea that Sheol is located in the *deepest part of the earth*. The verb meaning "go down" is often used in connection with this place, as are similar verbs. Jacob, inconsolable when hearing the report of the alleged death of his son Joseph, announces that he will go down mourning to his son in Sheol (Gen. 37:35). Evidently he thinks of his son as being already there, but there is no joy in the thought of reunion with him. With respect to his little son Benjamin, he also declares that if anything happens to him, Jacob's gray hairs will be brought down to Sheol in sorrow (42:38). Sheol is down in the earth and is accessible when the earth's surface opens up. Incidentally, it is normal for all men to go down to Sheol when they die, but extraordinary for this to happen while they are still alive (Num. 16:30). Hannah praises the Lord and sings:

> The Lord slays and makes alive;
> He brings down to Sheol and raises up.
> The Lord impoverishes, and he makes rich;
> He brings low, he also exalts. (I Sam. 2:6-7.)

David on his deathbed bequeaths a legacy of blood to Solomon by instructing him to bring down with blood the old age of Shimei to Sheol, and not to allow Joab's hoary head to go down to Sheol in peace (I Kings 2:6, 9). The list is almost unlimited; all passages make it clear that Sheol is below the surface of the earth.

The abode of the dead is a place of *darkness and decay*. It is a land of blackness, of shadow, gloom, and deep darkness (Job 10:21-22); a place of darkness, where one's father is the pit, and one's mother and sister the worm of decay (17:13-15); a place of ruin and destruction (26:6). All men go there upon death: rich and poor, kings and counselors, slaves and taskmasters, rulers and subjects, small and great (3:13-19; Ezek. 32:18-32). Sheol is insatiable; she swallows her victims without discrimination or restraint. The faithless, arrogant man, it is said,

> enlarges his appetite like Sheol,
> Is as insatiable as death. (Hab. 2:5.)

There are four things, says the wise man, that are unsated: Sheol, the barren womb, the parched earth, and fire (Prov. 30:15-16). As Sheol and death are never satisfied, so the eyes of a man are never satisfied (27:20). Sheol is a land of no return. All men go there, but none return to the land of the living.

> A cloud dissolves and it is gone:
> So is the one who descends to Sheol; he will not ascend:
> He will not return again to his house. (Job 7:9.)

> And I shall go the way that I shall not return. (16:22.)

In Sheol man is no longer remembered (24:20). It is better, therefore, to be a living dog—a mangy cur upon a dung heap—than a dead lion; for the living know they will die, and the dead know nothing at all. Neither are they remembered any more; their hates, their envies, their work in the land of the living, are gone and completely forgotten (Eccl. 9:4-6).

Man cannot worship God in Sheol. In that underworld there is *no praise of God*.

> Is it for the dead that thou wilt do wonders?
> Will the ghosts arise to thank thee?
> Will thy grace be recounted in the grave?
> Or thy faithfulness in Hades?
> Will thy wonders be made known in the darkness?
> Or thy righteousness in the land of oblivion?
> (Ps. 88:10-12.)
> For in death there is no remembrance of thee.
> In Sheol who praises thee? (6:5.)

The spiritual activities of men cease when they descend to Sheol. Worship, prayer, and praise are the privilege of the living, not of the dead. Sheol is not God's realm, for he is the God of the living, even though he may save men from Sheol—that is, from death.

God delivers the faithful from Sheol, the psalmist declares:

> The cords of death encircled me;
> And the tortures of Sheol found me. (116:3.)

> For thou hast delivered me from death. (116:8.)

> I shall not die, but live
> To tell of the deeds of the Lord.
> The Lord has disciplined me severely;
> But he has not given me up to death. (118:17-18.)

> O Lord, thou hast brought me up from Sheol.
> Thou hast revived me from among those who go down to the pit.
> (30:3.)

> There is life in his favor. (30:5.)

Although all men are destined to descend to Sheol—and this place is, consequently, not a place of punishment for the wicked (Job 21:23-26) —yet the wicked especially will go to the underworld, and also all the nations who forget God and the individuals who are faithless to him (Pss. 9:17; 31:17; Job 18:14). These go to the place of death prematurely, whereas the righteous first live to a dignified and ripe old age. The disillusioned man whose intimate friends have reviled, slandered, and cheated him, breathes a malediction upon them:

> Let destruction come upon them!
> Let them go down alive to Sheol! (Ps. 55:15.)

They are not to have the privilege of waiting until senescence comes and the diseases of old age strike them down; they are to descend suddenly to the pit, the land of the forgotten. Such a fate for the wicked cannot reassure the righteous, because it is the ultimate fate of all. There is no hope for the upright in Sheol, although there is hope of a tree which may send forth new shoots after it is cut down, as in the case of the willow or tamarisk. But man dies and is powerless; he expires and where is he? God destroys the hope of man as water erodes soil or even hard rock with continuous exposure to the harsh reality of the utter hopelessness of death (Job 14:10-19).

In a splendid satire against Babylon an unknown poet of Israel imagines the stir and excitement in Sheol at the coming of a new permanent guest—the defeated Babylon, here personified (Isa. 14). This nation has trampled other nations in the past, but now is laid low, to the delight of everyone, even the denizens of the underworld. The shades—or *rephaim* (weak ones), as the inhabitants of Sheol were called—lift from their thrones the kings of the nations, who will taunt the newcomer, saying,

> So you too have become weak as we are,
> have been made like to us!

Her fate is gleefully described:

> Beneath you maggots are spread,
> worms are your covering.

This nation, which had caused kingdoms to quake and cruelly refused to release her prisoners of war, has a special place in Sheol reserved for her alongside of the trampled corpses! She will not rest in peace as do the other nations, because of her sins of pride and cruelty. Egypt too will go down to this abode of the dead, where she will lie with her own people, segregated from other national groups in death as in life (Ezek. 32:18-32). The men of Elam, Meshech, Tubal, Edom, and Sidon are to lie with the uncircumcised who have been slain with the sword, and are to retain their national identity.

This rather full description of Sheol and the numerous verses cited above make it a simple matter to give a general account of the nature of the abode of the dead. It is apparently a large, pitlike, cavernous area under the earth, down beneath the mountains, shrouded in darkness and occupied by the microscopic organisms of decay and by the weak, semiconscious shades of the dead, who know nothing of happenings on earth and have no communion with God. These shades are grouped as their full-blooded, fully conscious bodies had been prior to death—in social strata and classifications—but the evil results of such groupings are not evident in Sheol. The slave is no longer in bondage to the task-master, and the prisoner is free from his jailer. There is a kind of equality—and the peace of a sleep disturbed by uneasy dreams. Here men are doomed to remain forever. Thus Sheol is a concept of human destiny which is entirely without hope, and which appears to guarantee the finality and the unalterability of death as the ultimate fact of life.

BIOLOGICAL AND SPIRITUAL DEATH

May we draw from this gloomy picture additional information as to the meaning of death in the Old Testament? We can ask, How are death and human nature related? We have found that man, who is made in the image of God, is also made of the dust of the ground, and that his fate is tied up with this seeming duality of his nature. Sin is oc-casioned when man refuses to accept the fact of his weakness as creature and presumes to act as though he were entirely free, like God. Death is the penalty which man must pay for his sin and his creatureliness. His sin he wills; his creatureliness has been determined for him by the act of God at the time of Creation. Into the garden of his life came the tempter, whispering to him the possibility that he might become godlike and possess both knowledge and immortality. In succumbing to this greatest of all human temptations, he sinned irrevocably; and instead of receiving immortality, he received the curse of death. In this way, the nature of man occasioned sin, and sin brought death.

A kind of death that has nothing to do with sin is also recognized in the Old Testament—the death of *biological* breakdown and decay. This is the death accepted throughout the literature of Israel, against which no valid argument may be raised, since man is mortal and his body is clay. It withers like grass before the summer sun; it is as fragile as a cobweb; and it is as ephemeral and insubstantial as mist or vapor. Even at this, man's body was thought to be fairly durable in the early stages of his history. Only with the coming of the corruption which brought on the flood was there a recognition of the shortening of man's life span from hundreds of years to 120 years (Gen. 5; 6:3). Death—after life had been fully lived and had borne the fruit of stalwart sons and humble devotion to God—always came, not as punishment, but as the result of the creaturely weakness of man.

Along with this view of death may be considered the conception of death as a judgment of God, the details of which in its outward mani-festations do not differ from the death of old age. Inwardly, however, and *spiritually* this death is different. It came as the result of defying

God's will in man's sinful rivalry of the Most High. It entailed the alienation of the spirit of man from God and the tragedy of an incomplete and frustrated life which such a separation always brings. There is no evidence for the conception of spiritual death as such in the Old Testament, but the ingredients for the formation of such a conception are present. Under circumstances in which the supreme loss is the loss of God through unfaith and disloyalty, the only kind of death that counts is the death of faith and the power to respond to the Creator in love and righteous living. This is the deeper meaning of judgment in Israel's literature. Death as judgment for sin is the termination of those ethical relations with God whereby loyal obedience and spontaneous worship are made possible.

The true life of man lies in the fact that he is made in the divine image, possessing in his freedom the capacity for righteousness and love and creative power. Through the possession of this capacity he resembles God and shares to a limited extent in his power. Sin is the overassertion of this power, which act paradoxically deprives man of his birthright as a son of God. The rebellion which is sin denies the divine sonship of man and the weakness of the human creature, and thus deprives man of a redemptive life with God, without which real life is ended. The judgment which comes because of sin, then, produces death by denying to man the fulfillment of his spiritual needs, the satisfaction of which depends upon humble submission and complete obedience to his Creator. The physical death which follows this spiritual death, in the absence of repentance, is the confirmation of God's judgment upon the proud spirit of man. "The soul that sinneth, it shall die!" (Ezek. 18:4, K.J.V.) Ezekiel was abrogating the old proverb relative to the deferment of punishment for sin to a later generation. He pressed home, as did Jeremiah (31:30), a true insight into the destructive effect of judgment for sin upon the spiritual life of the individual.

Man is both a creature of dust and a bearer of the image of God; by reason of the former he is mortal; by reason of the latter he is divine. Only by living on the level of his divine sonship can man truly live. At this point, the Old Testament reaches a position which unconsciously transcends the bleak pessimism of its conscious utterances on death, and prepares the way for later developments which appeared under the influence of Zoroastrianism and Greek thought. Some of these later conceptions may be seen in the intertestamental literature of the Judaism of the first two centuries before, and the first century after, Christ. But even in these writings—with their wealth of ethical insights, their messianic and eschatological ideas, and their strong expectation of the kingdom—may be traced the unfolding of beliefs already present, at least embryonically, in the Old Testament canon. The fundamental idea of the close connection between man's destiny and God's will is certainly in the canon, as is the belief that death is a form of divine judgment for sin. None of the canonical material tries to make a distinction between physical and spiritual death; such a distinction could not logically be made in view of the typical anthropology of the Old Testament. Man is essentially a unitary organism; he is not divisible into parts which could have independent existence. Notwithstanding this fact about his nature, the more compelling fact as to his complete dependence upon God—to which his traditional faith and his continuing religious experience testified—led him to express a confidence in God by means of which the tyranny of death could be overcome.

Such a confidence, when recorded in literature, can come only from a regard for the individual as having worth in his own right. Death has the appearance of being a *highly personal* matter: it comes to an Abel, an Abraham, a Jacob, a Moses, a David. It is to each man a disaster of absolute proportions, terminating once and for all the activities of his body and brain, and severing all contact with the world of sensory experience. The pleasure of movement, of sight, taste, and sound; the joy of beauty in line, form, and color; the excitement of the intellectual quest for new truth and for new forms of old truth—all are wiped out in a moment when the consciousness of the individual ceases, and death comes. True as this is, the people of Israel, when reproducing the facts of their life and faith in literary form, include the experience of death as a matter of course, but allude to it most often in the broadest of terms. Even as the interest of God was directed toward the national community, and as the history of his dealings with men meant the selection, guidance, and preservation of this community, so death was viewed as overtaking whole groups of men. This is what the prophets meant as they announced the annihilation of the nation. This is the conception of the poets who personified foreign nations and expressed their joy at the prospect of their defeat and ultimate ruin (Isa. 14:1-27; 15–20; Jer. 46–51; Ezek. 25–30). The apocalyptists, in the canon and outside of it, similarly picture mass death for sinful peoples in a mighty struggle at the end of history. Multitudes will gather in the valley of decision for the day of slaughter. The harvest is ripe! The wine-press is full (Joel 3:13-14). Let the slaughterers begin their work!

Since the community constituted the frame of reference for Israel's writers, even death was viewed in this *national setting*. It was thought to come because of the nation's sin, or because of the sin of the nations who were Israel's enemies. This means that death on a national or even international scale was controlled by God, whose righteousness was a determining factor in its use as a means of punishment. Natural causes, such as plague, famine, earthquake, were never looked upon as directly responsible for widespread death; these were merely the means selected by God for vindicating and upholding his righteous will. God's power to bring death was, in the eyes of the biblical thinkers, a convincing validation of their claims concerning his power over the universe and over men. The death of the individual, according to this point of view, was important to the degree that the fate and welfare of the nation were affected.

Jacob, as we have seen in another connection, was elaborately and extensively mourned for seventy days; Moses' death called for thirty days of lamentation, and that of David was recounted largely because it provided an opportunity to report the last will and testament of this king and Solomon's bloody compliance with it. Isaiah was in the temple, possibly at the time of King Uzziah's funeral obsequies, when his dazzling vision came to him. Jeremiah found it necessary to tell the nation not to mourn for Josiah—who had been killed at Megiddo—because other and more critical events, from the political standpoint, were brewing (Jer. 22:10-12). When the fate of the nation is in the balance, even the death of such a noble king as the reformer Josiah could not distract the attention of the prophet to the nations. This point is driven home by an incident in the book of Ezekiel:

> The word of the Lord came to me, saying,
> "O mortal man, behold! I am taking away from you the delight of your eyes by a sudden stroke; but you shall neither lament, nor weep, nor drop a tear. Sigh in silence; make no mourning for the dead; wind your turban round your head, and put your sandals upon your feet; cover not your beard, and eat no mourning bread."
> That evening my wife died; and in the morning I did as I had been commanded. (24:15-18.)

The sorrow of the individual must be suppressed in the face of a greater sorrow—that occasioned by the disaster about to befall Israel.

If death is primarily a matter of *individual* emphasis, however, its bearing upon the nation's history and destiny is of secondary importance. The man who sins will find himself cut off both from God and from life. This is *his* death, and not the death of the whole community, no matter how closely the individual is involved in the nation's life. We would expect, therefore, that the Bible's growing awareness of the worth of the individual would be accompanied by a changed conception of death. Is this the case? Before an answer is attempted, the main facts as to the rise of individualism should be recalled. Through one political defeat after another the integrity of the nation was slowly disintegrating, and through ethically self-conscious prophetic criticism of religion a clearer knowledge of the demands of God became available. Accelerated by the sufferings of the Exile, these forces promoted the rise of individualism, not as a full-fledged doctrine, but as an emphasis qualified by other emphases as elsewhere noted.

With this new emphasis was there an attendant revamping of the prevailing conception of death? The two great prophets of individualism—Jeremiah and Ezekiel—have nothing whatsoever to say about death in its relation to the individual. They evidently accepted the general belief and saw no contradiction between it and their new teaching concerning the individual. Their individualism was necessarily conditioned by the cultural patterns which defined for them the nature of man, society, and death. They saw each man as a spiritually sensitive and ethically responsible person, but always as sustaining lines of relationship with other men and with the community of Israel—never in the magnificent and artificial isolation of an absolutistic individualism. The destiny of each man was the destiny of the entire group. Yet this individualism anticipated a later interpretation of death, as well as of life, in its fearless enunciation of the seat of genuine religion—the heart and spirit of the individual. This meant that real death must start with the corruption of this personal locus of faith, the destruction of love and obedience to God in the heart of a man by the perversion of the will. Individualism accents the spiritual character of death, without ignoring its biological reality.

The description of the abode of the dead impressed us by the hopelessness of the concept as a means of solving the problem of man's fate. We saw how the mood of despair symbolized by Sheol is logically related to the nature of man as creature, made of the dust of the ground. We observed that death has profound spiritual implications, as it is visited upon men in judgment upon their sin of rebellion and as it deprives them of communion with God—the highest of life's activities. Thus there is a serious contradiction between the idea of death in Sheol, which is out of God's reach, and the idea of death as the judgment of God, brought about and controlled by him. Death cannot be both without and within the sovereign control of God. Somewhere along the line of religious development we should expect to encounter attempts to resolve this contradiction, if not by logic, at least by the application of a religious faith which desires unbroken communion with God. Let us now explore these possibilities.

HOPE OF RESURRECTION

The most obvious of the possibilities whereby death can be conquered or brought into the sphere of the activity of God is a resurrection from Sheol. Since all must descend to this place sooner or later, their only hope for life with God is a return from Sheol. But Sheol is the land of no return; the road to Sheol is a one-way road. On the other hand, the sovereign God of the whole universe, creator of heaven and earth, of the heavenly bodies, the continents, and of all life upon them, cannot be forever held back by the bars of death. He who overturns mountains and levels valleys, who uses mighty nations, and is the Lord of history, reaching to the skies and down to the depths for the vindication of his holy will, may one day reach even into Sheol and order the dead to arise. A limited number of passages bear upon this possibility. Let us first examine a few which suggest the power of God to bring the dead to life, perhaps even before they have gone down to Sheol.

One of these has to do with the leprosy of Naaman, a Syrian general, to whom the remarkable ministry of Elisha has been reported. Being a man of social standing, Naaman writes a formal letter to the king of Israel, apparently requesting the help of this holy man. The king's agitation concerns us here. He exclaims, upon receiving the letter: "Am I a god to kill and to make alive, that this man is sending to me to cure a man of his leprosy?" (II Kings 5:7.) This impatient remark conveys the existence of a general belief that only a god or God can bring the dead to life, or cure a fatal disease. We may compare also the stories of the deeds of Elijah and Elisha—some of the exploits of the two men are strikingly similar—and observe that each of these prophets is said to have brought to life or resuscitated a widow's child. The language is not too clear, but it is clear enough to warrant the conclusion that a holy man brings a dead person to life (I Kings 17:17-24; II Kings 4:17-37). We are interested neither in the technique used nor in the credibility of the result purportedly achieved. Our interest is simply in the recorded statement that men of God worked to restore life. We may refer also to the incident associated with Elisha's grave. A burial party was at work in the cemetery, when they suddenly spied a band of Moabite raiders. Without ceremony they flung the corpse they were about to bury into the grave of Elisha and hurried away from the danger zone. The corpse revived and stood on its feet as soon as it touched the bones of the holy man (II Kings 13:21).

A disputed and textually corrupt passage in Job (19:25) need not occupy us long.[1] Job's utter despair of his life and his yearning for death have already been mentioned in the above discussion. In this passage he asks his friends to have pity on him because he has been struck by the hand of God. He asks them why they are not satisfied with witnessing his physical breakdown, and why they keep opposing and torturing him "like God." Then he addresses the world in general, uttering the hope that the words pronouncing his innocence might be inscribed deeply and imperishably on a rock. Even this does not satisfy him; and he announces a fleeting hope that after he is dead, God himself will stand upon his grave and witness for him to the world that Job is a righteous man. Job does not expect to be raised from the dead; he expects only to have a moment of consciousness in his grave so that he will be aware that God has at last vindicated him to all mankind. Other interpretations have been given for this passage, but none which is truly critical supports the hope of a real resurrection, a view which would be entirely in contradiction to other passages in the book of Job.

Other references which appear to point to release from Sheol are really declarations of faith in God, who will deliver from death—that is, postpone its coming by overcoming a man's personal enemies or by healing a disease which might prove fatal. They are such passages as these:

> But God will ransom me
> From the power of Sheol, when it seizes me. (Ps. 49:15.)

> My flesh also dwells in security;
> For thou wilt not abandon me to Sheol;
> Thou wilt not let thy godly one see the pit.
> Thou wilt show me the path of life.
> Fulness of joy is in thy presence. (16:9-11.)

> Let the wicked be put to shame;
>   let them wait for Sheol. (31:17.)

> Into thy hand I commit my spirit. (31:5. Cf. Luke 23:46.)

In the light of this hope for deliverance from death, the best that man can expect from God is length of days. This is expressed by one who describes a new heaven and a new earth in which men will rejoice forever. In the new Jerusalem there shall be heard no more "the sound

---

[1] On this passage see S. R. Driver and G. B. Gray, *The Book of Job,* Vol. II (International Critical Commentary, 1921).

of weeping, nor the sound of crying," for the youngest one to die will be at least a hundred years old (Isa. 65:19-20).

But in two canonical books reference to a real resurrection is undeniable. These references, understandably enough, are contained in apocalyptic material; for they appear as aspects of a general world upheaval introducing a new order, at a time when the earth and even prevailing intellectual conceptions might well be shaken from their foundations. In one of these books we read that the Lord is to come to punish the kings of the earth and to compel the Gentiles to reverence him. Then he will come to the holy mountain and destroy death forever. In so doing, he will "wipe away tears from every face" (Isa. 25:8) and bring back to life the spirits of the departed.

> But thy dead will live, their bodies will rise,
> Those who dwell in the dust will awake, and will sing for joy;
> For thy dew is a dew of light,
> And the earth will bring the Shades to birth. (Isa. 26:19.)

These who are to return to life are God's dead, the faithful sons of Israel who, with the living exiles from Assyria and Egypt, will worship God on his holy mountain. Thus, at one blow faith shatters the orthodoxy that is no longer adequate, and destroys the gates of Sheol for the release of the righteous. Logically the ideas in this passage are inchoate ones, flashing into consciousness without much support from reason in the moment of an intense awareness of the redemptive activity of God for the salvation of his people. The concept of a resurrection is not really formulated; its logical difficulties are ignored in a thrilling realization that somehow God is the conqueror of death. These verses are an affirmation of faith, not a dogma of theology.

We may now examine the visions of the book of Daniel. The historical background of this book has already been treated. The tortures and tears of the early Maccabean period, and its martyrdoms and betrayals, were the fertile soil for the growth of new thoughts about life and death. In this book young Daniel symbolizes the purity and fidelity of a devout Jew who overcomes all temptations and is saved by his God in times of great tribulation. As Daniel is delivered from the den of lions and from a fiery furnace, so the faithful during the persecution of Antiochus Epiphanes will be given courage to endure horrible death by a renewal of faith in the God who can conquer death and give them everlasting life. After a dreadful time of danger and fear the kingdom will be given to the

people of the saints of the Most High—
Their kingdom shall be an everlasting kingdom. (7:27.)

Lest those who suffered martyrdom during the persecution are deprived of a position in this kingdom, "many of those who sleep in the land of dust shall awake, some to everlasting life" (12:2). Others will also arise "to everlasting reproach and contempt." In Sheol these faithless renegades who denied Israel's God in fear of torture and death cannot receive the punishment they so richly deserve. Therefore they will "awake" and suffer everlasting contempt in the land of the living. The risen martyrs who set the example of courageous fidelity will shine "like the stars forever and ever."

Thus, rather unexpectedly, near the end of the canonical period of Israel's religious activity and thought we encounter statements that death will be destroyed, the inhabitants of Sheol will return to life, and that some who rise from the dust will be punished by ignominious treatment when the kingdom is given to the faithful, whereas others will be exalted like the stars in brightness. These brief references do not tell what will happen to the Gentile or to the unbeliever, or whether all men will experience a resurrection, or what the requirements for such an experience are. We know simply that God has overthrown the grim enemy death, and that his kingdom is bound to come. It will be constituted of the living and of the risen who once were dead, and will continue everlastingly with Zion as its center. Therefore it is presumably both a material and a spiritual kingdom, solidly grounded, however, upon faith in God.

Only as we relate the idea of a resurrection in Daniel and in Isaiah to the faith of the entire Old Testament does it become understandable. This faith rests upon repentance for sin committed against God, a full acceptance of his sovereignty over the personal and social life of man, and obedience to the divine will. The conquest of death, now seen by these late apocalyptic writers to be within the power of God, demands repentance and obedience as the evidence of true faith. A real resurrection, as the product of salvation, can come, then, to men of faith. Daniel's account of the resurrection of the wicked and the apostate seems to be incidental to his main line of thought and certainly shows a qualitative difference from his allusion to the resurrection of the faithful martyrs. The wicked are to endure eternal reprobation, a fate impossible of realization in the underworld.

Why was the hope of a resurrection so *slow* in coming to Israel? Is not Sheol an intolerable concept for this people who led the way in their noble monotheism and their union of ethics and religion? These questions are provoked by the incontestable fact that throughout most of Israel's religious history the world's great monotheism appeared and flourished without benefit of a doctrine of immortality. The late emergence of individualism is one explanation for this remarkable circumstance. The restraining effect of the idea of community delayed its coming and directed the trends of religious thought toward the social situation and toward compensation—through social channels—for the lack of the idea of personal immortality. Through sons and grandsons a man's ego could be projected into many generations to come. His name could live on, and his piety could be transmitted, through the devout lives of his children. This was his hope and his answer to the question of self-realization beyond the grave. As he viewed the history of his people and mused upon the dreams of the prophets and seers, he also found fulfillment in a vicarious and anticipatory sharing of the nation's future glory. The kingdom of God was on the way; his sons' sons would share in it; that sufficed.

Opposition to the pagan cult of the dead served also to divert attention from the question of life after death. This cult's association with foreign gods was a source of contamination. The cult and its gods were tarred with the same stick and must be shunned. An additional factor in delaying the appearance of the idea of immortality in Israel was the typical monistic view of man. Man's visible, physical organism was indispensable to life: it was not separable from the rest of his nature. The evidence of the senses proved conclusively that this body perished at death. How could a future life be conceived, then? The writers of the Old Testament—except for the latest ones—had little or no opportunity to be influenced by Greek thought. Their orientation was toward the rest of the Semitic world, whose culture they shared. So the Hebrew eschatology of the individual was as unpromising as that of such countries as Babylonia or Assyria. A final circumstance helps both to explain Israel's evident indifference to the thought of immortality, and to provide a substantial basis for its postcanonical and New Testament development. This has reference to Israel's intense piety, her faith in a living God, the worship of whom was the chief delight of her saints. Caught up in the rapture of their adoration of God, they found their present unspeakably precious, and beyond this experience they had no desire to move in their thinking. They had eternity in their hearts, even though they had no immortality in their creed. But this was the religious experience which transformed Israel's eschatology ultimately and paved the way for a doctrine of personal survival.

IMMORTALITY AND FAITH IN GOD

The testimony of these men of God is noteworthy. One of them says, "I believe that I shall see the goodness of the Lord in the land of the living" (Ps. 27:13). His God will show his lovingkindness and demonstrate the goodness of life, even though it does end in the grave. This goodness of God and of life fills the poet with wonder:

> O Lord, thy goodness extends to the heavens,
> Thy faithfulness unto the clouds.
> Thy righteousness is like the highest mountains,
> Thy judgments are a great deep.
> Thou savest man and beast, O Lord.
> How precious is thy goodness, O God! (Ps. 36:5-7.)

Even though this goodness does not extend to Sheol, it rejoices the heart of the believer. When a man is so thoroughly content with the presence of God, why should he speculate idly about his future fate beyond the grave? If man trusts in God, he need not fear. Neither life nor death can separate him from the God of love and everlasting mercy.

> Commit your way unto the Lord,
> And trust in him; and he will act. (Ps. 37:5.)

> For the Lord loves the right,
> And he does not desert his saints. (37:28.)

> Thy grace is better than life. (63:3.)

> And having thee, I wish nought else on earth. (73:25.)

And further,

> Precious in the eyes of the Lord
> Is the death of his saints. (116:15.)

This expresses their assurance that God loves and watches over them even unto death.

Man may dwell upon the thought of the brevity of his life. It is short and frail, like a dream, or grass, or a cobweb, or like yesterday. Its length is only seventy, or at the most eighty years, so men should learn to make use of their days in the service of God and in obedience to his Law. If God permits the good days to equal in number the bad days before life is over, man cannot complain. And if he "establishes" the work of the faithful, God deserves praise (Ps. 90). The conviction as to the enduring quality of righteous acts is the only sense of permanence a man needs for his life. Such a life motivated by this assurance adds its weight to the total goodness which God is creating in bringing the kingdom to men. Another writer testifies that God rescues from pestilence, terror, demons, and death. As to any one of these, "it will not come near you" (Ps. 91). God will satisfy him with long life and thus show his salvation.

When a mortal man thinks of the brevity of his life, comfort comes in contemplating the God of his creation, who will survive the work of his hands. God is always the same, and his years have no end, although the heavens may perish (Ps. 102:26). Such a God will establish his servant's posterity in peace (102:28). God saves by forgiving sin, healing sickness, rescuing from the pit, and crowning men with grace and mercy. He of eternal grace and righteousness remembers that men are dust or grass that withers (Ps. 103). How, then, can he fail men, even at the time of death? In an exquisitely sensitive piece of writing we are taken into the mind of God as he plans creation. His purpose is clear—to create the earth as a home for all living things. From the fountains that flow in the valleys the wild asses quench their thirst; grass grows for the cattle, and wheat for human food. Even the young lions share in nature's bounty, "seeking their food from God." He provides for every need (Ps. 104). In death will he not make man a conqueror?

In view of these considerations the prospect of existence in Sheol did not greatly matter—the life of worship, service, devotion, and obedience in the land of the living was a full one. Furthermore men's hope for the future took concrete form in the idea of the continuing covenant community. This hope rested for its realization upon faith in the God of salvation; he alone justified it. Such a faith made possible a life with God—a life of quickened conscience, heart-warming communion, and creative social relationships. This life was valued as having incomparable worth. It was inevitable that such an experience as this should finally be conceived as extending beyond the grave. Its power and its value were too great to be frustrated by the belief in Sheol as the end of everything. After all, Sheol was the unchanging abode of the dead, whereas God was the God of the living, who through faith in him might transcend the annihilation of death. Life with God, suffused with the radiance of his holiness in temporal relations, assumed the quality of an eternal relationship through the sheer logic of daily experience, even though an ideology of immortality had not yet appeared. So the belief in the possibility of a bodily resurrection, recorded in Isaiah and Daniel, was supported by the witness of man's

THE THEOLOGY OF THE OLD TESTAMENT

experience of a precious communion with God in faith's attack upon the finality of death. The acid test of *religious experience* joined forces with the new idea of a resurrection to overthrow the dominion of death and Sheol. In the meantime, an empirical demonstration of the continuing goodness of God foreshadowed this eventual victory, and ideas already present in Israel's religion prepared the way for the arrival of an explicit doctrine of salvation for the individual beyond death. What are some of these empirical and doctrinal intimations of immortality?

The most prominent of these ideas has to do with the nature of God as *eternal*. From age to age, from generation to generation, he is the same. He survives and is independent of his mighty work of creation in the natural order. The old order of nature changes and is folded up like a garment to be replaced with a new one, but he is from everlasting to everlasting. In his being are comprehended the mystery and immensity and wonder of life. This God of eternal justice and mercy climaxed his work of creation by making man in his own image. We have seen that this act bestowed upon man spirituality, freedom, and the capacity for obedience and worship, in distinction from the other levels of conscious existence which God had made. The fact of man's creation means more than his resulting weakness and humble dependence upon God; it proves that man is like God and has a destiny unlike that of lower orders of life, a destiny which is related to the purpose of God in creating man. The loving, creative God has singled out man as worthy of sonship, and has accordingly endowed him with the capacity for acting like a son of God. Does not this potential sonship point to a relationship transcending death? To the degree that the individual is of great value in the sight of God, this question might well receive an affirmative answer.

By the fact of his creation in the image of God, man has been given a stature and a dignity beyond that of any other living beings. God has made him but little lower than divine beings. The highest compliment ever paid to his greatness is the opportunity given him to choose the good and to reject the evil. In possessing this opportunity, man is revealed as an ethical being, the conserver and promoter of righteousness and compassion in the world. Conceivably the God of justice could find other effective ways to conserve ethical values—they could survive and flourish in his being without the help of man—but here they could appear only as ethical absolutes, untested and unrealized in social experience. As far as man is concerned, ethical values—such as unselfishness and justice—are revealed in the conflict within a personal self and between such selves. Unselfishness is a meaningless term unless it is related to a personal center of consciousness possessed of self-awareness. The human discoveries of goodness and love and altruism belong to the divine-human adventure in the exploration of values, and will be cut off—no matter how long that event is deferred—if physical death terminates the human enterprise. This truth convincingly shows how the presence of ethical values in the Old Testament anticipates the Judaeo-Christian idea of immortality.

The worth of man as a worshiper is also relevant to our problem. It is man's chief end and his greatest glory to adore the Most High, who is his maker and redeemer. By such adoration he most fully realizes his function as a person. In the moment of worship, when his whole being is open to the cleansing and quickening touch of the Spirit of God, he justifies his creation. And on the part of God this worship in which man engages, not only wins the divine approval for work of creation which is well done, but implies for God that absolute godhood which makes worship imperative. Worship is a proof that God is God. Often the reader of the Old Testament runs across such words as these: "They shall know that I am the Lord." This is a knowledge which calls for an acknowledgement of the supreme Lord of the universe through the act of worship and the exercise of the will in deeds of righteousness. Man who is righteous is also man who worships the righteous God. May not this worship and this power to worship hint at the immortality of man? He is a person, the object of the wrath and the love of God; he is a moral being, able to further or to frustrate the good purposes of God; he is a worshiper, exhibiting his manhood by magnifying the God who made him. How can Sheol hold him, or the gates of death prevail against him?

8. The Problem of Evil

A LARGE measure of man's activity is devoted to the conquest of evil. The evils of poverty, unemployment, hunger, war, pestilence, flood, sickness, and death largely account for the elaborate social institutions and technical skills which man has developed through the ages of his history. This problem of evil is central in the cultures, ideologies, mythologies, philosophies, and theologies which have appeared during man's social evolution. The nature of reality as men daily experience it involves the fact of evil, which constantly harasses them in one way or another. This fact cannot be ignored nor dismissed with a cliché or an impressive psychological formula.

The solution of the problem of evil, at least in intellectual terms, has a direct relation to conclusions as to other equally serious and pressing problems of man's life and destiny. One's conception of evil cannot be divorced from his view of ultimate reality and the highest good. So the problem before us must be examined in the context of the problems of God, of man, of sin, and of salvation. Evil is not an isolated phenomenon; it is always experienced in relationship with something else, such as the good to which it is opposed or the universe which permits its continuance. So by the men of Israel, whose thought furthered mankind's understanding of this problem in a remarkable way, evil was seen in the setting of a total theological viewpoint, whose salient features this book seeks to outline. But before noting how this theological frame of reference affected Israel's various solutions of the problem of evil, we must identify general attitudes and particular teachings on the subject in the Old Testament.

In order to comprehend how the Old Testament treats this problem, we should consider the several ways in which the problem of evil presents itself to man. In the first place, evil may be viewed as an affliction caused by the caprice or anger of superhuman or divine beings who must be avoided or placated. Whether these beings are called spirits, demons, devils, or gods, they are responsible for the evil that befalls man. This belief calls for complicated taboos and rituals of sacrifice, especially in more primitive societies. The problem is merely one of avoiding tabooed objects and observing the ritual. Another explanation of evil is the view that it originates as punishment for disobeying a higher power, which is conceived as controlling man's destiny in some sense. The proper attitude, in this case, is to accept punishment as meaningful and necessary, and to seek to avoid disobedience in the future. This concept is rational and ethical to the degree that the divine power has a rational and ethical nature. Again, evil may be regarded as inherent in man's nature, and therefore as ineradicable save by the grace of God. On the human level the reaction to this belief is one of futility and despair. Man can do nothing. Another attitude, not necessarily involving religion, might be that of stoicism, based on a recognition that evil is man's lot, and he must suffer afflictions which he can neither understand nor remove. This brings us close to the fatalism of the Moslem, although the latter's vigorous theism imparts meaning to the evil that must be endured.

In India, particularly, still another viewpoint has been emphasized—the conception of evil as illusory, resulting from an error in thought. The problem is solved when right thinking is used as a corrective. More modern in tone is the view that evil is due to natural forces, to man's ignorance, or to both. The obvious solution lies in greater knowledge and better control of nature to reduce the evil and suffering in the world. This can be achieved by the full use of the resources of science. Finally, evil is amenable to an intellectual solution and may surrender before the onslaughts of theologians and philosophers. It is this form of the problem which is most familiar to modern students of religion, and most congenial with their general outlook.

In which of the above categories may we place the Old Testament conception of evil? Since they are not necessarily mutually exclusive, it is appropriate to place it in several. The evidence which may be adduced as to the prominence of any one of these must be determined by an examination of the biblical text. Evil resulting from the caprice or anger of the higher powers is certainly within the purview of Old Testament writers, although, just as certainly, not the most prominent element in their thinking. Anger is apparent, it is true, but it is usually anger against unethical conduct and therefore not capricious. Evil as punishment for wrongdoing is a viewpoint to be found in much of the literature. Evil has its mysterious aspects, but this situation is not conducive to despair as a rule, for God exercises responsibility for it; it has an explanation, although this may exist only in the mind of God. In a modified form, evil considered to be in part the result of man's own nature also has a place in Israel's thought. There is little speculative thought in the literature of ancient Israel, so that logical reflection over the problem of evil is largely confined to the wisdom literature and, in particular, to the book of Job. Finally, one finds no basis for a belief that evil is illusory or unreal, or that the acquisition of knowledge of the processes of nature will solve the problem.

It is a singular fact that a careful scanning of the pages of the Old Testament reveals an astonishing *indifference to suffering* and to the effect of evil upon men's faith in the divine goodness. Evil as such is not ignored; it is accepted usually without question and without curiosity as to its origin. Human suffering on a vast scale is recorded with the objectivity of a modern newspaper writer reporting on communal massacres in India. The Bible is not greatly interested in pain. Sin is the evil which preoccupies its writers. Suffering is described with calm, if not clinical, detachment. In individual cases—in Job, Jeremiah, and the Psalms—cries of agony are recorded when pain is intense, but on the whole suffering is uncomplainingly endured. Israel was schooled to suffering. So stern was her life in the earlier period that her historians by contrast called Canaan a land flowing with milk and honey. Famine, plague, drought, and war were deadly enemies, producing suffering on an enormous, incomprehensible scale. Except for repetitious pronouncements that these evils were the result of sin, no explanation of the widespread suffering they brought is offered. How may we account for this?

Awareness of pain and attacks upon it require an awareness of the individual. Pain in the aggregate is hard to feel; individualized pain strikes home and arouses protests as well as questions about the divine government of the universe. Statistical data as to the starvation of millions in Europe may not move us: the story and picture of a single child dying of malnutrition may stir us to compassionate action. Agony of the body and mind is an individual and a qualitative, rather than a quantitative, experience. In Israel the individual was consciously or unconsciously dedicated to the service of the community. Israel's welfare was paramount; the individual's pain was irrelevant aside from this larger goal. This subordination of the individual precluded preoccupation with his suffering on the part of religious thinkers of the day. In the literature which they produced, a seeming hardness of heart and insensitivity to suffering naturally followed. We obtain few glimpses of the tragedies of common men who starve, sicken, and die. Even the great ethical teachers of justice—the prophets—who were the champions of the poor and the abused in the social order, evince no deep compassion for the individual leper, slave, or orphan. They report on mass misery but fail to give an emotionally sympathetic account of it.

Many pictures of sheer misery are presented to the reader of the Old Testament—the harrowed widow of Zarephah mourning over her dead son and pleading for his restoration; Hannah on her knees, praying agonizingly for the gift of a son; Uriah walking into battle to his death knowing that David has seized his young and lovely wife; Moses standing over the body of the Egyptian he has slain in a fit of passion; the three women—Naomi, Ruth, and Orpah, who love each other, parting in anguish; Egyptian mothers by the thousands awaking one terrible morning to find their oldest sons dead; the patriarch Jacob shocked by the news of his son's death. Other sections picture the crowds in besieged Jerusalem, gaunt and starving, groping in the filth of the streets for a bit of food; the defeated Jews marching naked and barefoot into captivity, being spat at and taunted by the Edomites lining the highway; a traitor hanging on a scaffold, through the cunning of a beautiful Jewish-Persian queen; a man on a dung heap, reviled by friends and neighbors and forsaken by God; a brokenhearted prophet redeeming his faithless wife from further prostitution by buying her publicly in the market place; two women claiming the survivor of two infants, one of whom has died in the night; a blinded giant with bulging biceps, bringing death to himself and to thousands of his enemies by causing their temple to crash to the ground. These pictures are all the more impressive because of the unconscious art which produced them. It is not evident that the artist had any intention of portraying human misery: he was simply depicting life as he saw it, or acting as a propagandist for his religion. In no instance did the writer sketch the anatomy of pain or unmistakably reveal a genuine sympathy with his suffering characters.

However, the Old Testament is by no means silent on the subject of evil. It often pronounces a clear and positive word, and even its silences may be highly eloquent. Now let us trace briefly the references to the problem of evil, and indicate their value for arriving at the distinctive Old Testament teaching, if such a result is possible. Then we will be in a position to assess the significance of what this literature fails to say on the subject.

EVIL AS PUNISHMENT FOR SIN

The *J narrative* is simple in its dramatic form, but thought-provoking in its theological and anthropological implications. In comparison with the later priestly account of Creation, which tells how God gives man dominion over living things, the J story shows how man is given a chance to secure dominion over *himself*. He is given the choice of good or evil, life or death. With the struggle within man's soul and the tragic outcome of that struggle this narrative concerns itself. Evil appears, not so much as an extraneous force or supernatural power,[1] as the inner pride of man, who defiantly sets himself against his Creator. Man is a creature molded from the dust of the ground, a tiller of the soil, who may raise his eyes to the skies and sense his kinship with the universe. Because he rejects the moral demands of this kinship and chooses evil, he is cursed along with the ground on which he is condemned to labor in sweat and tears all the days of his life. The writer makes it clear, through the message of the tree of life and the tree of the knowledge of good and evil, that to taste life with its beauty, knowledge, sensuous pleasures, temptations, and opportunities for self-expression carries with it the possibility of untold evil. Evil came to Adam in the form of toil, banishment, and death. Yet, within life is the freedom to reject evil and to choose the good.

In the narrative of the flood the same theme of the evil consequences of disobedient conduct is found. This story reveals that man's wickedness was great, that the bent of his thinking was always evil, and that he continuously chose to reject the will of God and to follow his own desires (Gen. 6:5). So he had to be destroyed by a flood. This makes it clear that God's noble experiment—man—had failed, and to that degree God had failed. It had proved to be precarious in the extreme to endow man with freedom, yet God had taken the risk because there was the possibility that man's freedom might make him a lover of the good and a hater of evil. Man's freedom was not the cause of evil; it was its opportunity. A great flood came and destroyed most of mankind. Watersheds, flood control, reforestation, erosion—had they been known to the biblical writers—or rain and snowfall would have been ignored in searching for an explanation for this disaster. God had caused the flood in order to uphold his sovereignty and his righteousness. Similarly the tale of the tower of Babel discloses how a disruption of the force at work in building the city of Babylon occurred, so that the project had to be abandoned. The workers did not quit because of a wage dispute or because they desired a closed shop. They quit work because God made it impossible for them to understand one another—their languages were scrambled by a miracle. Their pride in their work was ruinous, since it challenged the supreme authority

---

[1] The figure of the serpent may represent a mythological being used by the J writer as an adversary of God, although hardly—contrary to the church fathers—as the figure of the devil.

of God. Evil is again revealed as the result of the God-defying misuse of freedom. So it is also in the story of the two cities of the plain—Sodom and Gomorrah. Destruction in the form of fire and sulphur was sent upon these cities because their sin was "grave" (Gen. 18:20).

The fascinating Joseph stories may be ascribed to the work of both J and E—the writers of the Yahwist and the Elohistic sources. These are strikingly effective in their classic delineation of human character and feeling, and in their portrayal of the fundamental tragedy of human life. In these stories the slavery, imprisonment, and suffering of Joseph and the grief of Jacob, his father, are depicted in moving scenes. But these experiences, tragic as they were, were God's means of carrying out his purposes in history by the selection, enslavement, and deliverance of a nation which would be the means of bringing redemption to all men. Reviewing these misfortunes in the life of Joseph and his brothers, the writer makes Joseph say, "God accounted it good" (Gen. 50:20). The evil that befell certain individuals, when viewed in the wider perspective, was really good. This judgment may also be passed upon the unhappy experiences of the Hebrews in Egypt and during their desert life, to say nothing of the misfortunes which overtook the Egyptians when they refused to let Israel go. (Exod. 7:14–12:28).

A reference to the *priestly works* in the canon may be made at this point. All of these writings—principally Leviticus, Numbers, and Chronicles—agree in attributing evil to sin. Dire punishments are to be inflicted upon those who live at enmity with God. Some of these evils to be sent because of sin are enumerated in the book of Leviticus: fever, consumption of crops by enemies, war, crop failure through drought, ravages by wild beasts, pestilences, dispersion among the nations (Lev. 26:16-40). Confession, however, will avert these disasters. This is also the truth involved in the Elohistic story of the golden bull or calf (Exod. 32:30-35). After giving vent to an outburst of furious anger against the Israelites, Moses tries to turn aside the wrath of God from them, saying hopefully, "Perhaps I may make atonement for your sin." In Numbers (21:4-9) there appears the familiar story of the stinging serpents. After these had killed many people, the survivors came to Moses and, after confessing their sin, requested him to "pray to the Lord that he remove the serpents from us." Even serpents were used by God to punish his erring people.

The priests wrote their codes and histories with little creative literary imagination, but with a firm belief in the principle of retribution. They held that the disasters and afflictions which came to men were caused by their sin in violating the will of the holy God, particularly as this was revealed in the sacrificial system of the temple. Defeats in battle, premature death, a loathsome disease, the loss of a kingdom—all came to pass as the prompt reaction to the violation of a taboo or the breaking of a law of God. The sovereign power of the holy God of Israel would not be defied with impunity. When evil struck, sin was undoubtedly present, so close was the connection between the two. It simply remained to search the codes and customs of the religious community to discover what the violation was. It was a neat, watertight causal system, impervious to the evidence of new experience, and firmly founded upon an unquestioned theodicy.

THE DEUTERONOMISTS

Nowhere in the Old Testament are the theological presuppositions and historical method of biblical writers more easily traced than in the work of the Deuteronomic school.[2] With emphatic finality, the sequence —sin, enslavement, suffering, repentance, prayer for salvation, the coming of a deliverer, and freedom from servitude—appears like a refrain in many parts of this material (Judg. 2:11-20; 3:7-11). History moves in cycles; each of its periods duplicates the spiritual crises and events of its predecessor. But this cyclic movement is not meaningless, although the writer of Ecclesiastes (1:8) believed that the historical process was always turning back upon itself in vain repetition. It charts a momentous drama, based upon the single underlying theme of the divine justice and human sin, but continuously changing with new generations of actors and new world tensions. History is the product of the conflict between mighty forces, represented by the God of Israel on the one hand, and human pride and perversity on the other. Since God retains his sovereignty and man his stubbornness, this struggle doesn't end, and age after age witnesses the consequences of the evil which ensues.

A conception of evil in some form or other enters into all philosophies of history. In the dialectic philosophy of Marxism, evil lies in the presence of a bourgeois class of property-holding individualists whose overthrow is necessary to salvation. History consists of a class struggle rather than a struggle between God and man. On the other hand, history may be regarded as a movement toward a distant although attainable goal which will be reached through knowledge and active good will. Thus evil is ignorance and ill will, which are strangely present among men who are potentially good, but which may be explained by

[2] Deuteronomy and Deuteronomic editions of Judges, First and Second Samuel, First and Second Kings.

reference to man's biological and physical limitations. Ignoring environmental determinism, the Deuteronomist looks at man himself and finds that his desires and loyalties are evil in that they turn him from God. Kings of Israel and Judah, and the people over whom they rule, become apostate of their own free will and thus commit sin. This evil choice, repeated and multiplied endlessly, affects the course of history and brings in its train war, famine, and all manner of other disasters. The Deuteronomists distinguish two kinds of evil in their conception of history—the evil peculiar to man's freedom, which permits rebellion against God, and the evil sent by God as punishment for this rebellion. Taken together, these account for the history of mankind, if we may believe the Deuteronomists.

Such a conception of evil can be said to be materialistic only when evil's discernible effects upon men are considered. These effects, by reason of their very concreteness, tend to hide their ethical origin and the fundamentally spiritual character of evil. The biblical writers were aware of Israel's tendency to interpret religious experience materialistically and to evaluate religion as a matter of profit and loss. For this reason, they took pains to call the nation's attention to the divine source of both good and evil and to its ethical basis in the nature of God. The people were admonished to remember that material abundance is the gift of God; and when they enjoy the gifts of fine homes, large herds, and gold and silver, they must be careful not to say, "My own power and the strength of my own hand have gained this wealth for me" (Deut. 8:17). It is the power and the faithful goodness of God which have poured upon the Israelites these blessings, demanding—at the very least—the reciprocal graces of gratitude and loyal obedience. Conversely, when evils come—such as sunstroke, plagues, consumption, political disaster—Israel must remember that these are lesser evils than the supreme one of deliberately rejecting and denying its God. They are exhorted to "choose life . . . by loving the Lord your God, by heeding his injunctions" and by following him faithfully (Deut. 30:19-20).

THE PROPHETS

The great prophets of Israel devoted their lives to the overthrow of evil. They lashed out furiously against the evils of social injustice, political corruption, and religious idolatry, with never a doubt as to the reality or the intolerability of that which they attacked. Rulers, judges, priests, and merchants—and indeed the whole nation—were chastised by the whiplash of their biting scorn and burning indignation. The prophets knew evil and spoke with authority about it. Did they

233

have a theory of evil upon which they based their attitude and which explains their amazing vehemence? They were not philosophers, but they had an explanation for the evil of their world. To use the language of philosophy, theirs was a monistic conception of reality; its ultimate principle was transcendently good rather than evil. No dualism, as in Persian and Greek thought, disturbed their singlehearted devotion to the highest good, which for them assumed the form of a personal being. It is true that their writings sometimes exhibit traces of a primitive dualistic mythology reminiscent of a cosmic struggle between good and evil (Amos 7:4—"the great deep," possibly Tehom or Tiamat), light and darkness (Isa. 45:7—possibly Persian Ahura-Mazda and Ahriman). However, these appear to be incidental in the thought of the prophets. They actively repudiate as abominable to God intercourse with demons and demigods as well as gods of popular Semitic religion. There may be other powers in the universe, but these are always subordinated to the supreme power or laughed out of existence (Hos. 13:2).

The prophets were content to speak of evil in only two ways: the evil that men do when rebelling against God, and the evil that God sends as a judgment upon the rebellion.[3] Of evils that afflict innocent communities they do not speak, except casually without any apparent realization that a problem has been created. Perhaps they were unable to conceive of innocent communities, since they placed all men into one of two classes—the righteous and the unrighteous, a division of humanity which cuts across community lines. Membership in either of these groups is determined by men themselves, as they make real choices and by their daily decisions align themselves on the side of the God of justice or against him, so determining their destiny. Men's right to enter one camp or the other is not questioned by the prophets, yet the vigor of their protests against evil testifies to their belief that evil choices are not inevitable, and that once they are made, their disastrous effects may be ameliorated or avoided by genuine repentance. When evil is chosen, punishment may be swift and terrible. God, the creator of the natural order, is able to use it to support the spiritual order. Calamities come, and they have their meaning in the light of this fact. They are both punitive and redemptive, as Amos indicates when he acts as the spokesman of Yahweh:

> Indeed, it was I that gave you
> Cleanness of teeth [famine] in all your cities,

[3] See pp. 191-94.

. . . .
But you did not return to me. (4:6.)

God sends famine and plant diseases to the fields of the farmer (4:9), in addition to other disciplinary measures, in order to maintain his moral government of the world and to persuade men to return to the paths of righteousness.

Evil is not an intellectual problem, since the righteousness and power of God explain it, provided that the group rather than the individual is the unit of reference. Isaiah has a simple formula:

Happy the righteous! for well shall they fare;
. . . .
Woe to the wicked! ill shall they fare. (3:10, 11.)

God's blessing rests upon men who humbly serve him. The corollary of this truth is transparently clear—his wrath pursues the wicked and proud of heart. Under the influence of the hardships accompanying the fall of Jerusalem and the Exile, the prophets were compelled to re-examine the premises of their thinking and to take account of new difficulties for faith. For example, Israel was finally conquered by the Babylonians, and both the nation and its faith were threatened with extermination. Was not this fate out of all proportion to Israel's sin? How could God choose and guide this nation through the tortuous course of its history, only to destroy it? How could the righteous be happy in exile? How could they sing the songs of the Lord in a foreign land?

The demands of such questions as these stimulated the prophets of the exile to make creative reaffirmations of their faith, in which they reckoned with the meaning of national adversity in relation to the promises of the covenant God who was Israel's savior. One of them came forth with one of the most potent ideas ever conceived by the mind of man: the idea that the terrible evil afflicting Israel was *God's way of redeeming the world*. In defiance of all the canons of logic and the testimony of human experience, he boldly announced that the nation's suffering and misery had a spiritual purpose—the healing of the nations. In the anonymous author's poem the nations speak in the third person:

Through his stripes we were healed.
. . . .
And the Lord made to light upon him [spiritual Israel]
the guilt of us all. (Isa. 53:5, 6.)

Then God speaks,

> Through his affliction shall my servant ... bring righteousness to many.
> (53:11.)

Israel, redeemed and purified by its suffering, becomes the servant of God, whose tragic punishment wins the nations of earth to the cause of righteousness. In this conception evil has a holy mission—the redemption of the world. Thus the idea of vicarious, redemptive suffering is born.

Jeremiah, whose keen sensitivity to the demands of God and to the sins of men sets him in a class by himself, is known for his contribution to the idea of individualism. His is a tempestuous soul, capable of flashes of violent anger, moods of black despair, and moments of ecstatic communion with God. He is the first prophet on record to give expression to impatient anger against God because of the personal sufferings to which his ministry subjected him. He anticipates the later question of Job when he cries,

> Why is my pain unceasing, my wound incurable,
>   refusing to be healed?
> Wilt thou really be to me like a treacherous brook? (Jer. 15:18.)

And again,

> Why came I out of the womb,
> To see trouble and sorrow? (20:18.)

In spite of his acute suffering Jeremiah does not theorize about the origin of evil and pain, for his is a personal complaint about God's treatment of him as an individual. Forced to undergo extraordinary hardships and severe travail of body and soul, this prophet breaks out into agonized expostulations to God. Jeremiah's was the kind of experience, nonetheless, which was essential to the rise of radical inquiries concerning the origin and nature of evil and its effect upon man's faith in God. Men are usually too content with the good that they enjoy to waste time speculating about the evil which besets others. It is only when it strikes them individually that they raise their voices in protest and begin to question their own beliefs. When the solidarity of the human group starts to disintegrate, and the individual becomes maturely self-conscious, then he is free to attempt a reconciliation of the divine providence and the world's misery, as well as his own.

Another prophet—a contemporary of Jeremiah and likewise a shrewd observer of startling international events occurring toward the end of the seventh century—witnesses the spectacular rise of a new power in the Near East, and asks why God keeps silent when the Chaldeans swallow up the righteous. Will God tolerate this situation forever, and never put an end to Chaldea's bloody campaigns? he asks. Is there any justice in a world which permits a wicked nation to win victory after victory and allows it to tyrannize over righteous people such as the Hebrews? What advantage has a nation in adhering to the one God if he fails to protect it against its enemies? With such questions as these in his mind the prophet watches and waits, hoping for an answer from God. Finally an answer comes to Habakkuk:

> Verily, the wicked man—I take no pleasure in him;
> But the righteous lives by reason of his faithfulness. (2:4.)

Here the term "man" must be interpreted in its broader social sense so as to include the national groups involved in the prophet's situation. In these words, echoing down the centuries, we are told that God is on the side of the right, no matter what the appearance of things. In loyal trust in God, the righteous man and nation will find life and salvation. This trust is the assurance of faith that God will not suffer his people to be afflicted continually; he will wipe out evil and finally set his people free from their enemies.

In a similar vein the various writers of the elegiac anthology found in the book of Lamentations affirm their faith that God is good, and that he metes out to man his just deserts. These poets witnessed or had access to firsthand records of the horrors of Jerusalem's siege and dawnfall. They are exceptionally well qualified to discuss the problem of evil, if opportunity to note its dreadful effects is a qualification. They describe in gruesome detail the famine and resulting cannibalism produced by the siege in the city. They depict the visible horrors and also those that are audible—the awful wailing of the bereaved, the moaning of the starving as they search for food, and the weeping of the aged as they witness the breakdown of organized government and the ruin of the sacred city of David. They describe their own feelings of torture in seeing the defilement of the temple and the shame of the Exile. They, of all men, are driven to deal with the problem of the divine justice in relation to evil.

When they ask, Why has this happened? there is only one answer—Israel has rebelled sinfully against her Lord (Lam. 1:18). This terrible situation has come about through the action of a righteous God because of the hideous crimes and unmentionable sins of the city's inhabitants.

> It was for the sins of her prophets,
>   the iniquities of her priests,
> Who shed in her midst
>   the blood of the righteous. (4:13.)

It is by the decree of God that this evil has come (3:38), but "he does not willingly afflict, nor grieve mankind" (3:33). Thus the whole book of Lamentations re-emphasizes the teaching of the prophets: that the Lord of the universe is both righteous and merciful, and maintains his sovereignty by vindicating his justice in sending punishment and rewards to men in accordance with their deeds and attitudes.

THE PSALMS

The book of Psalms contains heart-rending accounts of deep personal sorrow and despair. All manner of suffering is recorded in this book: mental and physical abuse by enemies, the writhings of spirit caused by the taunts of the flagrantly impious, torture of heart in the face of unjust accusations by associates and friends, sickness, the fear of death, and physical deprivation. In many of the psalms God's tardiness in entering the situation and setting things right is loudly bemoaned. These psalms make up a diary of many a sick soul, revealing his pain and pleading to be made whole. This diary is a monument to the power of faith. In spite of the concentrated misery of soul—and of body—revealed in this book, it also consistently testifies to the power of a triumphant faith capable of overcoming evil. Every psalm strikes a note of victory, although each in its particular key. All of the psalmists agree that

> The Lord is good to all,
> And his mercy is over all his works. (145:9.)

A major source of concern to these men is the observable fact that their theory of evil does not always correspond with the evidence of human experience. A number of the psalms point out that the wicked seem to enjoy life, and imply that this is hardly appropriate if God really is in his heaven upholding his righteousness. The wicked prospers and gets along in life so well without God that

> All his thought is, "There is no God."
> His ways prosper at all times. (10:4-5.)

One psalmist suspects that there is not much point in man's moral struggle, for man is like the beast that perishes. Wise men, along with foolish and brutish men, come to the same end, although the psalmist expresses the hope that fate will be kinder to him, and that he will be delivered from death when it seizes him (49:10-15). In the face of tangible refutation of his belief on every hand, the psalmist never questions the final goodness of God, even though he may be undergoing severe persecution or suffering of body so intense as to drive him to heap maledictions upon his enemies. One psalmist writes, "Burning rage lays hold of me because of the wicked." (119:53.) The psalmist rests the case of the problem of evil when logical arguments appear to be of no avail, and relies upon God to solve it in his own way. Of one thing he is sure—"The Lord reigns; let the earth rejoice!" (97:1.)

THE APOCALYPTIC LITERATURE

In the latter part of the Old Testament period there appeared a type of literature known as the apocalyptic.[4] This literature always reflects periods of danger in the life of postexilic Israel. It is characterized by a vivid and picturesque style, figurative and often cryptic language, and a sense of terrible urgency. The author's world is breaking up. Familiar political alignments, social relationships, and the cherished intimate life of his community are in immediate danger of destruction. The nations are at each other's throats, and Israel is caught in the bloody conflict. With the powers of darkness in the ascendancy the situation looks utterly hopeless. But for the apocalyptist and all men of faith it is at this very time of dark gloom and fear that God gloriously reveals himself. Through violent, catastrophic acts he suddenly enters the scene of history, triumphs over the forces of evil, and delivers his people. This is the hope and belief of the apocalyptic writer as he contemplates and shares the suffering of his generation in a time of severe persecution. The organized wickedness of the world is wholly unable to withstand the might of the holy God of Israel, when he comes to bring righteousness to the earth. Evil is doomed because a good God rules the world.

In this conception of the conquest of evil the full impact of evil is so keenly felt that there is no possibility of solving the problem by a redefinition of terms. Evil was not a matter of definitions to the Jewish victim of persecution, stretched upon a rack in order to be made to renounce his faith. Such a victim was in a position to learn the cruelty, the insanity, and the utter ruthlessness of evil. He could see it organized, supported by resplendent Greek culture, and rationalized by a godless, humanistic philosophy—as in the case of the author of

[4] See pp. 179-80.

the book of Daniel, who wrote when the Jews of Palestine were being martyred by the Greek-loving Syrian, Antiochus Epiphanes. He knew evil as physical pain, as the threat of spiritual disaster, and as national defeat. For him there could be no easy intellectual solution of its problem. Indeed there could be no solution at all on the human level. The enormity and complexity of evil baffled the human mind as its cruel malevolence distorted the human body, so that man's powers were quite unable to cope with it. Only one recourse remained—trust in God, the King of kings and Lord of lords, whose "kingdom . . . shall never be overthrown" (Dan. 6:26).

THE WISDOM LITERATURE

This survey of selected books whose teachings bear upon the problem of evil must, above all, include the wisdom literature, in which category it is customary to place the books of Proverbs, Ecclesiastes, and Job. The importance of these books for our purpose comes from the fact that they contain conscious reflections upon the conduct patterns and the meaning and value of life. While Jewish in their origin,[5] they have a universal outlook, and concern themselves with human life in general rather than the life of the Jewish community. They reflect and are influenced by the movement toward individualism which appeared in Judaism during the exilic and postexilic periods. Two of these books are unorthodox in their bold assertions with respect to good and evil and God's relation to the problem. These are Job and Ecclesiastes.

In the book of Proverbs there is little or no evidence of the existence of doubt regarding God's evenhanded distribution of justice and rewards in the world. Scores of sayings affirm with assurance that God always rewards the wise, the prudent, the temperate, the charitable, the industrious, the honest, and the merciful. There is a close correlation between the good that a man does and the goods that he receives as a reward for his meritorious conduct. God always prospers those who seek wisdom diligently and pursue it. There is one hint that misfortune may have a beneficial effect on its victim, and is not merely punishment for wrongdoing: "Whom the Lord loves he corrects" (Prov. 3:12). There is also a suggestion that it is not always easy to continue believing in God's righteous control of the world; the wicked apparently do prosper on occasion and arouse the envy of their neighbors. So one proverb contains words of reassurance to the anxious righteous in the community:

[5] See R. H. Pfeiffer, *Introduction to the Old Testament* (1941), p. 682. Here the belief that Job came from a southern source—S—is affirmed.

Fret not over evil-doers,
Nor be envious of the wicked;
For the evil man will have no future,
The lamp of the wicked will be put out. (24:19-20.)

That is to say, in spite of appearances the wicked are doomed; before too long, they will be destroyed—their lamp will be put out—and justice will be vindicated. This is the conviction of the entire book and of the community whose beliefs it so cogently expresses.

Unique in viewpoint is a short essay appearing possibly about 300 B.C., composed, in its original form, by an elderly and wealthy sophisticate residing in Jerusalem, with time on his hands for dabbling in philosophy and the problem of human existence—perhaps he was influenced by Epicureanism and Stoicism.[6] Observing the ceaseless round of nature and the lack of equity in human society, he is compelled to conclude that the commonly held belief as to the nature of evil is not justified by actual experience. For example, he notes that there is one fate for all; both the wise and the foolish perish (Eccl. 2:14; 3:19-21). The only reward for toil is trouble! The oppressed receive no relief, and the wicked prolongs his life (7:15). There is no real retribution. So the man of sense is advised to be not overrighteous (7:16).

This "gentle cynic" does not deny the existence or the righteousness of God; but he declares, in effect, that it is useless to try to know the secret of God's justice and control of the world. This is a vast and impenetrable mystery, which it is futile to explore. So man may as well give up and resign himself to the not unpleasant task of eating, drinking, and being mirthful, with the disturbing realization that even this will turn out to be a highly unprofitable matter. The contribution of this pessimist is his effective criticism of contemporary conceptions of evil. He incisively declares the presence of a real incongruity between popular belief and common experience. Nonetheless he skirts the problem of evil and never penetrates to its core. Faith is unable to influence this writer's logic, perhaps because his God is conceived as a transcendent, deistic creator instead of a merciful redeemer. God's power and justice are intellectually perceived, but his mercy and love are unknown to our disillusioned philosopher. Perhaps the obvious cold detachment of his investigations of life accounts for this. He commits himself to no challenging crusade for the furtherance of human good, and there is no passion for God or for justice in the lines which he pens. In this respect he is to be distinguished from the other thinkers

---

[6] See A. H. McNeile, *An Introduction to Ecclesiastes* (1904), pp. 39 ff.

of Israel, who fling themselves into life, and find in their struggle new light on the meaning of faith.

The canonical book most frequently associated with the problem of suffering and evil is the book of Job. Without examining the question of the unity of this book, we may simply state that it falls into five main divisions—the prologue-epilogue (1–2; 42-7-16), the dialogue (3–27; 29–31), the Elihu speeches (32–37), the Yahweh speeches (38–42:6), and the poem on wisdom (28). Omitting this poem, let us consider the significant teachings of these sections in the order given.

In the narrative at the beginning and end of the present form of the book—designated as the *prologue-epilogue*—we are informed that God and the Satan enter into a contest over the genuineness of the goodness of a certain man called Job. The Satan is given authority to test this man by inflicting upon him suffering through the loss of possessions, children, and personal health, as well as social status. Job survives the test successfully. He says to his wife:

> Should we, indeed, receive good from God,
> And should we not receive evil? (2:10.)

After his time of suffering is over, Job receives back from God what he has lost—cattle, children, wealth, and community esteem. This denouement of the drama clinches the argument for the truth of the formula that ultimately righteousness and true piety are rewarded. This is the orthodox answer to the question, Why do good men suffer? This answer, of course, does not carry us beyond the solutions found in the books already included in this survey. Evil enters the world on the authority of God, apparently for the purpose of testing men, and to punish those who are sinful. As for the Satan, he does not symbolize a cosmic power of evil rivaling God's: he is merely one among many heavenly beings dependent upon and deriving his power and authority from the supreme Ruler of the universe (1:6-7, 12).

The *dialogue* is the heart of the book of Job, presenting in the form of long speeches and replies by Job and his three friends the author's thinking, in noble language which—even in the English translation— justifies the book's inclusion among the classics of our culture. Disregarding the question as to whether the author created the figure of Job in order to voice his own personal experience or used Job as a literary device for the dramatization of the problem of evil, we may examine the essence of the speeches ascribed to this character.

In desperate straits Job loudly laments the fact that he was ever born, and bitterly complains of the life which God has "fenced in."

Disease afflicts him constantly; innocent, he is harried by God, terrified by dreams, and doomed to die. God, his accuser, jailer, and judge, as well as the tremendous power behind the physical universe, cannot be reached by his helpless victim. This mighty God has stooped to torture Job without cause. How can he be a just judge with an impartial outlook? Is God acting like a vindictive man, searching for the guilt which does not exist, knowing full well that Job is guiltless? Is it not shockingly incredible for God to turn upon this suffering mortal in irrational fury, after having watched over him lovingly in his earlier years (10:12)?

God, who has wisdom and power, is the ruler of history; he makes the nations great and he destroys them. Job knows all this, he protests; but he wants to speak to this God and not to listen to the wordy platitudes of his unfeeling friends. He knows he is innocent, and his feeling of tragic frustration comes from the fact that he cannot get God to hear and to believe his protestations. Instead God devises false charges against him. The belief that God will eventually slay him, after he is sated with torturing his victim, is unaccompanied by any hope of a life after death. In spite of this, Job retains his integrity as a man and stoutly maintains:

> Lo! He will slay me; I have no hope;
> Yet *I will defend my ways to his face*. (13:15.)

Piteously he cries out,

> Unto God my eye weeps,
> That one might plead for a man with God,
> Even as with a man for one's friend.
> For a few years will come,
> And I shall go the way that I shall not return.
> My spirit is broken. (16:20–17:1.)

To his entreaties God has turned a deaf ear, and there is no prospect of finding a friend who will be able to intercede for him.

Persecution continues, and his friends, family, and even his wife turn away from him in disgust and loathing. In a desperate search for a solution to his problem Job is momentarily consoled by the fleeting thought that when he is in his grave, he will be permitted a vision of God—at last his friend—standing upon his grave and vindicating him to all the world (19:25-26).[7] But this hope is vain; the wicked live,

---

[7] See p. 218.

grow old, and amass wealth; godless, they are prosperous. He seriously doubts that they are always punished. And in the end both good men and wicked men lie down in the dust together. Job's chief predicament is expressed in the words,

> O that I knew where I might find him,
> .   .   .   .
> I would set my case in order before him. (23:3, 4.)

However, he cannot find him, no matter how eagerly he searches. God the redeemer hides himself behind the universe which he has made. God has chosen to abuse him, and no one can stop him from persisting in his attacks, which weaken Job's spirit and overwhelm him with sorrow and black despair. (23:16-17).

With rising indignation at the boldness and irreverence of Job's accusations against God, the three friends give vent to their feelings of outrage and hasten to the defense of their beliefs. The first, and perhaps the oldest (15:10), of these—Eliphaz—announces that faith in the God of goodness brings its sure reward of health and long life. It is true that no mortal can be altogether righteous before the immortal God, and that man must expect to endure the normal hardships of human existence. God wounds, but he also heals. By his own words Job is condemned; these words prove that his wickedness is great. Recognizing this, he should turn to God and find peace. By humility and a just life he will be released from his wretched state.

The second friend—Bildad—urges Job to seek God, who never perverts justice. The irreligious man perishes, but the good man God befriends and abundantly blesses. In the imagery of the Oriental poet he insists that "the light of the wicked goes out," and his name is completely forgotten. Far from comforting Job or helping him with his problem, Bildad is content to reiterate the essence of the problem as Job himself has worded it: man, the maggot, can hardly be justified with God, the mighty creator from whom nothing is hidden, and whose awful power none can comprehend. How can Job expect to receive a reply to his petition from such a Being?

Finally, Zophar states that Job is even guiltier than his sufferings indicate. How can he presume to understand the ways of God? His domain extends beyond the heavens and reaches farther then Sheol. His earth-shaking and fear-inspiring actions are self-initiated and infinitely beyond the control of puny mortals. Nevertheless this God does give heed to evil; he does not remain aloof from man's moral struggle. Zophar restates the worn clichés of his associates: the wicked man's triumph is short; he will sooner or later die a miserable death, being snatched away in the night. If Job will but beseech God in true humility and put away evil, he will yet be saved.

The so-called *Elihu speeches* are undoubtedly the work of a writer who had before him the dialogue practically in its present form. Specific allusions by this writer to its argument show the handiwork of an individual who was dissatisfied with the viewpoints of the three friends and Job, but who had nothing particularly original to contribute from his own thinking. The reader is informed by Elihu that God is great as well as righteous. In his greatness he is unaffected by both sin and righteousness among men. Moral acts affect men, but they do not affect God. This does not mean that he fails to punish the unrighteous. On the contrary, no evildoer can escape his wrath, and no righteous man will be afflicted. Job cannot call God guilty, as he has evidently tried to do, for he judges the wicked impartially. Job has been tried by suffering so that he might learn to shun evil. If a sinner prays in a repentant mood, he will be rescued from death. Job's rebellious attitude is in itself sinful and prevents the divine forgiveness.

With the impact of an earthquake and with a logic as overwhelming, the words in the *Yahweh speeches* destroy Job's resistance and annihilate his arguments. God ironically inquires where Job was during the period of the Creation and asks what he knows about the mysteries of the natural order—the earth, the sea, the light, the lightning, snow and hail, rain, stars, lions, goats, wild asses, wild oxen, creatures whose ways are strangely different from the ways of men. In comparison with God, of course, Job knows nothing and is utterly powerless. Thus the incontestable superiority of the Almighty is fully established, and the absurdity of Job's attack upon God is made manifest. The ways of God cannot be challenged, much less can there be any argument between him and Job, since argument presupposes the equality of the contenders before an impartial umpire. God proceeds to deny his own guilt and, by implication, to assert the guilt of Job. As a consequence of this flood of celestial oratory to which Job has a chance to make but a feeble reply, he finally admits his insignificance and declares that he has been reduced to silence. Job says that he has spoken foolishly and promptly repents, declaring that he has seen God (42:5-6). This may be the author's effort to show how, by a powerful demonstration of the divine transcendence, Job's will to resist is broken, and he repents, thus preparing himself spiritually to see God and to yield himself to him. As to this, the language is not clear nor decisive; but it does suggest a solution of the problem of evil, namely, faith in a God who is always merciful and just, even though empirical experience tends to prove the contrary.

When the material in the book of Job is summarized, the congruity of its various ideas with one another and with those of other canonical books is recognizable. One main thesis is steadily propounded and maintained—God's rule of the world is a just one. The corollaries of this proposition are self-evident: righteous men receive preferential treatment from a righteous God, and evil men are invariably punished. Upon this belief practically all of the Old Testament writers are in agreement. The figure of Job is the great exception; this man stands out as the great Jewish protestant on this issue. He vigorously protests the smug assumption that religious beliefs need not be subjected to the test of experience, that there is no organic interaction between theology and ongoing human life. In the name of the undeserved suffering of his character Job, the author of this book insists that the facts of life must be considered when God and evil are thought about. It is doubtful that he proposed a new theory of evil; it is certain that he attacked the one that was popularly held in his day. By so doing he exposed the prevailing fallacy of adhering to a generalization which no longer truly represents all of the available data from experience. The retention of an orthodoxy which had grown out of a concept of social solidarity in a period when an emphasis upon the individual was emerging illustrates this weakness which he held up for critical discussion.

EVIL AND THE NATURE OF GOD AND MAN

We are now in a position to make a concluding summary of the extensive data resulting from our investigation of the problem of evil in the biblical sources. First, it should be noted that evil comes when man chooses to disobey God, whose will is righteous, and who demands righteous conduct on the part of men. Evil is therefore associated with the act of the will which causes men to defy God. It is also a word for the act of God when he sends punishment for man's sin. In both instances, evil is viewed as moral, or as having definite moral implications. This is always the significance of evil in history, in the opinion of the biblical writers. Nations and their institutions flourish or perish as they seek to do the divine will or to flaunt it. Further, evil also has disciplinary value: it chastens men and restores them to a life with God. This is not a prominent idea in the Old Testament, but its presence reveals a recognition that not all evil is punishment for sinful behavior.

THE PROBLEM OF EVIL

In many of its aspects evil is a mystery whose secret is in the mind of God and beyond human reason.

Evil in the thought of the Hebrews is not an eternal principle in the universe, engaged in an unending struggle with a principle of good, as in Zoroastrianism. The occasional appearance of the Satan or of minor demons has little significance in the religion of Israel. Israel's faith is strongly monotheistic; and if a conception of ultimate reality may be inferred, this is a monistic conception rather than a dualistic one. Men do not ask in the Old Testament: Why are evil choices made? Is there a superhuman force predetermining such choices? It is true, there is the serpent in the garden; and to the degree that it induced man to eat of the fruit from the forbidden tree, it influenced man's choice. Or we see the Satan in the book of Job, bringing evil upon Job. But even here his power cannot be brought into play without the consent of God. Throughout the literary records of Israel one finds no real belief that the power making for evil is outside of man; there is unanimity in asserting that this power resides in man himself. This was seen particularly in the utterances of the prophets, but no book is completely indifferent to this truth.

Modern students may reason that God the creator of man must be responsible for man's ability to choose evil, and therefore responsible for evil itself; but the biblical writer was so interested in confronting man with his moral and religious responsibility that he had no interest in such logical exercises. He frankly worshiped a God who sent both good and evil upon men, and usually set aside the question of how a good God could be a sovereign ruler of a universe containing evil. For him the only conceivable solution of the problem had to start with faith in the holiness and the righteousness of the living God. He began his attack upon the problem of evil with a stupendous assumption—a righteous God rules the whole universe! This God is the God of Israel. Upon the rock of faith in such a God he stands, unshaken by the tides of evil which sweep around and over him. War, plague, famine, irreligion, personal affliction beat upon this rock, but it stands. So say the historians, the prophets, the psalmists, the apocalyptists, and the wise men of Israel. Some of them state that evil overtakes Gentile nations because they are enemies of the Jews and of their God; others declare that evil comes to the wicked Israelite too, for his own injustice or faithlessness. Thus even in the biblical books which do not consciously face the problem of evil there is a lively interest and an active, although sometimes narrow, faith in a just God who controls and uses evil for his redemptive purposes.

This discussion shows that the problem is intimately connected with the nature of God in the Old Testament. He is involved as creator of man, conserver of justice, and ruler of the universe. In the first capacity, he imparts to man a measure of his own freedom, thus making possible decisions that may be either good or evil; in the second, he upholds the moral order, rendering good for good and evil for evil; and in the third, he uses his power over nature to provide a physical basis for the development of spiritual and social values among men, and as a means of rewarding goodness and condemning wickedness. The fact that physical disaster befalls whole communities without any apparent regard to the possibility of the presence of good people in them attests to the dominance of the idea of social solidarity in Israel, but by no means invalidates the concept of the moral majesty of God. It simply places the idea in the framework of biblical thought.

Earlier sections of this chapter have shown that the natures of man and of evil are also related. Man's freedom led to his downfall, and, if we recall the J writer's position, to the whole course of civilization, with its murders, lusts, and proud human accomplishments of hand and brain. Adam and Eve made their choice with open eyes and doubtless with the unmistakable words of divine prohibition still ringing in their ears. Urged on by pride, hunger, and personal desire, they ate the fruit of the forbidden tree. So the era of suffering opened for them and for their descendants. For the latter it was not inevitable evil, but evil brought on by deliberately repeating the disloyalty and disobedience of their ancestors. This was a voluntary, not a mechanical, repetition, practiced freely as an alternative to the good that might have been chosen. Israel's habitual choice of evil was a real choice, as all the records agree. To bring man to his senses and to dissuade him from his evil course, God was compelled to afflict him severely.

As has already been stated in the chapter on the nature of sin, man's physical nature is not the reason for his sin nor for the evil that appears as its result. His proneness to yield to the lusts of the flesh results from his eagerness to escape the problem created by the conflict between his spiritual freedom and the limitations of his physical nature. His sin consists in *choosing* sensuality, not in the possession of a body which makes sensuality possible. His body becomes the occasion for evil when he tries to overcome the feeling of frustration caused by the limitations it imposes upon the expression of his self-will and pride of spirit. So he immerses himself in the pleasures of the body. Only the judgment of God in the form of punitive action can eradicate this self-centeredness and remove the need for escaping into sensuality.

This interpretation gives to evil a marked ethical character, since it is associated with man's will rather than with his body. The locus of evil is thus determined—the human spirit. The problem presented by evil, therefore, is the problem of regenerating man's spirit by means of judgment and the forgiveness of God. The evil that remains in the world when the effect of man's ethical evil is eliminated from our thinking need not concern nor disturb man, for God can deal with it adequately, in his own way, and in his own time.

Man as a spiritual being is both ethically self-determining and religiously dependent upon his Creator. This feeling of dependence, when not corrupted by cultures and thought systems of man's own devising, may lead to a nonrational reliance upon God when reason fails. The mental processes peculiar to Old Testament thought always involve this context of faith in God, a faith which is held to be possible because of man's creation. Reason may falter when exploring the deeper problems of man's existence, while faith goes on, not to penetrate the darkness, but to declare that beyond the darkness is light. Man's capacity for faith constitutes the basis for the general Old Testament attitude toward the problem of evil. This may be observed in the books of Job and Habakkuk, and in other books as well. No matter how fearful and threatening the evil besetting men may be, man will "live by his faithfulness." So evil is strangely transmuted into life-giving power by faith in the God of Israel. The man of God need not fear evil when it comes, because he can be sure that God means it for good. When a man repents and believes with his whole heart and soul and mind, he has achieved a personal solution of the problem of evil. This is the distinctive teaching of the Old Testament.

HAVING searched the Scriptures, have we indeed found the words of eternal life? Having examined the books of the Old Testament and recorded their testimony as to the meaning of Israel's faith, have we found a faith which can convince men today of its truth, which can thrill and enthrall them by its mighty power? Perhaps the answer to this question has already been found as one by one the fundamental beliefs which constitute the theological framework of the religion of the Old Testament have been identified. It may be that identification is equivalent to validation. Certainly that is the method of Israel's religious teachers. They are largely exhorters who are convinced of the axiomatic nature of the teachings they vigorously proclaim. They are not interested in adducing proof in the modern sense. However, the mind of modern man is not that of the biblical writer; and it requires a rational demonstration—in so far as that is possible—of propositions whose truth is asserted. This is particularly the case when the alleged truth pertains to the supreme values of human existence, as in religious creeds. Hence this chapter will build upon the foregoing chapters, which have sought to set forth the nature of Old Testament beliefs, and will explore the question of their credibility and validity.

This task requires, first of all, examining the problem of the *unity* of Old Testament theology. If we grant that each of the basic ideas treated in this volume is self-consistent, is it possible to conclude that they fit together in a living, organic whole? Do we have one theology or several theologies as a result of our survey of the literature of the Old Testament? If the latter is determined, the entire effort has been fruitless, for there is then no theology of the Old Testament; at the best, we possess simply a more or less interesting assortment of miscellaneous ideas. On the other hand, if the ideas previously described tend to fit into a single pattern—without distortion or violence to any one of them—so that their interrelationship is undeniable, the fact of unity cannot be doubted.

It is already evident that no single element in the theology of the Old Testament exists in isolation from all other elements. The great realities embodied in this theology have of necessity been interpreted as dependent upon one another for their full definition. We may well ask: How does this happen? What is the explanation of this organic and logical unity? What principles may be utilized to account for the appearance of a single theological viewpoint and system in a literature covering a thousand years of history? It is begging the question to assert that a belief in revelation settles the matter by positing a divine Personality, whose antecedent will and holy purposes with respect to man, his sin, his destiny, and his salvation, are one in his mind before they are spread upon the pages of Scripture. In truth God provides the unity, for the Old Testament contains his revealed Word, which cannot be self-contradictory. But as long as we accept the reality of the human wills and personalities of the Old Testament authors, we must seek our unifying principle in the area of human experience and history. This position does not preclude the concept of revelation, but it relates it concretely to the experience and activity of men.

UNITY THROUGH HISTORICAL CONTINUITY

From this standpoint reference may be made to several principles conceivably contributing to the unity of Old Testament theology. The one most readily coming to mind is that of historical continuity. While changing with the passage of time, yet—like an ever-flowing stream which constantly receives into itself new materials from its shores and bed, but remains fundamentally the same and retains its distinctive features—Hebrew religion through the centuries perpetuated itself as a distinctive way of life and belief. To be sure, it grew and changed under the influence of new environmental conditions and new personalities, but its identity never disappeared. From the time the Hebrew people first became conscious of their common destiny in their life in Canaan until they achieved a new understanding of their purpose in history in the Exile, they were essentially the same people, with the same modes of thought, the same spiritual outlook, and the same fundamental religious view of the universe. In this survival of Hebrew culture there is nothing unique for the historian. In the life of any people the customs, social patterns, and general world view of one period are carried forward into succeeding periods to such an extent that the persistence of the old in the midst of the new can be readily recognized.

The various documents of Hebrew literature come from one thousand years of history, yet they all record with a measure of fundamental agreement—if not with entire uniformity—the hopes and fears of one continuing community. The individuality of the approach made by each writer to his task cannot obviate the clear evidence as to his consciousness of, and reliance upon, the thrilling history and the distinctive faith of his people. With a strong Oriental loyalty to his group he drew upon its traditions, history, and piety in the preparation of his material. This feeling of dependence upon his people's past provides the assurance that each writer—no matter how great his genius or forceful his personality—would act as a transmitter of culture from one generation to the next. A notable instance is the work of Amos, a rugged radical if there ever was one, who never gives the slightest indication that he regarded his ideas as new and revolutionary. His task, as he saw it, was to remind the people of the stern, ethical character of the God of their fathers, the God who had brought them out of Egypt and had enabled them to conquer the Amorites. In his radicalism he was theologically highly conservative, in the best sense of that term.

It was especially in the area of religion that the Hebrews maintained a distinctiveness that resisted the inroads of time and change to a remarkable degree. This made possible permanence in the midst of change for their major theological positions, since these were the indispensable and persisting symbols by means of which the nation could retain its special identity, its faith in its destiny, and could win in the struggle for survival against enormous odds. There is a great difference between the God of the J writer and the God of Second Isaiah, but there is also a deep likeness. For both men God was the righteous, redemptive, self-revealing Creator of mankind and the Lord of history. It was faith in such a God—from which they often wavered—that gave courage and confidence to the Hebrews, and a meaningful relatedness to the events of their tragic history. Thus the very fact that the Hebrews consisted of one highly self-conscious, continuing, historical community lends plausibility to the supposition that there was and is only one Old Testament theology.

CANONICAL UNITY

In addition to the unity determined by the fact that the Old Testament is the record of a single, self-conscious, historical community, surviving through the vicissitudes of its eventful history, the principle of canonical unity has value. As commonly used, this term means a unity established by the process and experiences of canonization, the end result of which was the recognition of the books of the Old Testament as having special sacredness and authority for the community of Israel.

Canonization is a process, rather than a decree of court or council, and in this process the literature is unconsciously subjected to severe testing as it is used to meet the personal and social needs of the group. While much of the process is unconscious, at times it is deliberately directed by writers or editors who try to adapt the biblical text to the needs of their contemporaries by inserting additions or interpolations into it. This means that prior to the official canonization of the Old Testament books the literature was continuously articulated with the ongoing life of the Israelite community. The writings were augmented, supplemented, and interpreted through the years so that they became both the record of the words and thoughts of their original authors and also the appropriation and adaptation of these words by the continuing religious community of Israel. In as much as the life of this community retained a basic identity as it changed, the adjustments it made in the biblical text through editing and rewriting tended to show the possession of a common historical faith. In this manner the canon makers, including the anonymous multitudes and the individual editors and writers, exemplified the interdependence of the community and its sacred literature. The impact of one upon the other is apparent, whether we consider the original composition of each book or its alteration through transmission and use.

An objection to the idea of canonical unity may well be raised. Is not such unity superficial and misleading? When the theology of the Old Testament is to be determined, must not the original autographs—in so far as these can be recovered—be its source? Are not scribal glosses, editorial additions and deletions immaterial evidence upon this question? This objection might readily be sustained if the secondary material were, in fact, mechanically superimposed upon the primary text. But this is not generally the case. Admittedly, the thought and meaning of the author are frequently altered by an editor or scribe, intentionally or unintentionally. Attention may be called to the book of Hosea, where the stern words of the prophet are often practically nullified by promises of deliverance. For many of the later readers of the prophetic books in the Old Testament period, the sternness of the prophets' words was unendurable, and additions more in conformity with human desire were demanded. Yet, even these bold alterations of the text are not theologically in contradiction to the content of the original book, for the later editors accepted practically the *same* religious beliefs as the original writers. Hosea's concept of God included both the idea of justice and that of mercy, as doubtless did that of the interpolater. The difference between the two is one of emphasis in the treatment of a particular idea or situation. Seldom does an editor or redactor conceive of the ideas of Jewish religion in a manner that is radically different from that of his source. After all, although belonging to two possibly widely separated periods of Jewish history, they are both the products of the same religious culture.

In a similar fashion the more substantial editorial work of such writers as the Deuteronomists serves to reinforce and supplement, rather than invalidate or nullify, the meaning of the original sources used. A good example of this may be found in the books of Kings. In these books the editors carefully select from their sources the facts which best illustrate their purpose and theological viewpoint, and then proceed to write a history that presents political and social data in an amount that is painfully meager, but which projects a conception of God and of history that is crystal clear. Their theological position is worked into the discussion so effectively that it becomes an integral part of the composition. In the writings which are reworked rather than composed by the Deuteronomists their theological position is equally apparent. Their belief in a righteous God of history, who punishes for wrongdoing and forgives when men repent, is quickly recognizable, not because it appears in sharp contrast with the literature they are editing, but because it is clearly and succinctly stated. As a matter of fact, the Deuteronomic doctrine of God and history is a prophetic concept whose presence may be traced in many other parts of the Old Testament.

These and other writers simply made sharply explicit what was already largely in their sources. Their oversimplified theological formula, wherever applied—in the case of the Deuteronomists—makes it possible for the modern student to detect a relationship of underlying religious belief between the authors of the autographs and the editors, which identifies the distinctive faith held by Israelites of many generations. By their continuous adaptation of biblical material to contemporary needs, the editors and revisers of the Old Testament succeeded in producing a text which tended to subordinate local and particular interests and allusions to the more general requirements of a faith applicable to all generations. So fragments of tribal history existing in the form of folklore, for example, were brought together in order to reflect a more nationalistic conception of Hebrew society (Gen. 49). Of great importance is the fact that the editors of the several books and documents, because of their religious motivation, promoted the process of canonization. They acted as interpreters of earlier writings to their own day. Whatever basic theological agreement may exist between the several editorial schools probably owes its existence both to the conscious dependence of one school upon another and of all schools upon the religious needs of a community constantly changing but retaining distinctive religious and cultural characteristics. In this manner, canonical unity may be regarded as the partial result, at least, of the unity achieved by the interpretative work of the biblical editors.

UNITY THROUGH WORSHIP

The preceding discussion makes it clear that canonical unity was achieved for the fundamental principles of Old Testament religion by means of the religious experience of the continuing community of Israel. These principles defined for the worshiping community and the worshiping individual the meaning of the object of faith and of experiences connected with a God-centered life. As these meanings entered the worshiper's consciousness through the exercise of memory or through attention to the spoken word of prophet, priest, or choir, they came as a living, unified truth, not as separate experiences. It is of the nature of such worship to see truth in its wholeness, to penetrate to the oneness of things, and to be moved by the totality of meaning which the world assumes when man worships. In the moment and the act of worship man sees God in relationship to himself, to his fellows, to his sin, and to his destiny and salvation. This does not mean that his mind is illumined by a sudden influx of clear-cut ideas on these subjects. Rather it means that he intuitively comprehends that a true God is really at work in his sinful self, producing results of a concrete kind. In such a situation a unitary theological position is implicit. Unity is achieved and convincingly demonstrated in the compelling religious experiences of Israel's great seers and saints.

Isaiah in the temple in the year King Uzziah died was a man entranced, beholding a holy God who was also righteous, discerning the awful consequences of his people's sin against that God, and his own share therein, and finding release for his soul only by surrender and obedience (6:1-8). This dramatic moment would be meaningless without the context of a single, distinctive theological viewpoint, representing the deep personal faith of the prophet. The theological implications of this tense experience are evident—a God of transcendent holiness and ethical judgment, man who is his sinful creature, a nation of men who are doomed save for sincere repentance, and a social hope based upon full conformity to the will of God. Not primarily by intellectual effort, but by the direct experience of God did Isaiah approach the realities of religion. It is doubtful that either he or any other spiritual

255

guide of Israel consciously worked out an integrated theological position which he called his own. But he and many others continuously reacted to certain religious beliefs—or the realities which these beliefs symbolized—with such assurance and passion that to deny their acceptance and appropriation by these individuals would be precarious in the extreme.

The high moments of Israel's religious life—as in the case of the prophet Isaiah—were occasions for furthering the comprehension of the whole meaning of this nation's faith, on the affective, the intellectual, and the ethical sides. Whether we think of the nation's celebration of the New Year's Day, adapted by Israel to her own needs from her Canaanite neighbors, the spring Festival of the Passover, or the later Harvest Festival, these were occasions for presenting dramatically to the minds of the people both the great Hebrew traditions and the reality of the God whose historical activity they were supposed to recount. With changing emphases from one generation to another, these community celebrations were powerful means of exalting the great principles of the people's faith and of transmitting them to posterity. The greatness of God the redeemer and judge, his inescapable demands upon his people for ethical behavior and loyalty, Israel's special privilege and obligation because of the covenant relationship, and her social hope of the kingdom were proclaimed and exalted by means of song, myth, and ritual before the assembled multitudes.

Such liturgical and tangible means of promoting religious education had a conservative influence upon the faith of Israel and served to perpetuate religious beliefs and cultic practices that had originated in early times. This conservation of religious values was high-lighted in times of crisis, when social and cultural pressures threatened to wipe out what was distinctively Jewish. Such a threat was present in the early postexilic period, for example. Politically dependent and surrounded by alien cultures, the Jews of this period developed a technique of cultural resistance which enabled them to survive as a cultural community. This technique involved both sociological and ideological factors, assuming the form of opposition to marriages with foreign women, on the one hand, and a stern insistence upon the exclusive worship of the God of Israel, on the other. Emphasis upon the one God and the one people became strong in this period, as we may find by examining the character of the postexilic revisions of pre-exilic books. So Hebrew history confirms the effectiveness of political or military misfortune in intensifying Hebrew faith and in crystallizing the convictions associated with it. This in turn so shaped and sharpened the tenets of Old Testament theology that they were more readily transmissible through the community's educational processes. Thus national adversity and defeat also contributed to the circumstances promoting the unity and the distinctiveness of Israel's theological beliefs.

INDEPENDENCE

Having examined the evidence which justifies the conclusion that there is a unity in the theology of the Old Testament, let us face the question as to the independent character of this theology. If there is but one theology of the Old Testament, after secondary and incidental ideas have been properly subordinated, is this theology really distinguishable from other contemporary systems of religious thought? Any discussion of the problem of validity raises the question of uniqueness, and this in turn poses the question of relationship with other ideologies of biblical times. If the theology is not distinguishable to any marked degree from these, it cannot be said to contain any self-validating truths, for it is then dependent upon, or otherwise related to, another system or systems which support it and give it meaning. Perhaps it derived its major doctrines from the Semitic world, of which Palestine was an integral part. There is much evidence to support this view in the results of archeological excavation, in the studies of the historian of religion, and in the work of the student of comparative Semitic languages.

In common with the rest of the Semitic world, the Hebrews used religious terms and performed religious rites showing their cultural affinity with the Babylonians, the Arameans, the Assyrians, and other ancient peoples. The use of a divine name meaning power, the prominence of the creation myth, the emphasis upon fertility in the popular religion, the use of certain agricultural seasons as the occasion for worship, and the general sacrificial system illustrate this affinity. The remarkable material in the Ras Shamra tablets confirms this conclusion as to the cultural homogenity of the Hebrews with their other Semitic neighbors. This has been so fully demonstrated by biblical scholars that there is no longer any room for argument. It is then proper to look with skepticism upon any easy assumption respecting the uniqueness of Old Testament theology. Nonetheless it is this very relationship which Israel's faith sustains with the beliefs of other Semitic peoples that makes possible the conclusion that this faith is independent and strikingly distinctive.

A large number of inscriptions and artefacts from the Semitic world make possible the reconstruction of ancient religious systems which were current in Old Testament times and earlier. Some of these directly affected the work of the biblical writers. Probably little actual borrowing occurred. Rather, the writers of non-Israelite materials and the biblical authors themselves drew upon a common culture formulated at an early time in myth and legend. It was not by his repudiation of this heritage that the biblical writer won fame. Instead it was through his skill and intelligence in appropriating the values of this cultural background and in placing them in a new and distinct setting that his signal success was achieved. For purposes of illustration the myth of the flood may be chosen. Here a familiar theme—that of a flood inundating the earth and wiping out practically all mankind—is utilized for the purpose of confronting man with the heinousness of his sin and the awful reality of the judgment which is sure to come upon him. The story becomes a terrifying portrayal of the absolute righteousness of God and, paradoxically, of an assurance of the divine mercy and forgiveness. When, however, the Babylonian epic is examined, a crude polytheism in which the gods are depicted as sensuous and self-centered is encountered. The sublimity of the Hebrew account is entirely lacking. There is no need to labor this point. A direct reading of the Babylonian myth and a comparison of its contents with the story in Genesis will easily confirm what is written here.[1] This holds generally when other mythological and religious texts of non-Israelite origin are compared with the relevant parts of the Old Testament. In ethical sensitivity, conception of sin, and definition of the way of salvation Israel towers far above her contemporaries.

While dependent upon her cultural environment in the Semitic world, Israel demonstrates with particular cogency the inadequacy of theories of cultural determinism. Her theology stands on its own feet; it is self-sufficient and undeniably independent. This notable phenomenon may call for an explanation; it can hardly require demonstration beyond a simple comparison of the available data. Such a comparison leads to results and conclusions which are supported by statements respecting the uniqueness of its teachings contained in the Old Testament itself. It firmly and insistently claims the special character of its origin and of its religious ideas. According to these claims, Scripture originated in God's disclosure of his will and plans for men's salvation to Israel only. Man, in the last analysis, had nothing to do with this origin save as a recipient and a vehicle for transmission. The writers of this literature sharply rejected any suggestion that their ideas were really theirs; for, they insisted, did not the word of the Lord come to them? Man's

[1] See Barton, *op. cit.*, pp. 273-77.

word and man's culture have no significance in revelation, they believed.

The Old Testament also provides grounds for determining the independence of its religious ideas from their general cultural milieu in its highly conscious repudiation of competing cultures and beliefs. The teachings of other systems are false and intrinsically evil, it maintains. Foreign gods, such as Bel, Nebo, Chemosh, Tammuz, Ishtar, and many others, named or alluded to anonymously; the cultic practices connected with their worship, such as astrology, necromancy, soothsaying, witchcraft, and intercourse with their devotees—all are condemned in no uncertain terms. The religion of the Old Testament is viewed as exclusive, unique, a thing apart, and it must be protected from contact with foreign corrupting influences at all costs. This is the attitude of the Old Testament itself, whenever it is articulate on this subject. With this belief the modern biblical student may agree, although he may have certain reservations in his assent. Israel's characteristic and fundamental faith *is* a thing apart in the inherent nature of the truths which it affirms, and in comparison with what was accomplished by the thinkers and leaders of the faiths prevailing in lands adjacent to Palestine.

BASES OF EVALUATION

By the use of principles drawn largely from the literature of the Old Testament, the essential unity of this literature's theology has been established. This theology is found to be remarkably independent of its cultural environment and possessed of a truly distinctive character. This discovery may permit the student to take the next step and to affirm, not only the special nature of Old Testament theology, but its *permanent validity* as well. He is impelled to take this step by the disturbingly challenging character of the religious ideas he has found, and by their startling claim of uniqueness and indispensability for the salvation of mankind. When the scholar comes face to face with the realities of Old Testament faith, he is under strong compulsion to shift his objective from the task of identification and description to that of evaluation and validation.

This is unavoidably the case, since the data with which he deals consist of intellectual propositions about religion and of unqualified assertions as to their ultimate truth. The ideas themselves are so phrased by the biblical writers that they challenge open rejection or complete acceptance. The ideas assume, in the very form they take in the record, that their validity is beyond the realm of doubt or debate. No sooner does the student raise the question as to the meaning of God in his sources than he receives from them the answer in terms that are final, absolutistic, universal in their implications. In a word, the Old Testament replies to the modern scholar's question concerning the validity of its recorded faith with an emphatic Yes. Its depiction of God and man, sin and salvation is true and forever valid for faith and conduct, the scholar is informed. Its positive language and passionate commitment to its basic assumptions which transcend and judge social and political ideals, furnish overwhelming evidence as to this. May we take this attitude as our own and accept the theology of the Old Testament as true and authoritative for us? This is an inescapable question.

To determine the normative nature of religious beliefs the *tests* of reason, experience, and faith are usually applied. These tests utilize primarily the disciplines of philosophy, history, and psychology. Their use permits inquiry into the compatibility of any given belief with the universe revealed by reason and science, enables the investigator to observe how this belief is confirmed or invalidated in the crucible of social struggle or personal conflict, and tests its relation to the religious community which gives assent to its truth and validity. A complete study should not exclude any one of these approaches; for together they represent the whole range of man's capacities for contacting his world and learning its meanings at the several levels of his experience —the physical, the intellectual, and the spiritual. With this in the background of our thinking, we are in a position to examine a few of Israel's beliefs for the purpose of determining their possible validity. The limitations of space will permit only a cursory treatment of the problem, although it is hoped that an approach will be suggested which will enable the student to pursue his inquiry further if he so desires.

THE IDEA OF GOD

We may therefore consider the question of the validity of the Old Testament's idea of God. The one living God, personal, rational, spiritual, righteous, holy, the creator of the universe, and redeemer of mankind—to him the Old Testament witnesses with deep conviction. Does reason support this witness? Reason enables the student to assemble the textual data and to define the nature of the God of the Old Testament. Does it make possible belief in him? To explore this problem is an obligation imposed upon the biblical scholar, from which he cannot absolve himself by referring the matter to specialists such as theologians; for the facts he has gathered include concepts of religion which are presented principally in the form of demands that these concepts be accepted, and that the truths they purport to identify be given wholehearted obedience. The student who refuses to take these demands into account on the ground that they belong, not to the field of biblical criticism and interpretation, but to the fields of theology and homiletics unfortunately fails to recognize that they are inseparable concomitants of the religious beliefs upon which they are based. Both the historical fact—the religious belief—and its inherent claim to possess authority over men appear in the biblical record in the same context and passage. A study of the idea of monotheism is out of the question unless the imperious summons of that God to men—"seek me and live!"—is also examined and evaluated. The source book for biblical theology thus proves to be a disturbingly personal document for the scholar, compelling him to scrutinize the Bible's astonishing claims and doctrines in the light of their possible ultimate truth.

As he considers the nature of God in the Old Testament, the student may discover that the idea of the *unity* of God is not rationally incredible. The idea of the unity of the universe, which transcends its pluralities on the various levels of evistence, conforms to rational experience. The complexity of the interacting systems of energies, organisms, and masses of matter constituting the universe reveals order rather than anarchy and supports a belief in the existence of an underlying unifying principle or power. The intricate mechanism of the universe is nonetheless a single mechanism, all parts of which have functions contributing to the activity of the whole. The oneness of God is not peculiar to biblical thought, of course. God as process, life force, the undifferentiated absolute, or the sum of the personality-making forces in the universe, may be viewed as one, but hardly as biblical. But in the Bible this idea of unity is vigorously proclaimed, and it is made the foundation of faith and conduct. It is not accidental that the oneness of Israel's God and the requirement of absolute, unqualified love for him are announced in the same biblical passage (Deut. 6:4-5). This oneness has both an intellectual and a religious basis. Reason seeks a unifying principle; faith, a single object of supreme devotion. Thus man's philosophical quest for ultimate reality and his historical worship of the one God have contributed to a deepening certainty that God is one.

The concept of God as *personal* brings us still closer to the biblical idea. The chief modern argument for this belief appears to be the necessity of thinking of God as at least as noble as the highest which men find in themselves. Man's experience of goodness, truth, beauty, love occurs on the personal level. This is where his thought about God must naturally begin. God is at least personal in his embodiment of these highest human values. A further argument comes from the rational necessity of projecting a supreme mind, of which the universe and man are expressions. Religious experience also points in the direction of a personal God. The worship and prayers of men presuppose a personal Being, and from these acts assurance is given that such a Being not only exists but actively communicates his purposes and reveals his will to men. It is in the realm of revelation and communication of purpose that the Old Testament particularly stresses the personal nature of God. Revelation is the interaction of mind with mind, the intercourse of God with man. Its principal medium is the divine Word, conceived as the thought of God transmitted to his human creatures. Its content is radically ethical and carries conviction, for it is associated with the personal will of the Almighty God.

As to the *righteousness* of God, modern man may have greater difficulty than did the ancient Israelite in holding this belief. Yet the moral universe he sees within himself seems to call for a supporting universe of moral values outside himself, calling upon him to perform incredibly heroic deeds and giving him the power of transcending self in moments of supreme sacrifice. If man takes the trouble to observe, he is made aware of the moral purpose which evidently runs through history, positively undergirding the good that men do and frustrating their evil deeds. Here man may see how evil begets evil in the wake of war, in the form of death, famine, economic revolution, the dislocation of whole populations, and the fear of renewed war. If righteousness resides at the heart of the universe, these are the results which reason would expect to find in history when war is waged among men. What faith and experience discovered in ancient Palestine man today finds tragically confirmed in his own world—it is a God of righteousness who rules the world.

The *holiness* of God, signifying his separate and unique individuality and the nonhuman power whereby his will is vindicated, is less congenial to the modern temper than is the divine goodness or righteousness; but reason and faith may agree in accepting this teaching also. There are times when the depth of man's failure and the completeness of his helplessness eloquently declare his need of a sovereign God, who alone can save. The mind of man, when grappling with the problems of existence and reality, is finally compelled to go beyond itself for an explanatory principle. In this search the hypothesis of transcendent power and being may be constructed as the unavoidable inference from observation of the natural order in the universe and of the human disorder in the lives of men upon this planet. This inference may be realized by faith as an ultimate fact of the nature of God, by means of which both condemnation and salvation are possible for man.

In the Old Testament God's sovereign holiness is linked with his righteousness and redemptive relation to men, so that it can never overwhelm or do violence to human freedom. Neo-orthodoxy—in so far as the divine holiness is believed to dominate and override the wills of men, who are thus rendered powerless to do anything about their own salvation—has departed from the biblical norm at this point. Karl Barth may adequately and accurately interpret Paul, but he definitely ignores or distorts the teaching of the Old Testament on this matter of the divine sovereignty and human freedom. As terrible as God's holiness is, it never is used to paralyze man's moral powers and to render him unable to make moral and religious decisions. God's grace does not tyrannize over man's will; rather it makes possible free and penitent decisions by confronting man with his sin and with the lovingkindness of the merciful Savior.

The God of Israel in his awful holiness exercises no dictatorial sway over the human mind; neither is he a kind of benevolent cosmic companion aiding and encouraging man in his upward climb, as modern moral and religious idealism seems to describe him. Contrary to this teaching—popular among certain liberals, especially in America—the God of the Old Testament is holy and transcendently righteous, sharply and severely condemning the evil among men and directing the course of history for superhuman ends which do not necessarily coincide with the plans and goals of men. Such a God is judge as well as redeemer, and his holiness makes it forever impossible to construct him in the spiritual or moral image of man. Faith declares that he is a God high and lifted up, when it confesses sin and cries out for forgiveness from a Being in whose presence man sees his utter unworthiness. It may be said that this view of God takes a mediating position between the extremes of neo-orthodoxy and ultraliberalism in insisting upon both the absolute power of God as sovereign judge whose holiness fills the earth and the redemptive love of God, whose word hurts and also heals the wounds of men. It may be added that this position is truer to the facts of man's nature than either of these extremes.

This brief discussion of the validity of Israel's idea of God makes it clear that this is a conception of unsurpassed value and of immeasurable importance for contemporary religion and life. Not only is it credible; it is mandatory as a belief for thinking men, desirous of adhering to an historic faith which is based upon an intelligent and sympathetic understanding of the Bible and of the modern world in which they live. In the last analysis, this faith is not arguable; its identification as the central passion and driving force in biblical religion and in subsequent Jewish-Christian history is sufficient argument. To discover the full meaning of this God is to fall down and worship him with the saints and prophets of old.

THE IDEA OF MAN

In its interpretation of man the Old Testament was unable to draw upon the results of modern research in the fields of sociology, anthropology, and psychology. In spite of this handicap the modern scientist or religious leader may not dismiss this interpretation with a shrug as being naïve. Much that he has since determined by laborious inductive research was known to the men of Israel centuries before the techniques of research were developed. One of the most striking of these intuitions about human nature is the concept of *unity*. In contrast with the more "advanced" view of the Greeks, the Hebrews believed that man was essentially one being, although he was able to function with his body, his spirit, or his mind as he reacted to the various aspects of his environment. He was not a body containing a soul or spirit, nor was he a soul temporarily inhabiting a physical body. He was a unitary organism, in which no fundamental dualism was to be found. In his psychological responses, for example, his glands and other biological organs were involved. We observe reference to his bowels, his kidneys, his liver, and his bones. Granting that this conception of psychology was by no means remarkable, since the Hebrews shared it with their contemporaries, we may observe that it remains closer to the realities of human nature as empirically described by the scientist than do theories of a more speculative nature.

Man as a unitary being cannot divorce the activities pertaining to the various sides of his nature from each other. Spiritual, social, physical, political, economic, or so-called secular interests belong together: they are simply different ways of describing the reaction of a single being to his complex world. The life of man is an organic whole. So the Hebrews saw in the fulfillment of the religious impulse implications for all of life and for every segment of it. This is the conclusion which modern science would have us draw also. Divided loyalties, compartmentalized beliefs, and excessive other-worldliness or this-worldliness produce distorted and maladjusted lives which are bound to be miserable and to bring misery to the world. A recovery of the consciousness of his oneness and an attack upon the forces that divide him are urged upon man by his scientific counselors and guides. This advice fits perfectly into Israel's thinking about man.

The Old Testament teaches that man's being and fate are intricately involved in the life of the community, and that he is at the same time a responsible individual who is personally obligated to establish right relations to God and man. In biblical thought the individual viewed as a solitary creature sustaining only artificial relationships with his group is an inconceivable abstraction. It defines man far more realistically and convincingly: biologically he takes his food from his mother's breast as an infant and receives from her a knowledge of his cultural inheritance; from his family and from wider social contacts he absorbs his awareness of loyalties, ethical standards, and religious faith, thus being thoroughly conditioned by the community that produced him. This view supports a thoroughly *scientific determinism*. On the other hand, biblical man is never completely swallowed up by his group. He retains his identity as a person and is required to acknowledge that fact whenever God calls him to repentance and obedience. At such times he becomes most painfully aware of the distinct reality of his own separate individuality. This supports a concept of *moral freedom* to match the scientific determinism.

Just as the theology of the Old Testament acts as a mediator between two extremes of modern thought, so its anthropology helps to reconcile the concepts of determinism and freedom on the human level. Man is determined by the fact of his creaturehood and his kinship with nature. Nevertheless he is free to choose his destiny as he faces the Creator in whose image he was made. He was made from the dust of the ground, but he was created in the image of God. Science confirms the first part of this affirmation; and it is unable to refute the second part, if, indeed, it does not seek to support it. By faith in man's creation Israel resolved the dilemma of freedom and necessity. In our day it is essential that science and religious faith accept this insight of the Israelites and give it concrete application in the life of the world.

THE IDEA OF CREATION

Is the biblical idea of Creation tenable in a day of geological science and biological research into man's evolution as a physical organism? Obviously the method of Creation as outlined in Genesis must be rejected. Does this mean that belief in man's divine origin should receive like treatment? Notwithstanding statements of avowed empirical theists whose method is that of scientific naturalism, the evidence at hand indicates that faith in Creation is a reasonable faith. The geologist or the biologist who maintains the foolishness and the quaintness of the biblical idea of Creation is a living denial of his contention. As a matter of fact, all science convincingly witnesses to the uniqueness of the mind and spirit of man and to the sheer untenability of a completely naturalistic or materialistic account of his origin. The mind of the scientist, or the saint, or the philosopher carries us inevitably to the hypothesis of a creator God rather than to a theory of amoebic life in primeval slime. Creation is the only hypothesis which can explain all of the levels and manifestations of life upon this planet. And faith transforms this hypothesis into an abiding conviction resting upon the revealed knowledge of God as creator and redeemer. Throughout history this faith has been confirmed time after time as men sensed their divine possibilities and rose to new heights of achievement.

THE IDEA OF SIN

A final doctrine of Old Testament theology—that of sin—may be presented in this part of our chapter on the problem of validity. On the negative side, this doctrine denies that matter is the locus of evil or sin. Sexuality, lust, or carnality are not sources of evil in man; they are merely external evidences of that which has its origin in the will of man. The physical scientist knows nothing of human sin in his research; but the theologian who subscribes to scientific naturalism may also know nothing of sin, not so much by reason of indifference to the subject, but because his presuppositions preclude its possibility. He could accept the biblical idea that the body is not sinful or the source of sin without following it in its discovery of sin in man's proud defiance of the will of God. Modern man and biblical man are agreed that the body is neutral as far as sin is concerned. Is there a similar agreement with respect to the location of sin in the human will? Our reply to this question will lead us to inquire what *psychology and ethics* as well as contemporary theologies say on this subject.

Behavioristic psychology finds in man's mental and emotional processes a series of stimulus-response reactions whereby adjustments are made to the environment for the sake of survival. Man is thus a mechanism with responses which are similar to, although more complicated than, those in lower forms of life. Failure to make effective responses may lead to disaster; it cannot lead to sin, unless sin is error or physiological sluggishness in the synaptic connections of the nervous system, which causes deferred responses. In this view, the human will has no real authority or even existence, since behavior is due to mechanical causes beyond man's control. Will is merely a poetic term;

it cannot identify the fixed purpose of a self which persists through change and passing time.

The psychology of the unconscious or subliminal self provides a better basis for comparison with sin as defined in the Old Testament, since it probes into the mind and the self for the discovery of dark desires and repressed impulses which may lie hidden there unnoticed by consciousness. As is the case in the Old Testament, Freudian psychology pushes to one side thoughts and desires which appear on the surface of consciousness, and searches for the deeper drives within the self. It regards as sin failure to recognize and expose the hidden element that wrecks the individual's life by stimulating various types of personality disorders. Likewise, in the thinking of Israel sin is not primarily the superficial act of disobedience, but the deeper, hidden power of a willful self determined to secure its ends in spite of the will of God. When the psychoanalyst gets to the heart of a personality problem, he may try to instill into the mind of his patient confidence in a power outside of himself, such as a friend or even God. This may be the beginning of a cure—salvation. Surrender to the majestic holiness of God and complete acceptance of his will is the biblical solution of the problem of sin. The main difference between the psychoanalyst and the prophet consists in the former's effort to arouse a weak will by quickening interest in a variety of ways, while the latter asserts that man's will is too strong and must be broken by the judgment of God, whose will alone can be supreme.

Ethical theory which asserts the reality and autonomy of the self also helps to shed light on the problem of sin in the Old Testament and in contemporary thought. This theory maintains the necessity of the organization of sentiment and desire around a common center as the only means of producing a mature ethical personality. This common center must have value beyond that attached to any particular desire in man's moral consciousness. Such a center, to command and unite the discordant elements deemed to have value for the individual, can consist only of the highest good. When this good has been enthroned, it becomes ethically wrong and disastrous to deny its authority. If we substitute God for this good, and sin for wrong, the similarity between biblical theology and idealistic morality is apparent. For both, the organization of life around a supreme object of devotion is the way to salvation. Contrariwise, organization around a lesser or inferior center, or lack of any organization, is sinful.

That sin is occasioned by an act of man's will in its revolt against God modern liberal theology will be inclined to agree. To it the idea of total depravity or even original sin is distasteful. The fall of man is regarded as a myth or a parable with considerable sermonic value, but not as an accurate account of the origin of sin. But the identification of sin in the will of man is in harmony with liberalism's high regard for the individual as a morally responsible person, capable of using his initiative and of achieving success along all lines of legitimate endeavor. The opposition of this school of thought to legalistic sin as evincing little recognition of the motives of men further favors its acceptance of the Old Testament conception, which emphasizes as the primary motive for sin the desire to glorify and to enhance the self. Only when liberalism forgets the God of Israel, whose blazing moral holiness illumines the dark corners of the self and exposes pitilessly its shams and weaknesses, is its conception of sin foreign to that of the Old Testament.

A survey of other basic beliefs of Israel's Scriptures could be added, showing how and why these also make their appeal and present their challenge to the mind and conscience of modern man. The truth of Israel's conception of salvation might be pointed out, for example, noting the teachings as to the justice, mercy, and lovingkindness of God, as well as his requirement of repentance and obedience imposed upon men, or the faith by which men seek him and find hidden sources of power, or the extension of his rule to the nations so that his kingdom of universal justice may one day come. There could follow an elaboration upon the meaning of death for the saint of Israel, picturing him coming close to a faith that not even death could break his fellowship with God, or pointing to his insistence that life after death can have no meaning apart from God. And evil could be evaluated in its Old Testament form to show that a righteous God rules the world, and that ultimately his kingdom of love will prevail through tribulation and in spite of evil. The objective description of these great ideas, which has been completed in the preceding chapters of this book, must suffice. It can only be concluded that the religious doctrines of the Old Testament are their own most effective validation.

RELATIONSHIP TO THE NEW TESTAMENT

However, one final method of validating these beliefs remains for consideration—that is, validation by applying the principle of conformity to the teachings of the New Testament. The older literature on the subject of Old Testament theology, when written by Christian rather than Jewish scholars, tended to use this principle almost exclusively. In fact, the very method of the writers predetermined the selection from the Old Testament of only those materials supporting, or believed to support, New Testament teachings or Christian doctrines. The Old Testament sources constituted, as it were, the basis for an introduction to the religious teachings of the New Testament. These sources had no voice or faith of their own. In view of this situation, which still affects the work of Christian Old Testament scholars, the question of the relation of Old Testament theology to that of the New Testament arises. Is the former actually dependent upon the latter for the explication of its meaning and value? If it is not, is there any vital relationship at all?

First of all, in aproaching this problem there can be no doubt whatsoever that a theology of the Old Testament indeed exists, and that it exists in complete independence of the New Testament. This book has been confined to the Old Testament sources, and to them alone. If a Christian bias has crept in, it has not done so because of the absence of an effort at conscious control. Such an effort is demanded by the exacting requirements of biblical research, whether that research be textual, historical, or primarily theological. To assert the independence of Old Testament theology is to insist that it is not to be treated as simply a background for the thought of the New Testament. As far as New Testament religious concepts are concerned, these came to birth and mature expression in the literature of Israel. To this pronouncement exception may be taken, but legitimately only with respect to ideas derived from Hellenistic sources. Even here it may be shown that many of these Hellenistic influences came into the consciousness of early Christianity by way of Judaism. It may be reaffirmed, therefore, that the fundamental structure of the religious ideology of the New Testament is found in the Old Testament.

This literature is the theologically creative literature of the Bible. It determines the major theological assumptions of the New Testament. Apart from the numerous direct or indirect allusions to, and quotations from, the Old Testament in the New Testament—which were consciously brought in to prove a point, or unconsciously made because its writers were thoroughly conditioned by Jewish concepts and attitudes—its basic religious teachings are taken from Israel's sacred writings. Not only will a recognition of this fact enhance the prestige of the Old Testament—a result much to be desired—among Christians; but it will provide a more defensible and intelligible basis for New Testament exegesis and interpretation.

We do not find one kind of a *God* in the Old Testament and another in the New Testament. In both literatures God is declared or assumed to be the mighty creator of the universe, the source of all life, the conserver and vindicator of justice, the merciful and loving redeemer, and the help of men in time of trouble. The New Testament adds nothing to the content of the idea of God which is not already present in the literature and faith of Israel. It is often argued that Jesus held a unique conception of God, by which is usually meant the fatherhood of God. We have seen, however, in Chapters 2 and 5, that the divine characteristics which the term "fatherhood" denotes are fully evident in the Old Testament. Among these are the ideas of compassion, lovingkindness, faithfulness, and mercy, shown toward the community of the faithful, both collectively and individually. For Jesus and for Jeremiah, God was merciful and also righteous. A full realization of this fact would help the student to understand Jesus' viewpoint relative to the meaning of history and of the divine judgment upon it.

It is highly improper to delete from the Gospels the apocalyptic sections—in which the writers vividly reveal how God's righteousness is upheld in the historical process, and how history's crises constitute a series of judgments upon men—when such a deletion stems from a belief that Jesus could not have thought in such terms. To reject these on the ground that they do not represent Jesus is to cut him off from the Judaism from which he came and to subject him to an uncritical and inexcusable process of modernization. The God of Jesus was a God of merciful forgiveness. This is the note sounded in the New Testament many times, and there is no reason to doubt that Jesus himself stressed this theme in his teaching ministry. But it must not be forgotten that this forgiveness was necessarily dependent upon the ethical nature of God. The salvation offered by this God demanded a deep-seated ethical regeneration as well as a radically new loyalty. The world catastrophe described in the apocalypses of the Gospels shows the vast outreach of sin in its involvement of nature and nations, and it exhibits also the revolutionary character of the processes of judgment and salvation which are set in motion by the God of wrath and love.

Modern students of the Bible would do well to view the New Testament's teaching concerning *man* in the light of the Old Testament idea. It is highly probable that Jesus viewed man in this way. He and the writers of Israel saw man as he was—a creature made of dust but in the image of God, free to choose the right and reject the wrong, created to worship his Maker and to live in communion with him, stubbornly sinning in seeking his own ends, and yielding to God's judgment and grace in the experience of redemption. Jesus saw man as a member of society, realizing his highest self in association with others; and he appealed to the great social principles of the prophets—justice, moral responsibility, and self-denial. He recognized the evil in men and harshly denounced it; he saw also the good and confidently appealed to it. He found no evil or corruption in the bodies of men, but taught the value of right motives as a means of controlling the lusts of the flesh. In these ways he manifested a genuinely Jewish attitude toward human nature.

Paul, on the other hand, seems to have developed a different conception of man, perhaps through his acquaintance with Hellenistic thought. At times he comes close to a Platonic dualism in his emphasis upon the physical and the spiritual natures of man (Rom. 7:18, 23; 8:3-5). However, it is doubtful that he fully adopted such a position, restrained as he must have been by his Jewish training. This is indicated in his attempt to explain the nature of life after death (I Cor. 15). In this attempt he holds to a Jewish belief in man's unitary nature, which permits the separate existence of no distinct self apart from the body. If there is survival after death, therefore, this must take the form of a bodily resurrection. In his anthropology it is apparent that Paul too is more Jewish than Hellenistic.

Further development of our thesis concerning the dependence of the religious ideas of the New Testament upon the theology of the Old Testament would require reference to the conception of the kingdom of God, which was Jesus' fundamental teaching; to the various ideas of sin and salvation; to messianic conceptions, by means of which the early Christians tried to formulate their faith in Jesus; and to the problem of evil, particularly as interpreted in the Gospels, the Pauline letters, and the book of Revelation. A detailed comparison could be made to prove that all of these ingredients of New Testament religion are substantially rooted in the teachings of the Old Testament. This task will not be attempted here, since it would carry us far beyond the purpose of this discussion, which is to show the extraordinary importance of an understanding of Old Testament theology for the student of the New Testament and of the Christian religion. This fact bears upon the question of validity, if it is assumed that the religious beliefs of the New Testament are themselves valid for modern man's faith and life.

THE PRESENT TASK

The faith of ancient Israel was formulated over a period of nearly a thousand years. In that time a nation was born, grew to maturity, and then disappeared from the stage of history, to be succeeded by a spiritual community which emerged from that nation's ruins. To that nation there came adversity, prosperity, victory, and defeat. The religious community which followed faced the hostility of alien cultures and peoples, the danger of inner moral decay, and the challenge of a world mission. For the nation there was political strife, international warfare, social conflict; for the community of believers there arose disturbing threats to faith—paganism, disloyalty, self-interest, and materialism, which engendered fear, intolerance and suspicion. Out of these situations there came abiding convictions which shaped the destiny of the Jewish people who adhered to them, and which determined the beliefs of myriads of Christians into whose scriptures the Bible of the Jews was incorporated.

Now we, the inhabitants of this planet—Jew and Christian, Moslem and Hindu, Shintoist and Buddhist, believer and unbeliever—live in a world which is witnessing a repetition on a far grander scale of the crimes and conflicts which plagued the Jews of biblical history. Opposing ideologies, conflicting economic systems, racial tensions, a frightening armaments race between nations, the fear of renewed war, and stark pessimism among the peoples of the earth mark our age. Can modern man lift his eyes to the hills with the assurance of the psalmist that there is the only source of help? Can the problem of human relations be solved unless men realize once again with the priestly writer that they have been made in the image of God, to worship him, to practice good will toward others, and to do justly and love mercy? Can confidence in the future be had unless men discover that there is in fact a destiny that shapes their ends, in the form of a righteous God of all mankind, whose kingdom is the goal of all history? Can the individual be redeemed from sin and despair until he experiences the presence of the God, who is compassionate and holy, able to guide him in love and to purify him in righteousness? Aside from an intellectual demonstration of the nature and the validity of the theology of the Old Testament such as has been attempted in this volume, there remains the task for student, minister, and layman alike of identifying for himself the content of Israel's faith and of experimenting with its great doctrines to meet the world's present need. Bold experimentation in the concrete situations which now confront men is the final and decisive test of the truth of Old Testament theology.

Selected Bibliography

I. General Surveys of Old Testament Theology and Religion

Budde, Karl. *The Religion of Israel to the Exile.* New York: G. P. Putnam's Sons, 1899.

Burrows, M. *An Outline of Biblical Theology.* Philadelphia: The Westminster Press, 1946.

Cheyne, T. K. *Jewish Religious Life after the Exile.* New York: G. P. Putnam's Sons, 1915.

Davidson, A. B. *The Theology of the Old Testament* (International Theological Library). New York: Charles Scribner's Sons, 1904.

Eichrodt, W. *Theologie des Alten Testaments.* Vols. I-III. Leipzig, 1933-39.

Fosdick, Harry E. *A Guide to Understanding the Bible.* New York: Harper and Brothers, 1938.

Knudson, A. C. *The Religious Teaching of the Old Testament.* New York: Abingdon-Cokesbury Press, 1918.

Köhler, L. H. *Theologie des Alten Testaments.* Tübingen, 1936.

Leslie, Elmer A. *Old Testament Religion.* New York: Abingdon-Cokesbury Press, 1936.

Oesterley, W. O. E., and Robinson, T. H. *Hebrew Religion.* 2nd ed. New York: The Macmillan Company, 1937.

Robinson, H. W. *Religious Ideas of the Od Testament.* New York: Charles Scribner's Sons, 1913.

Rowley, H. H. *The Re-discovery of the Old Testament.* Philadelphia: The Westminster Press, 1946.

Sellin, E. *Theologie des Alten Testaments.* Leipzig, 1933.

II. Books on Special Subjects

Albright, W. F. *From the Stone Age to Christianity.* Baltimore: Johns Hopkins Press, 1940.

Charles, R. H. *A Critical History of the Doctrine of a Future Life in Israel, in Judaism, and in Christianity.* New York: The Macmillan Company, 1913.

Cunliffe-Jones, H. *The Authority of the Biblical Revelation.* London: James Clarke and Company, Ltd., 1946.

Dodd, C. H. *The Authority of the Bible.* New York: Harper and Brothers, 1929.

————. *History and the Gospel.* New York: Charles Scribner's Sons, 1938.

Fullerton, Kemper. *Prophecy and Authority*. New York: The Macmillan Company, 1919.

Gray, G. B. *Sacrifice in the Old Testament*. New York: Oxford University Press, 1925.

Minear, P. S. *Eyes of Faith*. Philadelphia: The Westminster Press, 1946.

Niebuhr, H. R. *The Meaning of Revelation*. New York: The Macmillan Company, 1941.

Niebuhr, Reinhold. *The Nature and Destiny of Man* (Series I, *Human Nature;* Series II, *Human Destiny*). New York: Charles Scribner's Sons, 1941-43.

Oesterley, W. O. E. *Immortality and the Unseen World*. New York: The Macmillan Company, 1921.

———. *Sacrifices in Ancient Israel.* New York: The Macmillan Company, 1938.

Otto, Rudolf. *The Kingdom of God and the Son of Man* (tr. F. V. Filson and B. L. Woolf). Grand Rapids: Zondervan Publishing House, 1938.

Pace, E. G. *Ideas of God in Israel*. New York: The Macmillan Company, 1924.

Robinson, H. W. *Redemption and Revelation*. New York: Harper and Brothers, 1942.

Rowley, H. H. *The Relevance of the Bible*. New York: The Macmillan Company, 1944.

Smith, J. M. P. *The Moral Life of the Hebrews*. Chicago: University of Chicago Press, 1923.

Snaith, N. H. *The Distinctive Ideas of the Old Testament*. Philadelphia: The Westminster Press, 1946.

Wright, G. E. *The Challenge of Israel's Faith*. Chicago: University of Chicago Press, 1944.

Index of Biblical Passages

278

Index of Subjects

Aaron, 139
Abel, murder of, 165
Abraham, 30, 60, 131, 139, 165; call of, 137; selection of, 78; tested, 75
Absalom, death of, 202
Adam, 16, 54, 230
Adams, D. S., 19
Adultery, 135
Africa, 157
Agag, 168
Ahab, 167, 171; marriage of, 28
'Ahav, 126
Ahaz, 149
Ahijah, 172; conspiracy of, 167
Ahriman, 234
Ahura Mazda, 234
Albright, W. F., 175, 189
Alliances, foreign, 95
Altar, of God, 153
Amen, 130
Amen, God of, 130
Ammonites, 160
Amos, 24, 55; teachings of, 21
Anath, 187
Anathoth, 18
Anger, of God, 97
Animals, man and, 62
Animism, 18, 24, 48
Animistic: psychology, 41; religions, 33
Anthropologist, 64
Anthropology, 264; biblical, 214, 265
Antiochus Epiphanes, 219, 240
Apocalypse: in Isaiah, 116, 180; in Zechariah, 46
Apocalyptic books, renewed interest in, 179
Apocalyptic literature, 191, 239
Apocalyptist, faith of, 239
Apologia, of Job, 73
Apostate: kings, 233; nation, 122

Apostates, resurrection of, 220
Arabah, 115
Ark, 33
Arm of God, holy, 35
Art, Christian, 54
Artaxerxes, 128
Arvad, 161
Asceticism, 68, 204
'Asham, 85, 90
Asheroth, 169
Asia, 157
Askelon, 161
Assurance of God's help, 133
Assyria, 56, 67, 86, 88, 109, 111, 158, 183; God's rod, 112; gods of, 112
Assyrian alliance, 94
Astrological deities, 44
Aton, Egyptian god, 140
Atone, 135
Author and editor, theological agreement of, 253
'Avlah, 84, 89
'Awon, 84, 86, 101

Baal (or baals), 50, 76, 105, 112, 169, 187; functions of, 50; political power of, 51; priests of, 51; ridicule of, 51
Baalism, 31, 50, 51, 104, 109; defeat of, 199
Babel, story of, 110
Babylon, in Sheol, 211
Babylonia, 18, 94, 109, 158, 183; gods of, 112
Babylonian: flood story, 258; thought, 43
Balaam, oracles of, 141-42
Balak, 141
Barth, Karl, 263
Barton, G. A., 161
Basar, 64
Bashan, 46
Bathsheba, 171
Bauer, H., 187
Beasts, in Daniel, 191
Bedouin tradition, 157

Beersheba, 102
Bel, 259
Benediction (Num. 6), 130
Ben-hadad, 130
Benjamin, grief for, 208
Berdiaev, N. A., 175
Bethel, 18, 102; theophany at, 139
Bible: abandonment of, 15; ancient versions of, 13; relevance of, 15; study of, 13; ultimate truth of, 14
Biblical: criticism, 261; scholar, obligation of, 260
Bildad, 45, 189, 244
Biologist, 266
Blessings, material, 118, 138
Blood revenge, 136
Book of the Covenant, 99
Bower, W. C., 15
Briggs, C. A., 59
Broome, E. C., Jr., 40
Brotherhood, world, 186
Buddha, 24
Burial: ceremonial, 205; Egyptian, 205; importance of, 206
Burnt offering, 89, 170
Burrows, M., 17

Cain, 30, 199
Calamities: eschatological, 191-92; punitive and redemptive, 234
Canaan, 56, 60, 92; gods of, 112; settlement in, 137
Canaanite (and Canaanites), 20, 24, 157
Canonical unity, objection to, 253
Canonization: an experience, 253; a process, 253
Carnality, 109
Case, S. J., 175
Catholic, 17

morphic, 28; awareness of, 21; belief in, 150; biblical meaning of, 134; concept of, 23, 47; conqueror of death, 219; delight in, 205; dependence upon, 49; doctrine of, 254; eternal, 130, 224; freedom's c o n s e r v e r, 167; (giver) of fertility, 51; hostility to, 89; idea of, 22, 138, 260; image of, 272; immortal, 108, 244; Israel's, 27, 116, 120; J's and Second Isaiah's, 252; Jesus' idea of, 270; living, 22, 24, 25, 26, 27, 32, 42, 48, 80, 179, 223; majesty of, 103; man's image as, 34; meaning of, 23; New Testament's, 270; personal, 28, 31, 95, 261; presence of, 118, 125; primitive ideas of, 24; provider, 223; savior, 94, 117; self-determining, 29, 30, 130; source of Scriptures, 258; sovereign, 262; spirit of, 107, 141; spiritual, 39; supreme mind, 262; supreme reality, 16; transcendent, 263; unity of, 48-49, 177; will of, 76, 119. *See also* Creator, Covenant, Ethical, Faithfulness, Father, Goodness, Grace, History, Holiness, Judge, Judgment, Justice, K i n g, Love, Power, Righteous, Salvation, Trustworthiness

Gods, 77, 82, 134; agricultural, 109; astrological, 104; false, 87, 115; fertility, 28, 50; foreign, 26, 259; immortal, 205; worship of, 149

Golden age, myth of, 158

Golden bull (calf), 88, 137, 169, 231

Good, divine source of, 233

Goodness of God, 118, 128, 239

Gospels, 156; apocalyptic sections of, 270

Government: centralized, 92; divine, 172; theocratic, 166

Grace, 130, 153; active love, 129; faithfulness and, 131; fidelity and, 128, 131; God's, 84, 117, 126, 129, 175, 263; man toward man, 127; saving, 128; tyrannical, 263; unmerited love, 129

Graham, W. C., 64, 158

Gray, G. B., 218

Greek thought, 213, 221

Gressmann, H., 187

Grief of Elisha, 202

Group demands, primacy of, 204

Guilt: ceremonial, 134; consciousness of, 106; offering, 90, 99

Hades, 131

Halal, 85, 90

Ham, 56, 60

Hamas, 84, 90

Hamath, 115

Hanan, 129-30

Hannah: prayer of, 55; Song of, 209

Harris, Z. S., 187

Harvest Festival, 99, 256

Hata', 84-86, 101

Hazael, 130, 202

Hazor, Baal of, 28

Hermon, Baal of, 28

Hebrew. *See* History, Religion

Hegel, 175

Hellenistic period, 89

Henotheism, 18, 48

Hesedh, 127

Hezekiah, 62, 89, 104, 149

Historian, 64; of Hebrews, 17-18

Historical: biblical study, 18; method, 16-17

History, 16, 52, 156; apocalyptic idea of, 179; Chronicler's view of, 62; cyclic conception of, 175-78; Deuteronomic, 137, 177; d i v i n e-kingdom, 167; early Hebrew, 115, 137; end of, 180, 191; God in, 24, 27, 78, 166, 180, 253-54; Israel's, 17, 54, 61, 109, 157, 158; Israel's religious, 139; J's idea of, 176; Kingdom of God's, 164; Lord of, 79; moral purpose of, 262; national, 121; organismic conception of, 175; periods of, 177; personal, 54; philosophy of, 27, 174; political, 165; priestly view of, 179; prophetic idea of, 177; scientific, 174; spiritual, 164; stage of, 126; summary of Hebrew, 178; teleology of, 175; truth's vindication in, 159; unitary, 177; validity of theology and, 260; within a history, 164

Holiness, 35, 39, 120-21, 143, 145; early view of, 34; God's, 36-37, 112, 118, 143, 262; idea of, 33; magical, 33; moralization of, 37; practice of, 179; redemptive, 36; righteousness and, 38; transcendent power and, 48

Holy community, 101, 148, 154

Holy One of Israel, 35, 52, 87, 131

Homiletics, 261

Horeb, 55

Hosea, 55, 102

Hoshea, 94

Human need, 114

Idealistic morality, 267

Idol worship, 101

Idolatrous beliefs, 146

Idolatry, 26, 105, 109-10, 112, 115, 135, 147, 171, 178, 193, 233; condemned, 183; folly of, 103; as harlotry, 102; sin of, 101, 106

Idols, 25-27, 90, 104-5, 110

Ignorance as evil, 232

Illiteracy, biblical, 13

Image of God, 42, 65, 138, 153, 212

Imago dei, 82

Immanentism, 34

Immortality, 221-22, 224-25

Individual, 72; and community, 144; eschatology of, 221; responsibility, 72; sin of, 106; suffering of, 228; value of, 72, 224

Individualism, 221, 240; idea of, 73; Jeremiah's, 236; rise of, 216

Iniquity, 84. *See also* Sin

Innocent, suffering of, 234

Interdependence of ideas, 251

International: life, 157; rule of God, 185; scope of love, 184

nistic nature, 221; mortal, 108; Paul's conception of, 271; religious person, 78; sinner, 143, 153; son of God, 213, 224; unitary, 68, 214, 271; worshiper, 225. *See also* Creatureliness
Mana, 33
Manasseh, 104, 134
Mankind, 110, 114, 199
Marah, 87
Marduk, 41, 43, 53, 187
Market place of Bethel, 186
Marriage, 60, 184, 256
Martyrdom, 220
Martyrs, 179, 220
Marxism, view of evil, 232
Mathews, I. G., 17
Mathews, S., 175
Matter, sinfulness of, 68
Menahem, 161
Mercy, 62, 118, 120, 126, 130
Meshech in Sheol, 211
Messiah, 131, 157, 172, 195-96
Messianic: ideas, 213; king, 196; leader, 184; literature, 171; teaching, 15
Metaphors for God, 170
Micah, 30
Micaiah ben Imlah, 55
Michal, 55
Midian, 50
Mighty One of Jacob, 132
Migrations into Palestine, 160
Mission: of Israel, 172, 185: sense of, 154
Missionary document, 184
Moab, 88, 116, 141, 161
Moabite, 55, 184
Molten images, 51. *See also* Idols
Monarchy, 27, 30-31, 160, 166-68, 176
Monotheism, 18, 27, 48, 52, 221, 261
Montgomery, J. A., 187
Moral: consciousness, 95; experience, 31, 52; freedom, 76, 180, 265; judgment, 96, 99; law, 72, 96; majesty of God, 248. *See also* Ethical
Moralists, 96
Morals, 75
Moses, 48, 55, 57, 75, 134, 139; death of, 201, 202;

stories of, 165; theophany to, 137
Mount Carmel, 55, 76
Mount of Olives, 47
Mystic, 78
Myth, 21, 190, 258; in Genesis, 190
Mythology, 53, 187, 193, 234; Near Eastern, 175, 187

Naaman, the leper, 217
Naboth, 171
Nasa', 135
Nathan, 167, 171
Nation (and nations), 35, 122; breakdown of, 72, 216; deliverance of, 231; idolatrous, 159; Israelite, 78; prayer for, 152; reconstruction of, 138
National: feast days, 256; frustration, 158
Nationalism, 154, 183
Nationalist, 184
Naturalism, scientific, 20
Nature, 45-46, 194
Near East, 13, 20, 92, 187, 237
Nebo, 259
Necromancers, 206
Necromancy, 207
Neo-orthodoxy, 263
Nephesh, 64, 65, 66
Neshamah, 39
New Community of Israel, 138
New Covenant, 134, 138
New Testament, 23, 127, 157, 269
New Year's Day, 256
New Year Festival, 162
Noah, 56, 60

Oath, 25
Obedience, 143, 147, 150
Oesterley, W. O. E., 17, 59, 154, 162
Offenses, capital, 200
Oholah, 109
Oholibah, 109
Oneness of God, twofold basis of, 261
Orenda, 33
Organismic idea of history, 175
Orthodoxy of Job's friends, 244
Otto, R., 34

Padhah, 135
Paganism, 52, 109, 165
Pain and the individual, 228

Pakadh, 124, 126
Palestine, 13, 16, 45
Pantheism, 34
Pardon, 134, 135
Parents, honor to, 116
Particularism, 183
Particularist, Jewish, 184
Passover, 256
Patriarch, 56
Patriarchal stories, 169
Pauline idea of body, 109
Peace, 18, 118, 184, 186, 191, 194
Penitential psalm, 106
Pentateuch, 49, 139, 187
Peor, Baal of, 28
Perazim, Baal of, 28
Persecution under Manasseh, 104
Personal: communion, 118; religion, 118; responsibility, 144
Personality, 29, 82, 187
Pesha', 84, 86, 101
Pessimism, 213
Pfeiffer, R. H., 59, 240
Pharaoh, 87
Philistine, 55, 160
Philosophy: biblical, 20; Greek, 29, 66; Hellenistic, 64; humanistic, 239; validity and, 260
Phoenicia, 28
Phoenician, 187
Physics, 14
Piety, 15, 151-52
Plagues of Egypt, 139
Platonic: dualism, 271; thought, 108
Political kingdom. *See* Kingdom
Polydaemonism, 18, 48
Polytheism, 18, 188, 258
Poverty of Israel, 159
Power of God, 21, 32, 76, 180; mysterious, 244
Power, will to, 147
Punishment, 173
Praise, 79, 152
Prayer, 79, 144, 152-53; answer to, 135; conditions of, 153; David's, 67, 152; Elisha's, 152; essential to salvation, 153; Ezra's, 152; grace and, 128; Hannah's, 152; Hezekiah's, 152; ideological basis of, 185; need of, 80; private, 151; Solomon's, 67, 134, 152
Presuppositions: for bibli-